THE ODYSSEY OF A PARTISAN

by
Joseph L. Zygielbaum
Edited by Krista Burlae

*Joseph (Kuba Mordecai) and Adele (Rachel),
Wedding Photo, December 22, 1945, Poland*

*Joseph (Kuba Mordecai), center, Parade of Liberation,
Reichenbach, Germany, May, 1945*

Joseph, Wroclaw, Poland, 1945

Joseph, with Soviet Medal   *Joseph, Soviet Uniform*

Ryfka Zygielbaum, Joseph's sister, 19 years old, Warsaw, 1939 (Killed along with her mother and grandmother in Treblinka.)

*Szmul Artur (Samuel Mordecai) and
Golda Zygielbojm, Joseph's father and
mother, Chelm, Poland, 1918*

Zygielbaum Family Apartment, Warsaw, 1940

*Szmul Artur Zygielbojm (Samuel Mordecai),
shortly before his suicide, London, 1943*

Joseph and Adele, La Crescenta, CA, 1960

Arthur, Paul, Adele, and Joseph, La Crescenta, CA, 1965

The Odyssey of a Partisan

Original Copyright © 1988 by Joseph L. Zygielbaum

Copyright © 2016
Arthur I. Zygielbaum and Paul S. Zygielbaum

Original hardcover edition of this book published in 2009,
with layout and design by Blooming Twig Books LLC.
ISBN 978-1-933918-39-6

Paperback Second Edition 2016
ISBN-13: 978-1540444264
ISBN-10: 1540444260

All rights reserved. This book may not be photocopied for personal or professional use. No part of this book may be reproduced, stored in a retrieval system, or transmitted in any form or by any means (electronic, mechanical, photocopying, recording, or otherwise) without permission in writing from the copyright holder.

In Memory of my martyred parents and only sister:
Szmuel Mordko (Arthur) and Golda Zygielbaum
Ryvka Zygielbaum

And my wife's parents and little sister:
Israel and Rachel
Raizele
a few of the six million victims
of the Nazi Holocaust

Don't ever say that you are on your final way,
When angry clouds blot out the clear and sunny day,
Our yearned for hour, it will finally appear,
When we shall proclaim to the world that YES, WE ARE HERE!
This song was written not with ink, but human blood,
It's not a sing-song by a bird that's free and proud.
Among the ruins of their burning, crumbling towns,
A people sang this song with rifles in their hands!

Acknowledgments

I wish to express my deep gratitude to Rose Lenore Gold and my daughter-in-law, Sandy Zygielbaum for their unselfish dedication and long hours spent on the preparation of this manuscript.

I am especially grateful to my wife Adele and our sons Arthur and Paul for their patience and encouragement during the many months and years of writing this book.

Joseph L. Zygielbaum

Editor's Preface

I remember finishing this book for the first time in the middle of a rainy summer night in 2007. It was two a.m. and I was so affected by the piece that I had to burn off some energy, so I went for a walk in the rain. Was I in a partisan camp in Belarus? Could I turn around to a German at my heels, gun in my back? Or was I just in Lincoln, Nebraska after reading the memoir of a Second World War hero and survivor? This book is a true story. The author passed in the 1990's and his family has chosen to keep his words authentic.

My first read through this book left me stunned. And, it was still in an unkempt form, scanned from type-written pages to MS Word with so many grammatical errors and extra symbols in the text (from the scanning process) that my version of MS Word wouldn't read the errors. Even in such a raw form, the story drew me in, and kept me to the end.

I found myself in the forests in Belarus, wandering with the partisans as I read. I found myself understanding a perspective of the Second World War that is not well known. I found myself in awe of a man who could not only live through such ordeals, but live to tell them, to tell us what happened. That was what he wanted. He wanted people to know how it really was for Jews in Poland during the occupation. He wanted people to know about the hide-aways of partisans in the forest. He wanted his story told so that we would not forget.

I walked in the rain for two hours that night. It took me over a week to digest what I had just read: an unpublished story of a place and time that are fading from view and memory as the years tick by, from a person who lived through it; a story not otherwise told, of spies and heroes and losses that seem unfathomable to my

1960's forward life. Eventually, I came back to 2007 and asked myself: *what and where are the similarities today?* I believe that is what Joseph Zygielbaum wants his readers to ask. He wants a story told so that history remains in the past and does not repeat itself. *Odyssey of a Partisan* is his story, in his words.

Krista Burlae, Editor
Lincoln, Nebraska
September, 2008

Introduction to *Odyssey of a Partisan*

This is the true story of our father's extraordinary experiences during World War II. He finished the manuscript just a few years before his death in 1995. We have preserved the text intact, except for minor corrections to the spellings of certain place names, minor grammatical corrections, and such. None of the described incidents, settings or emotions have been changed. However, some names of individuals still living or recently deceased have been changed, to protect all parties.

The story itself describes something of our father's childhood in Poland and takes the reader through an odyssey spanning horrendous events from 1939 to 1945, ending just before his emigration with his new wife to the United States. We shall allow that story to unfold for the reader in our father's own words. However, the meaning of our father's story in the context of his life after the war would be lost without some further explanation.

In the early 1960s, our father was involved in the American Space Program. The prologue describes part of a work day in which he is trying to make arrangements for Soviet participation in an upcoming scientific conference. His telephone conversation with a Soviet official causes him to recall his war experiences and to consider how so many unlikely circumstances, including his very survival, had brought him to this episode.

The epilogue picks up his thoughts as this reverie ends. He pulls his car into the driveway of his home in Southern California. He happily anticipates an evening off before he has to once again take up delicate diplomatic issues.

So, what events brought our father to a world so far removed from the brutality of the war?

Our father had many secrets that died with him. Some of his sabotage work as a Partisan and a Polish army officer was done in coordination with the US Office of Strategic Services (OSS), the forerunner of today's Central Intelligence Agency. He was a mechanical engineer by education. By the end of the war, he had become fluent in most European languages. He had gained intimate knowledge of Soviet mentality, politics, strategy and technology, as he fought in Yugoslavia, White Russia (Belarus), Finland, and other countries. He knew vast areas of Eastern European and Soviet terrain. And he was, in Soviet eyes, a Red Army deserter.

For these reasons, and particularly his knowledge of OSS methods, the OSS did not want him falling into Soviet hands after the war ended. The liberation of Eastern Europe from Nazi occupation created an opportunity. Our father made a clandestine return to Wroclaw, where he met our mother, a Holocaust survivor, and reconnected with a few relatives who had also survived the Holocaust.

Our parents took over a farm in southern Poland, not far from our mother's hometown near Krakow, and were soon asked to train Jewish emigrants for the journey to Israel. They led a group of emigrants over the southern mountains into Czechoslovakia, where they separated from the group, making their way into West Germany. Our parents made contact with American officials, who made priority immigration arrangements. In December of 1946, our parents arrived, nearly penniless, in New York, where they were kindly housed by the brother and sister-in-law of one of the immigration officials. Their first son (Arthur) was born two months later. We heard many times that Arthur's first crib was the third drawer in a chest of drawers.

Our father did many odd jobs to get by. His first job was selling matchbooks on a street corner. For awhile, he sold shoes. He wrote articles for and worked in the print-shop of the *Forward*, a progressive Yiddish newspaper. Our mother took in neighbors' laundry.

In 1947, they moved to Los Angeles, where our father eventually got work as a machinist. In those days, mechanical engineering involved a lot of hands-on training in such skills. He eventually opened his own machine shop and was well-respected for his ability to make intricate products with high quality.

In 1950, their second son (Paul) was born.

In 1956, our father took a position in the machine shop at the Jet Propulsion Laboratory (JPL), operated for the Army Ballistic Missile Agency (ABMA) by the California Institute of Technology, near Pasadena, California. In 1958, the National Air and Space Administration (NASA) took over JPL as its preeminent research center for unmanned exploration of the moon and beyond. Our father manufactured components for rockets and communications equipment intended for anticipated space launches.

During the late 1950's, the United States was undergoing a controversial process to establish a government organization to build and launch space satellites. The ABMA and JPL were proposing to build and launch the world's first satellite, using a modified Army booster rocket. Instead, President Eisenhower selected the US Navy to develop a new launch vehicle and a satellite, called Vanguard. As history recorded, several attempted Vanguard launches ended in fiery failures.

Meanwhile, largely ignored by Western intelligence services, the Soviet Union moved ahead with its own program. The launch of Sputnik I on October 4, 1957, marked the beginning of the Space Race, shamed and shocked America, and put the Soviet Union on the world stage as a scientific and technological leader. It was also the day that our father's fortunes changed dramatically.

The Soviet success caused Eisenhower to give the go-ahead to JPL to undertake its project, called Explorer. Just 80 days later, on January 31, 1958, JPL and the army successfully launched Explorer I. That satellite carried a battery support structure built by our father in the machine shops at JPL.

Awakened to unexpected Soviet technological prowess and its military implications, JPL cast about for individuals who could translate mountains of Soviet technical, military, political and popular publications to extract intelligence. Our father was transferred to JPL's Technical Library.

Over the next five years or so, his technical and language skills propelled him into closely-guarded prominence in American intelligence circles. He became head of JPL's Technical Translation Department. He analyzed Soviet space and military programs and capabilities for NASA and the Department of Defense. He briefed Presidents Eisenhower and Kennedy on these topics. He participated in negotiations with Spain for the placement of a NASA tracking station, which is still in operation. We vividly recall news reporters interviewing our father at our home on the night that the Soviets launched Yuri Gagarin into earth orbit. He gave the reporters a tour of our garage, where he used short-wave radios to monitor Radio Moscow and other foreign stations.

Our father would disappear on trips sometimes lasting several weeks. On one such trip, which we had understood to be a civilian visit to Europe, he called our mother from Greenland. The plane carrying him home had had engine problems and made a precautionary landing at a military base. It wasn't until years later that we found out that his plane was a US Air Force transport and that he had been in Eastern Europe at a radio listening post during a Soviet space launch.

Our father had an abiding interest in space exploration. One of his proudest moments was when he received a citation from NASA for his analysis of data published by Soviet scientists after their first unmanned spacecraft landed on the moon. His analysis had formed the basis for engineering decisions regarding the design of the footpads on America's first moon landers, the Surveyor spacecraft series, and eventually for the Apollo manned landers.

This period of time, when America and the Soviet Union were locked in intense, but not necessarily overt, competition forms the background to the prologue and epilogue. One will appreciate the sense of irony and danger that never left our father's consciousness.

To complete the story, it is important to relate that our father left JPL for a company called Electro-Optical Systems (EOS) about 1964, where he did similar work under government contracts. After EOS was acquired by Xerox, he joined some coworkers in the formation of a new company, Data Dynamics, which lasted only a few years. His next step was to form his own consulting company, TerraSpace, which enabled him to continue his technical translation work under direct contract to NASA.

By the late 1960s, however, the American Space Program had entered a budgetary decline, and automated language translation was becoming more commonplace. NASA terminated their contract with TerraSpace and ended our father's direct involvement in the space program and military intelligence work.

He and our mother were forced to seek other income, and the only opportunity that presented itself was to buy a small bakery in a wealthy suburb of Los Angeles. Those were very difficult times from an economic standpoint. Laid-off aerospace engineers would come to the bakery door, begging for work, fearing starvation for their families.

Our parents owned that bakery for 12 years. The backbreaking labor and long hours took a toll on their health. The resulting loss of social interaction gradually caused many of their friends from the old days to drift away. In his later years, our father worked in hardware stores and furniture stores. He was always well-liked for his helpfulness and ready wit.

In the 1980s, our father was contacted by the Brotherhood of All Veterans Organizations (BRAVO), a group dedicated to building understanding between veterans of different countries, particularly those of America and the Soviet Union. The Soviet invasion and occupation of Afghanistan was nearing its end. American veterans of the Vietnam War reached out to these brethren, seeing the similarity of the tragedies they'd each faced. Our father was asked to make contact with a Soviet general to further the sponsorship of the group. This he did, speaking directly by phone with a general who knew exactly who our father was. His call was successful. It was deeply moving to see our father acting for peace with this former enemy.

Having been discarded, as he seemed to see it, by the American government after so many years of dedication and service was a turn of events that hurt our father deeply. He and our mother had chosen to adopt America, and he had contributed to the nation's supremacy in the Cold War. Even more poignantly, very few people ever understood the meaning of political freedom better than our father. Upon his death, some 25 years later, Dr. Eberhard Rechtin, a senior manager at JPL in the 1960s and later US Assistant Secretary of Defense and head of the Defense Advanced Research Projects Agency, would give a eulogy in which he said that our father had taught all his managers and coworkers what it meant to be an American.

Our family bears the scars of the Holocaust. War marks anyone unfortunate enough to encounter it. Genocide, the wholesale murder of your family, your friends, your schoolmates, and your community, is something from which no one can ever fully recover. However, our father once said, "Bravery in the face of death is common. There are a million stories like mine."

But in the end, our father's experiences teach us that one must keep self respect even in the darkest of circumstances. They teach us the importance of using one's intelligence to the fullest and maintaining one's will and spirit to persevere against all odds. That's the kind of man he was.

Our father passed away on May 2, 1995, after a battle with cancer that had lasted many years. Our mother, Adele, continues to honor him and cherish the 50 years they spent together. Having served under three flags, our father was buried with full military honors. His grave is marked with a simple stone, upon which are carved these words:

Joseph L. Zygielbaum
1919-1995
Beloved Husband and Father

Hero in War
Builder of Peace
Missed Forever

Arthur I. Zygielbaum
Lincoln, Nebraska

Paul S. Zygielbaum
Santa Rosa, California

September 2008

Part I:
Occupation and Escape

Prologue

Kuba Mordecai's face was that of a mild man. His dark hair was not as thick as it once was when it blew wildly in the biting wind of western Russia. His slight stature belied his actual capacity for dragging a machine gun through the mud of a Polesye swamp. His hands were those of a sensitive and educated man, but they also had held the gun that snuffed out the life of Steinbeck. Steinbeck was the man responsible for the murders of his wife and child in faraway Poland. A small gray flecked mustache adorned Kuba's upper lip and friendly, brown eyes looked at the world with tolerance and a slight weariness.

It was a day typical of warm, Southern California. The hot breath of the Mojave Desert a hundred miles away had already overpowered the cool breezes blowing in from the Pacific. Heat waves, generated by the warm sands rose like transparent serpents into the white-flecked sky. The San Gabriel Mountains sloped into the foothills so gently that ridges and gullies resembled the folds of a great brown blanket.

In the distance, a helicopter approached in its bright dress of orange and white. Closing quickly, the whirlybird turned into the long glide path that brought it over the exclusive Rockhill Girls' School. Drawing still closer, the craft made its long and circular landing approach which brought it over the waters of Lucifer Reservoir. The waters, ruffled by the propwash, lapped briskly against the gray concrete walls of the dam. The reservoir originated in the myriad small streams that descended from the Lucifer National Forest. The main stream often crested over thirty feet and occasionally claimed a life.

Kuba watched the whirling blades slow perceptibly as the helicopter dropped quickly beyond a great cluster of tan buildings. The installation was surrounded by a barbed wire enclosure. The structures all seemed to press against the hillside like so many huddled sheep.

The aircraft landed and Kuba winced as a loud shriek emanated from the rocket test pits high up on the mountain slopes. The blast was compounded by several locomotive whistles and a low-order explosion. The roar was caused by the testing of a small, two-pound thrust, rocket engine, a far cry from the six thousand pounder that was to follow.

The motor pool was at the bottom of the slopes where a large number of military vehicles were neatly lined up. Several mobile rocket launchers were among the standard ordinance equipment. In the nearby parking lot, many hundreds of automobiles stood waiting for their owners to return. The small foreign cars were huddled together in their spaces like little animals driven together by the behemoth American cars surrounding them.

The Missile Assembly Building (MAB) was in a central location among an aggregation of structures. Only a select few were allowed entry. On the asphalt beside the MAB lay several canvas-covered monoliths. The fabric could only attempt to hide the familiar shapes of ballistic missiles capable of carrying bombs that could instantly level fifty square miles of skyscrapers.

Adjacent to the MAB, the cooling towers of the great Wind Tunnels breathed vapor into the atmosphere. The mist was the only outward sign of the immense activity going on inside the Testing Facility. Hidden away in soundproofed vaults, the giant compressors howled and screamed throughout the day and night. The sound, above the level of human endurance, could not be heard outside, but the vibrations could be felt inside one's bones. The entire output of the red-hot hurricane machines was blasted through a twelve-inch pipe. The hypersonic velocity of the wind could melt a metal model of a spaceship in less than a second.

The Administration Building fronted the road that led to the main gate. Armed guards were posted at every entrance and in the halls of every building of the entire installation. Flanking the

Administration Building, coniferous bushes trembled in the hot breeze, resembling the wild hair of small boys.

The interior was a scene of sedate activity. The Director resided here, and together with his staff, did much of the planning that affected the nation's future in outer space. In an upstairs area, the Program Control Center provided the motion picture facilities, closed-circuit television, and color charts which told the story of each research program.

At the east end of the building, the Central Documents Control staff carefully recorded the travels of the most trivial classified document. In addition, the birth certificate of each new document spawned by a laboratory scientist was recorded here and watched until its demise.

Kuba walked to his office, which was hidden away behind a steel door in the Technical Documents Library. On his desk lay piles of Soviet technical papers. To his right, two dictaphones stood mute for the moment. He frowned as he considered the approaching International Geophysical Year Symposium. It was coming up next month, and representatives of the Soviet Academy of Sciences were expected.

Strangely enough, the Soviets had delayed confirming their reservations and Kuba had been asked by the Director to stir them into some kind of commitment. It should have been easy enough to pick up the telephone and ask for Professor Chertrov of the Russian Academy of Sciences in Moscow, and yet... It had been years since Kuba had last spoken to an official of the Union of Soviet Socialist Republics and time had seemed to cloud the old experiences with a kind of misty forgetfulness. And now, abruptly, the past cut through the fog with knifelike swiftness. He let his hand rest on the receiver. It had been the year 1941. Twenty years! Was it possible? The interval had not dimmed a single remembrance.

Another rocket blast from the test pits shook Kuba from his reverie. He hurriedly picked up the telephone receiver and asked the operator to please hurry his call to the Soviet Academy. "One moment, please," the operator requested, and then added, "Please go ahead. Professor Chertrov is on the line."

"Hello, Professor Chertrov," Kuba said in Russian.

"Hello..." the voice replied faintly.

"Can you hear me? This is Dr. Goldman," stated Kuba, using an alias.

"Yes?"

"Of the Pacific Rocket Laboratory in the United States."

"Yes?"

"We want to know if you plan to be represented in the IGY Symposium that will be held in the United States."

"Please repeat. I did not listen carefully."

"Can you attend the Symposium in the United States?"

"When will it take place?"

"On August 10. We have a telegram that says your people, Troyevsky, Stanislaus and Groyin will not be able to attend. Could you say whether anyone from your Academy will attend?"

"One moment, please." Professor Chertrov could be heard speaking quickly to another person. At last, he said, "Please explain which telegram you are referring to. I do not remember clearly."

Kuba took a deep breath and asked, "You do not remember sending a telegram?"

Professor Chertrov replied, "That is correct."

Kuba then asked, "Can we have your answer by telegram?"

Chertrov nervously attempted an answer, "...Today? We need time...because..."

Kuba still not understanding, requests again, "Can you repeat the last sentence, please?"

"At this time, cannot answer...already eighteen...late..."

Silence fell upon Kuba's ear and he stated "I cannot hear you."

More silence, then, the only answer was, "We will answer by telegram. That is how it stands."

"I understand."

"That is good."

"Goodbye..." then a click sounded. Kuba realized that the speaker had hung up. He took a deep breath and slowly exhaled, then lit a cigarette and turned off the recording machine. His hands were perspiring profusely.

After a few moments, the Director's secretary called and asked, "Has the Russian Academy of Sciences been contacted yet?"

"Yes, I just talked to them," Kuba responded, "but I don't know if I have much to report."

"Just a second," the secretary requested. In a moment she was back. "Dr. Crowden would like to speak with you."

"Hello!" the voice had a British flavor.

"Yes sir. I talked to Chertrov, but I can't say for certain whether or not they plan to send anyone. They're going to telegraph us, I think."

"Why did they not say one way or another? Did they not receive our telegram?"

"Yes...but...I think the fellow is afraid to say anything, at least until he checks."

"Oh come now. Surely he cannot get into trouble just making a commitment like this. You know how they keep saying they would like better relationships with the West."

"Believe me, Dr. Crowden. What they say and what they actually mean are not necessarily the same."

"Well...Keep at it and let me know."

Kuba hung up and locked his desk. Rising from his chair, he snapped the lock on his classified file and turned out the light. He walked out of the office, through the Technical Library and down the hall.

The participation of the Soviets in this symposium was of particular importance to the State Department, the UN and mostly to the President of the United States. It was to be a deterrent against the Cold War. Kuba found himself involved in a maze of international intrigue, which he was not quite ready to face. It was the year of the Republicans, and General Eisenhower was one of Kuba's favorite Americans. He was the first U.S. officer that Kuba saw after the defeat of Nazi Germany. He met President Eisenhower during a briefing he gave at White Sands Proving Grounds during the early days of rocketry in 1957.

Outside, the sun had not yet gone down and the white vapors from the city were filtering through the evergreen eucalyptus trees. He walked slowly to the parking lot and got into his automobile. Pushing the car's starter, he thought to himself, *Trees... how different they are from those in Poland, these dry and dusty plants thrust into the hot rocky soil of this California hillside.* He recalled the beautiful virgin forest of Poland, all birch trees and standing in water; where on the little islands of Wygon Lake a peasant could live out his life working the lush meadows without ever leaving.

Oh well, perhaps tomorrow he would decide whether to accept Henry McKeiver's offer to accompany him to Moscow. And, if he did, he might again see the Polesye and the Wygon Lake. Dr. Henry McKeiver was a young scientist involved in the development of satellite tracking systems, including radio-telescopes and antenna configuration. Henry was selected to represent the United States at the fifth IGY symposium to be held in Moscow in August of 1958. He prepared a sixteen-page paper for that occasion, and Kuba translated it into Russian. Kuba also gave Henry an accelerated course in the Russian language. During the last week of the Russian language instruction, Henry and Dr. Crowden suggested that Kuba accompany Henry to Moscow.

Kuba passed through the gate and waved at the guard in reply to the latter's salute. He turned north on Foothill Boulevard and began to reason about the trip to Russia. Kuba pondered on how he could even think about such a trip. Only thirteen years ago he escaped from that country to save his very life. Of course Stalin and his henchmen were gone, but the new regime was not any better. He was still his father's son and his American passport would not prevent the KGB from grabbing him on arrival in Moscow.

Kuba made his decision and tomorrow he would inform his boss. Traffic was heavy and Kuba was driving slowly. Memories flooded his mind and he recalled episode after episode of those past years during World War II.

Chapter One

While driving, Kuba thought about those first days in 1939, when World War II started. Every detail was vivid in his mind. It was on September 1, 1939, Kuba remembered, the day the world turned upside down and Germany began its march on Europe.

In 1939, Hitler had not cared how he fomented a war with Poland, providing he could get it started without involving France and England as well. One part of the dictator's hoax called for the shooting of a few Poles and dressing them as Nazi soldiers. The bodies were then to be planted on the German side of the border as evidence of Polish aggression.

At that time, Kuba was twenty years old and guileless. His young face still carried the unlined freshness of a student. He had graduated from the Warsaw Technical University only a few months before. His first job was with the enormous Lodz Textile Company, 150 miles from his home in Warsaw, and he was proud of his new position.

Kuba was a skilled machinist, trained in accordance with the European method used in engineering schools. Each candidate for an engineering degree was required to spend fifteen hours per week in a machine shop, welding shop, blacksmithing, etc. The training included the operation of engine lathes, shapers, milling machines and all other equipment used in the metal industry. After two years in college Kuba was qualified as a journeyman machinist. Now, war had come. What happens during a war? What does a young man do? Kuba hardly knew that he would launch upon a course that was to carry him to many places, through many a perilous experience and many loves.

Kuba's father was a member of the city council. He would know what to do. Surely everything would be all right. He recalled that his father had told him if war began the polish Army would not be able to hold Lodz for more than a day. As Kuba was returning home, he could see the barrels of anti-aircraft guns pointing skyward from many factory roofs. Printed signs everywhere proclaimed the fact that Germany had attacked Poland without warning. Kuba passed a brick faced wall on which a black-lettered sign proclaimed: "GERMAN AIRPLANES BOMBED WARSAW AND OTHER POLISH CITIES. THE POLISH ARMY IS DEFENDING EVERY INCH OF OUR SOIL. IT IS THE DECISION OF THE GOVERNMENT OF POLAND TO FIGHT TO THE LAST MAN." IGNACY MOSCICKI, PRESIDENT OF POLAND

The streets were becoming clogged with people the closer Kuba came to his home. The number of hand-drawn carts filled with household goods was increasing. Samuel Mordecai, a graying man in his late forties, met his son at the door. "Kuba, how is everything in town and at the factory?" Samuel asked as he embraced his son. "We were a little worried about you, because the son of Mayor Kwapinski was shot today by a German machinist from your plant."

"Oh, there was some commotion at the plant when the state police began removing some German nationals who started acting as if they were the masters of the plant and physically abused some Jewish and even Polish workers," Kuba replied.

Kuba picked up some letters addressed to him from a small table in the entry hall. His father looked at him with worry in his eyes and said, "Let's go into my study, I want to talk to you."

Kuba sat down in a chair next to his father and began to open his mail. There were two bulky envelopes. One was from the University of Warsaw containing his Bachelor of Science degree in mechanical engineering. The other was from the Ministry of Defense P.V. (ROTC) unit, containing orders for Kuba to report to his unit in Warsaw on September 3, at 10:00 a.m. He handed the documents to his father and lit a cigarette. He watched as his father read the documents. Samuel's face was tense as he read. He turned to Kuba and asked, "When are you leaving, Son?"

"I will try to get on a train tomorrow morning. That will give me a chance to spend some time with Mother and the rest of the family before I join my military unit."

Samuel got out of his chair, took Kuba's head in his hands and kissed him on the forehead. "Congratulations, Son, on your degree, and I hope that we will see you before the real war begins." Kuba embraced his father, kissed him on the cheek and looked deeply into Samuel's tear filled eyes.

Over the years Kuba saw his father only at intervals. His parents divorced when he was six years old. The times he spent with Samuel after that were always in the presence of his father's second wife, a known actress of the Polish stage. The divorce of his parents left Kuba with a deep feeling of bitterness, however he was too young then to fully understand the gravity and emotional impact on all people involved, particularly his mother and sister. He continued to cling to his father feeling suddenly that something grave and monumental was about to happen in the next few days.

Samuel Mordecai was not a tall man and did not possess great physical strength, but he radiated an inner strength and determination that could only equal that of a Samson. Even Samuel's strongest opponents could not withstand the stare of his steel blue, penetrating eyes. He was never told by anyone what should be done. Instead, he was asked what should be done, and he was always the first to do it. As a young man during World War I, he drank the water from a river believed to have been poisoned by the enemy in order to learn if it was safe for human consumption.

Samuel had risen from the depths of the Jewish people and reached the highest pinnacles of their dreams. Fighting seemingly insurmountable odds and without a formal education, he achieved the leadership of the largest political party of the Jewish people: the Jewish Labor Bund. Active in the trade union movement, he was elected a member of the Central Committee for the International Congress of Trade Unions in Poland. He was elected to the City Council of Warsaw, the capital of Poland, and later to the City Council of Lodz, the second largest city in Poland. Finally, he became a member of the Polish government in exile during World War II.

Kuba could not get on a train the next day. The German troops destroyed the railroad line to Warsaw.

September 5, 1939 was the fifth day of World War II, the day following Kuba's return home. The Nazi-German invaders were nearing the city of Lodz. The Polish Government ordered all men of military age to move east so that new fighting units could be formed. The only means of transportation available to Kuba and his father was Kuba's bicycle. At six a.m. that day, riding the bicycle, they left their apartment. Samuel sat on the frame behind the handlebars and Kuba pedaled, heading towards Warsaw.

"Father, please tell me what you think about the German invasion of our country. Is it possible for the Polish troops to withstand a German onslaught on our Eastern lines?" Kuba asked.

"No, my son! And if it becomes obvious that the Nazis might overtake us, remember that I might be a prime target and it will be up to you to save yourself as well as your mother and sister."

After a few minutes of silence Samuel spoke again. "You see, Kuba, we have to straighten out the front line so it will be easier to defend Poland. That means giving up the cities of Lodz, Lovich and some others in a straight line from the Baltic Sea to the mountains in the south. Even then, if we do not get any direct help from England and France, we will not be able to hold off the Germans for very long. They have built the most modern war equipment and we are still depending on our cavalry with their sabers to stop the powerful German tanks. Tell me, Son, are you afraid?"

"No, just very confused and worried about the events and our immediate future."

"Well, Son, this is the beginning of a second world war. Eventually it will involve the old alliance, France, England, the United States and the rest of Europe, including the Soviet Union in spite of their close relations and pacts with Nazi Germany. Looking at the situation as it develops from this moment on, I am sure that we will have to leave Poland because we are Jews." Samuel paused for a minute and then continued. "I hope that we all make it in time before it is too late. The old government of Poland failed badly and a new one will have to be set up somewhere in exile. By the way, you know that you cannot report to your specific military unit because the Germans occupied Krakow and all the surrounding areas including Nowy Sanch. It's possible we will find out something more specific when we reach Warsaw."

The land between Lodz and Warsaw was mostly flat and wooded with a number of farms and towns scattered here and there. Two roads crossed the land, both going towards Warsaw. One was the main highway which stretched from Silesia to Warsaw and the other, a secondary road, headed in the same general direction about three or four miles to the north.

Kuba looked at the familiar fields, freshly harvested. The landscape displayed even rows of stacked wheat and hay, like soldiers on a battlefield. Here and there, peasants were still tying bundles of wheat, looking up occasionally at the sky when the noise of squadrons of German bombers shattered the serenity of this seemingly peaceful morning. Then all hell broke loose...

The highway was a solid mass of people with refugees from Lodz and other cities. Most were on foot, quite a number on bicycles, and occasionally there were cars and horse-drawn buggies. Approaching the city of Lovich half way between Lodz and Warsaw, the landscape changed. A forest was on the left side of the road and an unharvested field on the right. Behind the field there was a green pasture on which cattle grazed. In the background a farmhouse was aflame, probably hit, Kuba thought, by a German incendiary bomb.

The stillness was broken suddenly by the roar of German aircraft. Flying over the treetops, they swooped down low over the highway and began spraying the refugees with machine gun fire. Screams and groans filled the air as people scrambled toward the forest and wheat field for cover. Hundreds of people were scattered over the road, most of them probably dead, and there were many wounded. Blood was everywhere.

Still bicycling, Kuba and his father were munching on sandwiches from a rooksack they had removed from their bicycle when the German planes appeared. Behind them was a troop of Polish Boy Scouts on bicycles, singing patriotic songs. The German plane passed and then returned, machine guns blazing. Kuba turned to the left and immediately drove the bicycle into a ditch. Lying next to him, Kuba's father held his hand. A German plane passed over them, "Are you afraid?" he asked Kuba.

"No," Kuba answered. "You are with me, and your courage somehow is mine."

"Come! Follow me, Kuba." His father got up and started running toward the forest. Kuba tried to lift his bike, but another wave of German planes swooped down on them. A Boy Scout, no more than thirteen or fourteen years old, dropped next to him, grabbing Kuba's arm and crying hysterically. Bullets were hitting the ground around them, sending sprays of dust into their faces. The Boy Scout gripped Kuba's arm tightly. Suddenly he let out a single groan. Then he lay still. Kuba saw that the entire back of the boy's head was gone. He felt sickened, staring at the gaping hole covered with blood and dirt. Finally, when the planes left, Kuba picked up his bike and went searching for his father. There was no trace of Samuel among the living, who again, were on the move towards Warsaw, nor among the dead and wounded who were left behind on the road and in the forest. After two hours, Kuba gave up the search.

Arriving in Warsaw at night, Kuba went directly to the apartment where his mother sister and other family members lived. There was his maternal grandmother, his Aunt Tamara and her husband Abram, his Aunt Hanna (Samuel's sister) with her husband, and his Uncle Rueben (Samuel's brother). All those people left their homes in order to be closer to relatives in face of danger. He told his mother about the events in Lodz and on the road and reported in detail on how he had lost sight of his father. They were left wondering about the fate of Samuel Mordecai.

Regina, Kuba's sister, clung to him and kept on asking numerous questions about their father. "What happened, Kuba? Do you have any idea where Father is?"

Kuba retold the events of their journey between Lodz and the vicinity of Lovich. Regina's beautiful face and dark blue eyes were focused on Kuba as she listened to his story. At some points she cried quietly. Golda, their mother, came into the room and started asking very pointed questions.

"Kuba, is your father still alive? What did he look like when you last saw him?"

"Mother, I feel with my whole being that Father is alive and making his way toward Warsaw. Last time I saw him he looked tired and very agitated as he ran to safety in the forest. That is all I can tell you now."

"Did he say anything about us before you became separated?" Golda asked.

"He talked about you and Regina as we were riding the bicycle. He even placed an envelope in my hip pocket for you," Kuba replied and produced the envelope, about which he'd forgotten completely. Golda opened the envelope and extracted two small pieces of paper -- notes to her and Regina from Samuel, as well as a number of U.S. ten dollar bills. She cried openly as she read the note and clutched the bills to her chest. In the note Samuel told her that the bills were actually Kuba's last month's wages from the textile factory. Samuel exchanged Kuba's wages into American currency and added some of his own for Regina and Golda.

The two women talked for most of the night, but Kuba fell asleep immediately. The following day, Kuba ventured into the streets in time to hear a broadcast ordering all men from sixteen to sixty-five years of age to proceed to the Soviet border where a new Polish Army was being formed. That evening, Kuba kissed his mother and sister, telling them, "Goodbye. I'll be back when I can."

"It won't take long," Golda, his mother cried. "In a few days you will return, and we will be together again."

Samuel Mordecai reached Warsaw via the secondary road two days later, convinced that Kuba had met death in the German ambush. His sorrow grew even greater when he found that Warsaw had been abandoned by the Polish government. His intentions were to continue moving to the east. However, after meeting with his old friends and leading members of the Polish Socialist Party, he decided to check in with the government officials of the city of Warsaw, determined to remain in Warsaw and take part in the defense of the city. He knew it would be a bloody fight. A small number of defendants would be hard pressed to fight against the mechanized war machine the Germans had deployed against the city.

The following day Samuel Mordecai met with the mayor of the city of Warsaw, Stefan Starzynski. They were soon joined by the leader of the Polish Socialist Party, Mieczyslaw Niedzialkowski who was a long-time friend of Samuel's.

"Gentlemen, we are facing a grave situation," the Mayor said. "There is virtually no military defense planned for our city. The Polish army is retreating toward the Soviet and Rumanian borders. The German troops are fast approaching Warsaw and we must decide what to do. The members of the government are already on their way to France and England."

After a long moment of silence Samuel began to talk. "Judging by what I have experienced on the road between Lodz and Warsaw, it is clear to me what the Germans will do to our people once they enter the city. We must defend Warsaw by all means. As you said, Mr. Mayor, there is hardly any military authority left here. Therefore it is up to us, the leaders of trade unions, political parties and the clergy to organize the citizens for the defense of Warsaw."

"I agree with that statement completely!" said Niedzialkowski. "I shall organize the Polish workers and the people of our Catholic parish."

"And I shall call a meeting of the other segments of our society, including the National Democracy Party, the ND," said the Mayor. "I know that this is not going to be easy. The ND has demonstrated their preference to the rule of the Nazis in former conversations."

"In order to give dignity to our people we must proceed with this plan and assure the participation of all citizens in the defense of Warsaw. If that preference is lost, then we may as well subside to the demands of the conquerors, the German Nazi hordes!" said Samuel.

And so, the leaders of the various organizations spoke at many mass meetings to the citizens of Warsaw. Fighting battalions were formed and weapons were obtained from the armory and the various military posts in the city.

Workers who never carried guns or any other weapons, suddenly manned cannons, machine guns, tanks and even small planes. They fought the German invaders in spite of heavy losses, until there was no more ammunition or any other means of defense.

Samuel and the other heroic citizens of Warsaw defended their city for twenty-one days. Finally, they were exhausted and without ammunition, food and water. They were overpowered by the German forces. The Nazis occupied the city, and the most bestially-planned, mass murder and genocide of an entire people began.

A few days later, the German Gestapo demanded of the Mayor of Warsaw that he select twelve prominent citizens to be named as hostages, responsible for the lives of the German troops in the city. Samuel voluntarily became one of the hostages. In their next move, the Germans ordered the formation of a Council of Elders or "Judenrat" for the Jewish population of the city. By that time, Himmler's plan for the extermination of the Jews in Europe was operating: the first step was to force the Jews into ghettos, thereby separating them from the rest of the population. After a few weeks of occupation, the Germans ordered the "Judenrat" of Warsaw to carry out the creation of a ghetto within designated streets and to enforce the resettlement of the Jews into that area. The majority of the Council, at a special meeting, decided to comply with the German request. Samuel Mordecai fought vigorously against such a decision, but to no avail.

After the decision was made, Kuba's father made the following statement: "A historic decision was made here. It seems that my efforts to convince you that we cannot make such a decision, which directly affects Jewish lives, were too weak. I feel I do not possess the moral strength and justification to participate in such a deed. Therefore, I hereby resign my mandate as a member of this council. I fully understand it is the chairman's duty to inform the Gestapo of my action. I realize the consequences which I will have to face personally because of this. However, I cannot act in any other way."

The statement made an enormous impact on the Council, and a new debate began. It was decided not to go along with the Gestapo order, but, instead, to inform the Jewish population of the fact such an order was received by the "Judenrat." Within an hour, special messengers spread the information among the Jewish population of the city.

The next day, over ten thousand Jews gathered in front of the Community Building in Warsaw, demanding clear instructions in respect to the resettlement order. Samuel Mordecai addressed the crowd of people. "Do not move voluntarily into a Gestapo-designated ghetto," he urged. "Remain in your homes until the Nazis remove you by force."

At the next Council meeting, a Gestapo representative requested that Samuel come to Gestapo headquarters the following day for a very important discussion. The meaning of this invitation was clear. Samuel Mordecai now had to go into hiding.

Two months later, by order of his party and the resistance movement of Poland, Samuel left the country, armed with forged documents and special urgent messages to the Free World. With enormous difficulty and many disappointments, he finally reached Brussels, Belgium.

Samuel arrived in New York on September 12, 1940, and began immediately to inform the American people and the Free World about the horrors in German-occupied Europe. On a speaking tour of the United States and Canada, he stressed the plight of the Jewish population in Poland and gave an eye-witness report on the beginning of the Nazi extermination of Jews. In a series of articles, published in the JEWISH DAILY FORWARD, he described in detail the life and suffering of the Jewish people in the ghettos and particularly in the Warsaw ghetto. The articles were reprinted by many publications. Kuba's father became the "ambassador" of the enslaved people of Europe and especially of the Polish Jews.

In the spring of 1942, Samuel Mordecai was appointed to the Parliament of Poland, the Polish National Council. He moved to London, England, where he served in the Polish government for more than one year. During that period, he conducted an enormous campaign to stir the conscience of the Free World, with the hope that special action would be undertaken by the Allied Forces to stop the mass slaughter of the European Jews. He delivered hundreds of speeches over the BBC and on the floor of Parliament.

He talked with Prime Minister Churchill, President Roosevelt and underground leaders of occupied countries. Frequently he addressed the people of Poland by radio, and he was in daily contact with Polish underground radio stations. In his special broadcasts over the BBC, he encouraged the Polish people to intensify their resistance against the Nazi oppressors.

On April 19, 1943, the Germans made their move to liquidate the Warsaw ghetto. At two o'clock that morning, SS troops, equipped with tanks, artillery and every conceivable weapon, moved into the ghetto. The ghetto awakened to the biggest, bloodiest uprising known to mankind. Although poorly armed, mostly with homemade Molotov cocktails, every man, woman and child became a soldier and went into battle. They had no hope of survival. Their only purpose was to show the world and the Nazis that Jews can fight and kill the killers. The main purpose of the desperate fight was to die with human dignity, not like sheep. It was the most desperately gruesome and suicidal struggle by brave men, women and children and comparable in history, only slightly matched by the defenders of Masada. Out of a population of over half a million, only sixty thousand people remained alive.

In his office at the Polish Ministry of Interior in London, Samuel was reading through the latest radio reports from the Warsaw ghetto. He expected to soon see a special courier from the Polish underground, Lieutenant Jan Karski. The news from Warsaw was critical. The fighters were dying everywhere, in cellars, sewers and streets. Karski reported the actual situation in the ghetto to Samuel with specific instructions from the desperate fighters to the outside world. His eyes blurred with tears as he read their message: "LET THEM GO TO ALL THE IMPORTANT ENGLISH AND AMERICAN OFFICERS AND AGENCIES. TELL THEM NOT TO LEAVE UNTIL THEY HAVE OBTAINED GUARANTEES THAT A WAY HAS BEEN DECIDED UPON TO SAVE THE JEWS. LET THEM ACCEPT NO FOOD NOR DRINK; LET THEM DIE A SLOW DEATH WHILE THE WORLD LOOKS ON. LET THEM DIE. LET THEM DIE. THIS MAY SHAKE THE CONSCIENCE OF THE WORLD.

Samuel Mordecai's answer was direct and extremely honest. "Mr. Karski, I will do everything I can do to help. Everything! I'll do everything they demand. If only I am given a chance!"

Again Samuel spent the next days trying to impress on the conscience of the world and its leaders the urgency of the Polish Jews. When he realized that all channels of contact to implement some kind of a rescue for the Jews of Poland were exhausted, he knew that only one recourse was left to him. The demands of his tortured people in the Warsaw ghetto must be fulfilled.

During the night of May 11, Samuel Mordecai wrote a number of letters, one addressed to the President and Premier Minister of Poland, another to the President of the United States and to the Prime Minister of England. His pen scratched across the paper, and occasionally he paused, deep in thought. "I cannot be silent," he wrote. "I cannot live while remnants of the Jewish people of Poland are dying in their desperate struggle. My comrades in the Warsaw ghetto took weapons in their hands on that last heroic impulse. It was not my destiny to die there together with them, but I belong to them and in their mass graves. By my death, I wish to express my strongest protest against the indifference with which the world is looking on and permitting the extermination of our people."

Again Samuel lay down his pen, pausing to open the desk drawer where his revolver lay. He took it from its holster and laid it on the desk, then took up the pen to continue the letter. "I know how little human life is worth today, but, as I was unable to do anything positive during my life, perhaps by my death I shall contribute to breaking down the indifference of those who may be able now, at the last moment, to rescue the few Polish Jews still alive from certain annihilation. My life belongs to the Jewish people of Poland, and I, therefore, give it to them, gladly. I wish that this remaining handful of several millions of Polish Jews could live to see the liberation of a new world of freedom... I believe that such a Poland will arise, and that such a world will come!" With that, Samuel Mordecai picked up the gun, determined that his tortured people in Warsaw must be heard. A moment later a gunshot echoed and he closed his eyes forever.

Franca was two years younger than Kuba. She was a voluptuous girl with an oval face, dark eyes and hair, his sister Regina's classmate. They met at Regina's birthday party in 1937. After that time they met on several occasions and their friendship turned to something more serious. Kuba became Franca's steady escort to all parties afterwards. Using his father's press card, Kuba took Franca to all performances at the opera, philharmonium and theaters of Warsaw. However, it was the outbreak of World War II that brought the two together more closely. Before Kuba left Warsaw, after his return from Lodz, he visited Franca's house. The family was in turmoil. Her father was at work at the newspaper where he was employed as a linotypist. Her older brother worked with his father and her younger brother was helping his mother pack and store their belongings. Franca's mother, an attractive middle-aged woman, opened the door for Kuba, embraced him and burst out into tears.

"Oh, Kuba, how is your family? When did you get home? We heard that Lodz has fallen to the Germans. There are some rumors that the Germans are only thirty kilometers from Warsaw. What will you do now? You are an officer in the Polish Army."

"I lost my father during a German aircraft raid near Lovich. I could not find him after the raid. My mother and sister are all right. I have orders to travel to the east where a new Polish army unit might be formed. I have to leave in the morning."

"Kuba, I am worried about Franca. I met some refugees from Piotrkov and they said that the Germans were raping young Jewish girls and placing them in whorehouses for the German troops. You are the only friend she has outside of us. I beg you, please take her with you. She will be safe with you because you two are almost engaged. By the way, what is your beautiful sister going to do?"

"Regina refuses to leave the city. She wants to stay with Mother and take care of our grandmother."

They were silent for awhile and Franca's mother cried quietly. Kuba put his arm around her and rested her head on his shoulder. Franca came over and put her arms about both of them, then she whispered into Kuba's ear, "Please take me with you, otherwise I might kill myself."

At home Kuba went through another effort to convince his sister to leave with him in the morning, but it was in vain. There was a peculiar gleam in his sister Regina's eyes at that moment— and Kuba experienced a unique feeling, that they would all be dead before this war was over.

And so, next morning Kuba and Franca left Warsaw. They soon fell in with some old school friends, one of whom, Velvl, had an infected leg. Kuba took his turn occasionally carrying Velvl. German attacks forced them to travel only at night. Kuba soon began to weaken from the poor diet and the endless walking and carrying. At dawn, at the town of Stotchek, Kuba and Franca lay down to rest. Franca rested her head on his leg. The sun was high when they awoke and the others were gone. They learned that their friends had taken Velvl into town for medical attention, but they never returned.

Plodding on, the tired couple reached the riverbank opposite the city of Brest-Litovsk, which was surrounded by Germans. The tide of refugees recoiled and turned back upon itself with no place to go. They heard a rumor that the Russians had crossed the border and were marching to the Vistula River. In the country near Shelekhov, the pair knocked on the door of a peasant's house and asked for food. To their surprise, the man provided a simple meal. The old man watched them sadly while the impoverished youngsters ate. "Unhappy is our land," he said. "The Germans are on one side, and the Bolsheviks are on the other. What are we to do, where are we to go?"

"Do you think we could stay the night?" asked Kuba. "We haven't had a good night's sleep in many days."

The old peasant regarded them with sad eyes, the wrinkles and furrows in his face deepened as he remonstrated, "The Germans are quartered three miles from here. They have told everyone that if any Jew is found in a home, the house will be destroyed and the village will be burned."

"What are we to do?" asked Kuba. Franca closed her eyes and rested her forehead against Kuba's shoulder.

"Well," said the old fellow, relenting, "there is a slit-trench in my courtyard. I dug it when the bombs were falling. You may sleep there, if you like." The pair found the trench. Camouflaged with a covering of planks and earth, it had all the aspects of a tomb. Nonetheless, the inside was filled with hay, which made it a little more comfortable.

The following days, Kuba and Franca were in the towns of Shelekhov and Maciejowice with a group of Warsaw Jews with whom they had joined. They were attempting to return to their homes. At the Vistula they saw soldiers blocking the bridge. Germans and many other soldiers could be seen encamped along the shore. Kuba left Franca and surreptitiously advanced until he was within a few yards of the guards.

"When can we go home?" shouted a civilian.

"When we meet our Kameraden, the Russians, on the Bug River," the guard replied with a smile.

"Then the war will be over and you can go home." The soldier's words smote Kuba like a blow. The Russians were not in Poland to help the Polish Army. They were allied with the Nazis. It was then he realized his great danger. The Russians would kill him because of his father's anti-communist views reflected in many public speeches and actions, and the Germans would kill him because he was a Jew.

That evening while Franca was resting, Kuba met a former neighbor from Warsaw who had just escaped from the other side of the Vistula. He told them of the nightmare of German brutality. It was the first report of the mass arrests of Jews and their summary executions. The dye was cast. They would have to proceed eastward and chance the Russians.

Back in Shelekhov, someone stopped Kuba in the street. He could not recall the man's name. "Are you Kuba?" the man asked. Kuba admitted his identity and was told his aunt was in the town. He and Franca accompanied the man to a private home where he met his mother's youngest sister. Kuba's aunt, Tamara, was about five feet tall, with long, black hair and an extremely smart expression in her black eyes. She was particularly close to Kuba, because as a twelve-year-old girl, she actually took care of the infant boy until he began his formal schooling. She had lost her husband somewhere along the way and was in despair. He related to her all he had learned up to that time. While they were talking, a German tank invaded the town, emptying the streets instantly.

"What shall we do now, Kuba?" Tamara whispered. "How can we get away?"

Kuba's eyes were aglow with inner tension. He looked at the two women with deep concern and came to a sudden decision. "Follow me quick. We are going to Lukov. It's only thirty kilometers away. We will make it."

They gathered their meager belongings and left the town through an alley and some unharvested fields. It was on the road to Lukov that Kuba began to realize his responsibilities. He was the man to whom these two women were looking for guidance and protection. His eyes had already assumed a new aspect. They reflected a little of the instinctive cunning of a hunted animal. They glanced continuously along the ditches of the road. They searched far ahead looking for possible danger.

Late in the afternoon a column of military vehicles appeared ahead of them. From a distance it was impossible to determine to which army these belonged. "Quickly, into the ditch!" Kuba said and led both women to the right of the road.

"Are those Germans?" Franca asked with deep concern in her voice.

"I hope not," Kuba replied as he camouflaged the two women in the bushes near the road. As the vehicles came nearer, they observed red crosses painted at the sides, designating a field hospital. The soldiers manning the trucks were dressed in khaki uniforms.

"That is part of the Polish army!" Kuba shouted and stood up waving his arms. Some soldiers waved their arms at him and the column raced on toward Shelekhov.

They continued walking all that day and late in the afternoon they came to a village. A large hay car stood in the center of the village and several soldiers stood nearby. From the distance, their uniforms appeared to be of the Polish Army, but as Kuba and the two women continued walking towards the soldiers, they were able to see the red stars on their caps. "Why, they are Red Army men!" his aunt exclaimed.

The soldiers stopped them and one, apparently the top-ranking member, asked in Russian whether they were armed. Kuba and the women did not understand the language, but, finally, they comprehended the meaning of the strange words. Franca and Tamara were pale and frightened. Kuba unfastened his coat and submitted to a search. After each of them had been searched and found to be unarmed, they were permitted to leave. The women were smiling with relief and they decided to spend the night in the village.

The farmer was about six feet tall, blonde with a heavy mustache. Kuba met him at the roadside in front of his farm. He offered Kuba and the two women some cold water, and they struck up a conversation about the general conditions in war torn Poland. "There are German troops coming around in the evening and checking the farm grounds for hiding Jews and Polish officers," the farmer informed them.

"Sir, we must spend the night here. We are on our way to Lukov, but it is very risky to be on the road at night. Could you somehow accommodate us?'

"That is very dangerous, but let me think. There is one possibility. I have built a bomb shelter behind the barn. If you think that you can endure close quarters for the night, I will take the chance." The shelter consisted of a hole in the ground, about ten feet wide, seven feet long and four feet deep. There was a wooden lid covered with dirt and grass, which hid the shelter when put in place.

The farmer fed them some boiled potatoes, and after that Kuba and the two women lowered themselves into the shelter, which was lined with fresh-cut straw and hay. It resembled a grave more than anything else. The farmer closed the lid and complete darkness encompassed the three tired travelers. Franca snuggled up next to Kuba, and Tamara was at the far right. It was a cold and rainy night and the three refugees were shivering under the green army blankets, which Kuba carried in his knapsack. It must have been past midnight when the heat generated by their bodies finally made it possible for Tamara to fall asleep. Kuba and Franca were awake. There were heavy foot steps above them and a

German voice asked, "Are you sure that there are no Jewish refugees on the premises?"

"So help me Christ the Saviour!" replied the farmer. Kuba and Franca could hear the barn doors being opened and a search began. It lasted for about twenty minutes and then the farmer spoke up. "Here is some pure vodka that I made last week. Enjoy yourselves, gentlemen," the farmer said with a chuckle.

"You keep your nose clean and you will not have too many problems!" the German voice replied.

The sound of departing motor vehicles broke the stillness of the night. Franca was not asleep. She kept on turning and finally embraced Kuba, her hands exploring his body. "Kuba I am so afraid," she said quietly.

"I know. I am also afraid and my brain keeps on thinking about ways to get out of this situation," Kuba replied as he began stroking Franca's head.

She cuddled up closer to him and Kuba could feel that she was shaking either from coldness or fear. "I have this feeling that the world is coming to an end, Kuba. I feel that there is no tomorrow for us." Now she had her arms around him, as if trying to hide herself from some danger by pressing her body into his. Her rate of breathing increased as she pressed her loins against his. "I know that we are going to die soon, my dear," she whispered.

"Oh, my darling, something will work out and might be we will be able to live in peace," he replied, not believing his own words.

Suddenly she took his hand and pressed it against her breast. Her lips were very hot as she kissed him on the mouth. Kuba responded and began moving his hands over her body.

"My Kuba, I want you now before it is too late," she whispered.

Kuba pulled her even closer to him, beginning to forget the graveness of their situation. She nibbled at his ear and began to pull him on top of her. "You think that we can do it now?" she whispered in his ear.

"Only if you keep very quiet."

"Oh, Kuba!" she whispered, and began pulling down her underwear. In spite of the biting cold and rain they made love. Kuba kept his eyes open and watched his Aunt Tamara, but she seemed to be deep asleep, oblivious to the activities that were taking place next to her.

During the night he heard voices...angry voices speaking in German. The farmer did not betray them, and insisted that there were no Jewish refugees on his farm. Finally everything quieted down and Kuba fell asleep.

Lukov looked more like a huge military camp of the Red Army than a city: red banners decorated the building, bonfires were burning in some of the streets and Red Army soldiers were sitting around them. Kuba and the women walked cautiously down the streets, staying in the shadows.

A large crowd stood waiting at the railroad station. There were people of all ages including children and infants. The pavement was cluttered with bundles of their belongings and some children were playing around them. Franca and Tema (short for Tamara) were sitting on their bundles, quietly observing the people and the Soviet troops.

Kuba leaned against a lamppost and lit a cigarette. Suddenly he felt a tap on his shoulder. He turned around and came face to face with a young Russian soldier. "Pan, may I have a Polish cigarette?" he asked politely.

Kuba chuckled at the word pan which means "Sir" in Polish and handed the Russian his pack of cigarettes. The soldier smiled and extracted one cigarette. He seemed the same age as Kuba.

"Where are you from?" the soldier said handing back the pack.

"Warsaw is my home," Kuba replied.

"That is a large and beautiful city", the Russian said. "I wanted to see it very much".

Kuba handed him some matches and said: "I have a feeling that you will some day, with or after the Germans." The soldier saluted and returned to his comrades. A group of Polish refugees were involved in a quiet discussion.

"Where are you going?" Kuba asked one of the people.

"To Brest-Litovsk!" the man exclaimed. "Haven't you heard that the Russians are handing Lukov over to the Germans?" The man's eyes were bright with fear.

"When?"

The man thrust his hands deeper into his pockets and answered with a shiver, "In the morning." At that moment, a contingent of Russian soldiers surrounded the crowd and ordered them into the station. It was already crowded with refugees. There was no room to sit, but once inside no one was allowed to leave.

After a two-hour wait, they were herded into some drafty box cars of a freight train, departed immediately and arrived in the city of Brest-Litovsk that evening. Brest-Litovsk, prior to this time, was a city of about a quarter-million inhabitants. Like Lukov, it now looked like a giant military camp. In addition to soldiers, there were refugees everywhere in all the public buildings and wherever there was space to sit or lie down to rest.

Kuba and the two women remained that night in the railway station. His glance wandered over the large room and took in the usual large clock on one wall. He noticed that it had been reset to indicate Moscow time and he observed two Soviet soldiers, each wearing broad, red markings on their caps, leading a few Polish soldiers toward one side of the station. He followed them to the door of a large room filled with Polish soldiers who, he later learned, were considered prisoners of war and were being consigned to special prison camps.

Kuba wandered around the station all that night. At dawn, he noticed a line of Red Army men at a station newsstand and he lingered to see what would happen. When the stand opened a half hour later, the soldiers clamored for newspapers. Kuba was amazed at their eagerness and his respect for them increased with this evidence of literacy. However, their interest was not in the printed word, but rather the utility of the paper. Each soldier carefully tore off a bit of a sheet, sprinkled tobacco into it and rolled it into a long cigarette. This ludicrous climax to what Kuba had expected to be a scene of soldiers wanting to read all the news about the home front, suddenly elicited an outburst of uncontrolled laughter from him. It could have been an invitation to disaster. Luckily the soldiers' attention was already diverted and he quickly walked away.

Kuba and his party went into the city the next morning and he met a few people he had known in Warsaw. The streets were jammed, despite the early hour, as the friends led the three to an apartment of a Brest-Litovsk friend. There they were introduced to a sizeable group of members of the Jewish Socialist "Bund." Kuba met two of his closest friends, old schoolmates, who told him about an astonishing event: they had arrived in Brest-Litovsk on September 19, 1939, the same day the Germans had handed the city over to the Red Army. An impressive military parade was held to celebrate the occasion, and a stand had been erected on the main street of town, decorated with red banners and swastikas. Nazi officers had stood side-by-side with high Soviet officers while first the Germans, then the Red formations passed in review. Military bands had played the Horst-Wessel song first and then the Internationale, after which the city was formally transferred to the Reds from the Germans.

A large group of "Bund" members were in Brest-Litovsk and among them was one of the best-known leaders of the party, Henryk Ehrlich. At first, these people felt free to do as they pleased, but that freedom was short lived. Only a few days later, the first large scale arrests of both Brest-Litovsk citizens and refugees began. The Narodnyĭ Kommissariat Vnutrennikh Del (People's Commissariat of Internal Affairs) or NKVD was seizing all of those known to have been Socialists. Also, the arrests of the Polish farm population, the so-called "settlers," began. All officials of the Polish administration were imprisoned and most of them were immediately shipped to Siberia in specially prepared trains. The owner of the apartment house in which the group had been living was also arrested at that time.

The atmosphere in Brest-Litovsk was fast becoming oppressive, so Kuba's group decided to leave the city, each independently. The next morning, Henryk Ehrlich, whose destination was to be Vilno, went to the railway station, only to be apprehended by the NKVD. He was never seen again. It was only later that Kuba learned that Henryk, together with the other well-known "Bund" leader, Victor Alter, were executed by the NKVD in December of 1941.

Kuba watched as train after train departed for Siberia carrying people who had made the "blunder" of belonging to the Polish Socialist Party. A large portion of the Polish farm population was spirited away to Russia. Many trains carrying refugees, who were going to the heart of Russia "to work," were leaving the troubled territories. All the volunteers hoped they would be given an opportunity to settle down and resume their lives as normally as possible. After the first week, however, most of them were convinced of the gravity of their mistake.

The narrow streets were packed with humanity. Normally Brest-Litovsk had a population of some 50,000, but now there were about three times that number in the city. Tamara met some of her friends, with whom she and her husband Abram left Warsaw. After a short conversation with them she came over to Kuba and said, " They are going to Kovel and Abram is there. I am going with them."

She embraced Kuba and Franca and kissed them. All three of them were crying openly, tears rolling down their cheeks. Tamara left with her friends, Kuba and Franca looking after her small figure, feeling completely lost.

Up to this point, Kuba's path had resembled that of a snail making glistening traceries with no sense and no direction, but now, the meandering trail suddenly stopped. They were faced with a choice. Should they go to Vilno or to Homel?

"What shall we do, Kuba?" Franca asked as they were munching on some dry pieces of bread.

"Well, that is a very difficult question. We must take into consideration the geographic and political locations and situations of the areas."

"What do you mean?"

"Look at it this way: Vilno is now the capitol of Lithuania, which is occupied by Soviet troops. There is a certain amount of liberal freedom there and some American welfare organizations like the Jewish Labor Committee, the Workmen's Circle and others are still permitted to operate. However, there are a great number of communist agents and spies there who hunt for members of the Polish and Jewish socialist parties. With my father's sharp anti-communist and anti-Nazi activities in Warsaw, you and I are prime targets for such agents."

Franca began to say something, but Kuba waved his arm sharply, closed his eyes as if to blot out the surroundings and continued. "Vilno is only a few miles from German-occupied territory. I do believe that Hitler will occupy the western parts of the Soviet Union before long. I would hate to be trapped in that mess."

"Then what about Homel?" Franca managed to ask.

"Now, that is a different story. Homel or Gomel as the Russians call it is located about five to six hundred miles east of here and about the same distance south of Moscow. Communist agents over there probably would not know about my father and in this respect we would be safer. However, that city is deep in Soviet territory and it will be almost impossible to escape from there."

Suddenly Franca put her arms around Kuba's neck, kissed him on the lips and said, "Oh my darling, let's go to Homel. You are a good machinist and engineer and maybe our people will escape from Warsaw and join us there."

So Kuba and Franca elected to go to Homel, where the Soviets had promised them employment. They never dreamed that most of the refugees choosing to travel to Vilno were transported to the United States through the efforts of the Jewish Labor Committee in America.

Chapter Two

Every click of the train's wheels carried Kuba and Franca deeper into the land of the Soviets, but it was still three days before they arrived in Homel. To their amazement, the Russians received them with a great display of hospitality. They bathed in a dilapidated bathhouse and then were treated to a dinner in one of the town's best restaurants. Everyone was friendly and pleasant. The inhabitants smiled at them as they passed. Everything seemed to be better than the refugees had expected.

Late in the evening, the group was called into the Lenin Railway Worker's Club, where the president of the City of Homel welcomed them to "free Soviet soil." He was a portly Russian, bold and with high cheekbones. He was dressed in a gray suit and necktie and he wore steel-rimmed glasses. He told them, "You shall live wherever you work, and you will be happy together with us all." After the president's speech, they were assigned to various factories. Kuba and Franca were sent to a peat works, located twelve miles from Homel. The peat works was really a tremendous marshy field, perhaps thirty square miles in area, where the peat was extracted during the summer and made into bricks. In the winter months, the bricks were dried and then used as fuel for heating numerous factory buildings in the city. Sixteen refugees were assigned to this peat-extracting plant but, because he was a skilled mechanic, Kuba was assigned to the machine shop as a lathe operator.

There was a village in the center of the peat works which housed the various shops, a store, a restaurant (cafeteria style), fire station, police and living quarters for the workers. The living quarters consisted of six barrack-like buildings. Four of these buildings contained thirty to forty beds each, where the single people lived. Two of these barracks were women's quarters and two men's quarters. There was no privacy of any kind. The men and women visited each other and often spent the nights in each other's beds. The other two barracks were divided into single rooms and the married people lived there, many with children. In addition there were several small houses in which the administrator and other high plant officials lived with their families.

The refugees were assigned beds in the various barracks. Kuba put his meager belongings under his bed in the men's quarters and went to check on Franca. She met him with tears in her eyes. "Kuba, I cannot stay here," she said. "These women are like prostitutes. They tried to get me to sleep tonight with one of the Russian men. You better spend the night with me here."

Kuba looked around the room. There were many men sitting on the various women's beds, involved in more than just social activities. The woman in the bed next to Franca's was a sturdy central Asian type, short in stature with black eyes and dominant breasts. She came over to Franca's bed and said to Kuba, "You are one good-looking Polack. Why don't you cuddle up with me under my blankets and we will find out if you like that skinny Polish girl better than me."

"No, thank you," Kuba said in his best Russian. The girl started laughing and turned away.

It was a most difficult night. Kuba hardly slept, sitting on Franca's bed and holding her in his arms. Franca finally fell asleep. At daybreak Kuba said to Franca, "I think we should get married today and obtain a private room."

"Oh, Kuba, please let's do that!" Franca replied with tears still in her eyes. Kuba spent the night with Franca. The following morning they were married by the resident magistrate. The ceremony lasted only ten minutes. Following the ceremony they were assigned a room in a barrack for married persons. The room contained a wooden bed and dresser, both unpainted. There was a sink with cold water and a two-burner gas stove. After they got settled, Kuba took Franca in his arms, kissed her on the lips and both started crying. It was a strange feeling for Kuba because he had not cried tears since he was a child. He suddenly realized the great importance of this step in his life and wished that his mother could have been present.

Kuba began to learn about Russian methods in the machine shop. The shop ran twenty-four hours a day in three shifts. At first, Kuba tried to produce products of the highest quality and to very close tolerances as had been his custom in Poland. The foreman praised him for his effort and he felt very happy, that is, until the end of the week when he received a very small sum for his work and could not believe his reward could be so slight for all his diligence.

"We are working according to the piece-system here," explained the foreman, "and you just do not produce enough." He continued, "Here in the Soviet Union, the methods are different from what they may have been in capitalist Poland. You will have to learn from the other operators how we work here!" Kuba was stunned. He told Franca the reason for the small sum he had brought. She looked at him in dismay, realizing they could not begin to survive on the pittance.

Kuba strode into the shop the next day with new determination and to observe one of the Soviet lathe operators. He stood behind a man whose production had been triple his own the previous week. Kuba peered over the man's shoulder and stared with amazement. At that time they were making bearings for the wheels of the narrow-gauge train that transported the wheel that carried the tool-bit into the metal of the peat bricks. Kuba watched intently as the man quickly turned bearings they produced and was amazed to see the cross slide move in and out with great rapidity as the bearings tumbled into the waiting bin. Unable to believe his eyes, Kuba picked up a bearing and placed it into the hole of one of the wheels that was ready. Any machinist knows a bearing must be machined to within one-thousandth of an inch oversize to fit properly. They are usually forced into the hole by tapping them with a hammer. The bearing he held in his hand simply fell through the hole in the wheel. He checked several more and found that they too fell through the hole.

Hesitantly, he asked, "Comrade, do you know that these bearings cannot last? They are far too small to fit in the wheel properly." The man laughed as he picked up a chisel. He made some notches on the bearing and then bumped it into the wheel with the heel of his hand.

"Ready," the man said with a laugh.

"But this wheel will be returned to us in a few days for repair," Kuba protested, disbelieving.

"That is none of my business," the man replied with a wink. "In the meantime, we'll make money."

Kuba stood silently. He recalled reading a news story telling of how Russian locomotives required an overhaul every month. Now, he could readily understand the reason for such frequent repairs.

Soon Kuba and Franca began to earn a little more money as they absorbed the Russian way of doing things. But a dreadfully cold winter set in and, as the months passed, the fearsome cold of Mother Russia began to steal down upon them; and in its intensity, grew steadily worse. The refugees, with their insubstantial clothing, were far too lightly clothed for the rigorous Russian climate. The only heavy garment Kuba and Franca had was Kuba's overcoat from Poland, still in good condition but lightweight. He was able finally, with considerable effort, to obtain some heavier material which Franca sewed into a dress, but their supply of both outer and underclothing was inadequate. As time passed, with only bread and flour to eat and the bitter cold, their physical conditions worsened. Meat was so expensive that only the wealthy could afford it. Soap was unobtainable. People traveled hundreds of miles to buy a bar. The resulting sanitation was far below any reasonable standard. Kuba made progress in his understanding of the "Soviet System" of production and his compensation had increased greatly since that first week, but they still could not afford to eat their meals in their own home. They ate in the factory cafeteria in order to save money, and even this slight cost left them with nothing from Kuba's weekly pay.

Every evening Kuba would go to work on the night shift at eleven-thirty and Franca would be asleep when he left. After kissing her gently, he would quietly close the barracks door and lock it from the outside with a padlock, lest someone steal their pathetically few belongings. One morning he returned from work at eight-thirty to find the lock on the door broken, the door ajar, and the room filled with a strange smoke, like heavy incense. He threw open the door and fell back before the nauseating cloud that filled the room. When the smoke had cleared, Kuba entered the room to find Franca unconscious. She continued to sleep even after he tried to awaken her. As the smoke gradually disappeared through the open door, Kuba glanced quickly around the room. All their clothing, his skimpy overcoat and even Franca's homemade dress, were gone. Even the garments Franca had worn the previous day and had draped over a chair at the bedside before retiring were gone. The tablecloth, towels and the few personal articles carried from Poland, all had been taken. Nothing remained of their meager furnishings.

Franca continued to sleep and when Kuba nudged her, she seemed to be in a trance. She looked at him uncomprehendingly while he asked her what had happened. "Please, Franca, tell me what happened here?"

"I don't know exactly. I have a terrible headache. All I remember is that I thought that you came home because the door was being opened, and then there was this terrible odor and after that I do not remember anything." Franca began to cry as she held on tightly to Kuba's neck.

Frantically, Kuba rushed to the factory to notify the NKVD representative of the event. In the meantime, the report of the burglary had spread through the barracks, and all their neighbors had gathered around.

One woman, a young, blonde Russian who lived with her husband next door, brought one of her dresses for Franca. "I heard some commotion early this morning, but I thought that was Kuba coming home from work," she said to Franca.

"Thank you very much for the loan of the dress," Franca said to the woman.

Kuba returned and the woman said to him, "Would you like some hot tea? I have it ready."

"That would be nice, thank you."

After a few minutes the neighbor returned with a teapot and some cups. She also carried a package under her arm. She poured some tea for them and then said, "I have here a piece of material which my mother sent me some time ago, but I am a poor seamstress. If Franca knows how to sew she might make a dress out of it."

"May I pay you for it?" Kuba asked.

"Oh no. We are all friends here. We must help each other when needed."

Within an hour, a large group of NKVD men and militiamen arrived. They spent nearly five hours interrogating everyone in the barracks, but they learned nothing. Having accomplished nothing, they looked quite bitter about not finding the culprits, and left, but not before they had drunk all the vodka Kuba's meager weekly pay could buy.

Now poverty really had them in its grip. Kuba had the work clothes on his back, and Franca had only the single borrowed dress. No one offered to help them in their sad plight and, of course, Kuba had to report for his usual duties that evening as though nothing had happened.

Franca made a beautiful dress out of the material that the neighbor woman gave her. She showed it off to the women in the barracks and they all liked it. Franca was quite skilled in sewing and she began to make dresses and do alterations for the women in the village.

Several days later, Kuba was summoned to NKVD headquarters, where he was brought before an officer. He could not believe that they had found his property. But as soon as he stepped inside the office, the Russian officer glared at him. "Where are the stolen goods?"

Kuba smiled, thinking the officer was joking, and answered in the same manner. Was it possible they had forgotten that he was the victim? "You should know more about it than I. After all, you are conducting the investigation."

The officer arose and pounded the table with his fist. "Answer when I ask you!" he raged, and demanded, "Where are those things?"

Kuba stood there, stupefied, unable to comprehend the man's words and trying to understand what was happening to him. The man crossed the room, came closer, and thrust his face forward, speaking rapidly, "You accursed people from the West! You think we are not up to your little tricks! You hid those things yourself! Now you make a lot of noise so that you may discredit the Soviet authorities."

"But that is not true. You people investigated this case..." Kuba started to say.

"Say another word and you'll never see tomorrow's sun. Understand? Now get out!"

Kuba returned home, feeling persecuted and disillusioned. Winter passed slowly and with the first rubles he earned, he bought a second-hand coat for Franca, making his own worn out work clothes suffice. He could detect a decided change in his Russian fellow workers. Their attitude towards him was as cold as the winter winds. There was neither sympathy nor assistance of any kind offered. The rigorous, icy winds of that bitter winter swept through the barren buildings of the peat works for many months before the cold began to lessen. Conditions did not improve for Kuba as he continued his work as though nothing extraordinary had occurred. He could not miss a day, for their very existence depended upon his unwavering attendance.

One day the foreman told Kuba to turn a small disc-like plate on the lathe. When Kuba finished the plate, he resumed machining the long shafts which had been assigned to his lathe, meanwhile observing the foreman and two workers at the end of the shop who were huddled over the wheel. He walked over to them and watched as the foreman worked with a pair of dividers on the face of the plate, trying to determine the location for forty-five holes in order to turn the blank into a gear. The shop did not have a milling machine for that purpose so they decided that holes should be drilled near the outer edge. They would then to use a file to form the gear teeth. But, try as he would, the foreman was incapable of determining the spacing between tooth centers with the dividers and the positioning of the holes.

"I know a direct and relatively simple method of determining the proper spacing," Kuba spoke up and the foreman gave him an ugly look.

"YOU know of an easier way?" the man asked with an incredulous look.

"Yes," replied Kuba. Then, using a piece of chalk, he calculated on a table the correct distance between the teeth. Returning to the gear blank, he prepared a layout, then with a center punch indicated the points where the holes should be drilled. Finished, he paused briefly, and then returned to his lathe.

In a few moments, the foreman approached him, as the other workers smiled behind the man's back. "What is your education?" he asked Kuba.

"I graduated from a technical college in Poland," he replied. Without a word, the foreman wheeled around and left the shop.

The next day, he stopped Kuba at the door. "You will not be working on the lathe. You are an engineer," he said, "and I have a good job for you."

Kuba was elated. At last things were to change. He was sent to rebuild a mobile conveyor, which was used to extract peat from the ground before it was shaped into bricks. His assignment was to design the gears requiring replacement. The machine was parked in a field about twelve miles from the shop. The thermometer there hovered at forty-two degrees below zero. Kuba had to travel by sleigh to the machine and, without gloves, his hands and fingers became numb. He wrapped some rags around his hands to ward off the cold air.

When he found the conveyor, Kuba reached into its vitals with his bleeding fingertips and the skin on his fingers stuck to the cold metal. In desperation, he tried to pick up the parts by holding them with the rags. He suffered miserably during those seemingly interminable hours of digging into the conveyor and recording the necessary data for the gears.

When he returned to the shop in the later afternoon, the foreman frowned, "You will become accustomed to working as the Soviet people work." Kuba knew that the foreman was punishing him for his humiliation in the presence of the other workers.

Time passed, and as conveyor repairs became his assignment, Kuba traveled in sleighs through the frigid fields to machine after machine, scattered over those snow-covered expanses. With only his flimsy worn clothes, no gloves, and hands protected only by the few rags he had scrounged, his situation grew worse each day. His hands toughened slightly, but his fingertips continued to crack and bleed. The pain in his heart was worse than the pain in his fingers for he drew even less pay than he had as a lathe operator. The bone-chilling cold did not lessen as he and Franca were slowly ground down between the glazed palms of Mother Russia.

There was a State holiday one day, and Kuba and Franca celebrated by eating in the shop cafeteria. An elderly-looking Russian, a fellow worker who was a blacksmith, sat across the table from them. He was about fifty years old and was dressed in clothes which were even shabbier than Kuba's, wearing nothing more than a light gray jacket over his overalls. His rough, red hands were so stiff he could hardly grasp the spoon.

"Comrade," Kuba asked in sympathy, "why do you not get yourself a sheepskin jacket to keep yourself warm?"

The man looked up quizzically. "My friend," he said slowly, "in the Soviet Union there are only twelve real sheepskin coats, and you will find them all in the Kremlin."

Kuba nodded. The blacksmith, he knew, had expressed the thoughts and feelings of the whole Russian people with those simple words.

As the winter season progressed, Kuba noticed that there were more and more strangers passing the peat works. He discovered that these people were refugees trying to escape from the labor camps to which they had been sent. They were like Kuba and Franca, whose fate was as bad and, in most cases, much worse than theirs. One by one, sometimes in little groups of two or three, the pitiful creatures would slip through, walking furtively and cautiously, trying to mingle with the crowds of regular workers. They were poor and starved, but dared not ask for any help or food. Many of them died on the road. It was easy for Kuba to spot these people, and without being detected, he began to help those that he could. Although he could not share much food with them, he often let one or two of them spend the night in his room. The escapees told him of their terrifying experiences at slave labor in the "Tayga" coal mines and in the timberland of sub-arctic Siberia. All of them gave similar descriptions of the hunger, the cold and the brutality of the Soviet supervisors. Like cattle, they were crowded into cold, barren rooms, furnished only with scattered straw mats so alive with lice that sleep was almost impossible. They were treated like prisoners at all times. Under heavy guard, they were forced to do the hardest of manual labor for long periods without a drop of water to quench the burning thirst which accompanied the starvation diet of black bread and cabbage soup. Torment and torture were the only attention given those who became sick with dysentery. One starved wretch described to Kuba how a friend had become sick with dysentery and could not lift himself to go to work. The friend's medication consisted of being stripped of his clothing and thrown into the snow to freeze. There was no doubt about it. They had been slaves.

Kuba and Franca now realized that they truly lived in a chamber of horrors. The stories they heard each day of the miseries of these helpless, innocent people would have filled several books. It was not hard to understand the desperation which drove them to try to escape, preferring to die by a possible bullet, rather than face the slow death which awaited them in the Soviets' refugee camps. They realized that, but for fate, Kuba and Franca could also have been sent to Siberia. They, too, might have been on that perilous road, risking death by the bullet rather than endure the living death in a Russian coal mine.

One night, Kuba held Franca's hand and looked into her eyes with despair. Without a word spoken, they knew they had to shake the snow of this accursed place from their feet. They had to return to Poland even if it meant their lives.

Chapter Three

From time to time, they received letters from Franca's mother, asking them to try to come to Lida, a small town in Poland, now occupied by the Russians. She wrote that many of their friends were escaping to Lithuania and from there to the United States. She sent money to pay their regular expenses and to clear up any debts they might have.

It was April of 1940 before they were able to obtain traveling papers. Conditions in Homel were growing steadily worse and they were elated to have this opportunity to go anywhere that would take them closer to Poland and away from the Russians. One dark spring night they slipped away from their room and joined one group among the steady stream of refugees, heading west toward Poland.

In Lida, there was a tearful reunion when they finally made their way to the address of Franca's family. As they took turns telling all that had happened since they last saw each other, Kuba could see where the tension, anxiety and fear had left marks on all of them. They sat up all night talking by candlelight. They discussed their present situation, tried looking into the future and digging through the buried memories of the past. Towards dawn, Kuba's father-in-law informed them that they could stay with him until they found quarters of their own. He showed them where they could hide if it became necessary. At the back of the house stood an old shed which had been used for many things for several generations. In recent years it was used by the landlord to slaughter black market beef. This had become common practice, since the war had caused such tremendous food shortages, and therefore Kuba was neither surprised nor impressed when he was shown the shed.

The blood-spattered walls and blood-soaked earth were, in themselves, excellent camouflage for the trap door hidden beneath the sand-covered ground leading to a damp and dark cellar. Kuba was not yet aware of the strategic role these and other hidden compartments were to play in the life and death of every Jew throughout Poland. Nor did he know how soon he was to have to use this very one himself.

In Homel, Kuba had succeeded in getting a work transfer to the railroad depot. He had brought with him the necessary permit and had no trouble finding work in the railroad yards. Franca, however, was not so fortunate and without a work permit, it was impossible to get work of any kind. They needed the extra money and were getting quite desperate when they heard news which seemed to be the answer to their dilemma. It was May 18, 1940, and the Russian authorities announced that due to the unprecedented population increase in the cities, it would be necessary for everyone to register so that new work permits could be given. They were told to register by nationality, address and trade so that each person could be assigned work suitable to his abilities. Few persons, he was sure, suspected at that time the true reason for this complete census. They cooperated quite willingly with the Russians, who, it appeared, were desirous of helping the workers.

The deception became all too apparent on the night of May 20. By this time, the address of every Jewish refugee had been made available to the office of the NKVD. In the early morning hours of this bloody day, Kuba's father-in-law, like all the others, was awakened by loud, insistent knocking on the doors, the sound of boots on the pavement and harsh commands to open the doors and submit to a search of the houses. Without ceremony, the occupants were placed under arrest and forced into the streets where all were compelled to march en masse to the center of town. Those who resisted or tried to escape were shot on the spot.

Kuba was awakened by his brother-in-law and told what was happening. He mistakenly thought that the NKVD were only seeking out young and eligible men like himself. At his brother-in-law's and Franca's frantic urging, he fled to their hiding place in the shed, but stayed above ground where he could see through the cracks directly into the front room windows. That was how he happened to see the police enter their house and, after a quick search of the place, push and shove his wife out into the night as they placed her under arrest. His first thought was to run to her rescue, but he immediately realized how hopeless that would be. He waited until it became quiet, then ventured back into the house where he tried to console Franca's grief-stricken mother. It was then that he decided to give himself up to the Secret Police, foolishly thinking that they would allow him to be with his wife.

In that one night, six-hundred-thousand persons had been arrested on former Polish territory. It marked the beginning of the mass arrests which took place throughout Poland with increasing ferocity and brutality. Thousands of old men, women and children were shipped at once to Siberia. Many of them were never heard from again. Young men and women, like Kuba and Franca were thrown into the old Polish prison and held for investigation.

There were thirty-nine men in his cell, which normally could not accommodate more than five persons. A single, naked light bulb burned over their heads, day and night, like a lidless evil eye. How many times Kuba longed to hurl a shoe at it! At four o'clock in the morning, they were allowed ten minutes out of the cell to go to the latrine— ten minutes for thirty-nine men! For the morning meal, they were given a chunk of black bread and some watery ersatz coffee. They split the bread into three parts in order to make three meals of it, and after drinking the "coffee," they ate the grounds. Besides this, they received only a thin soup.

After six weeks of this close confinement, they had become dirty, howling devils, their red-rimmed eyes glaring at each other like starving beasts in a cage. All but two of them were taken out of the cell. They heard a scuffling of feet and shouting of commands in the courtyard below their window. Through a tiny hole in the sheet of tin that covered the window of their cell, Kuba and his cellmate watched the activity. An examination of prisoners was under way, Russian style. Everyone had been ordered to strip nude, men and women alike and they were then subjected to a rough physical examination. God only knows how long some of them had been imprisoned in this hold. In the bright daylight, they looked like shriveled mummies. Their eyes were sunken and their hair as stringy as frayed rope.

There was a rumor circulating among the prisoners that their destination was to be a special camp in the Katyn Forest, near Smolensk. Kuba wondered why he and his cellmate had been spared. He expected an even worse fate, and shortly after midnight one of the guards came for him. His knees turned to water and he thought, "This is it!" He turned to look once more at the bare cell which now seemed like a haven. His cellmate and he exchanged glances in a silent salute. He was taken before an officer who was sitting on the corner of a chair, munching sausage and bread; that alone was torture to watch, for Kuba was desperately hungry. He could not concentrate on the officer's questions, but could think only of the food before him.

For the first time, he was informed of the charge against him -- illegal entry, a violation of paragraph one hundred twenty and something or other. In other words, espionage, for which there is only one punishment! What irony! A Polish Jew arrested in his own country for illegal entry!

Kuba's long confinement and starvation diet had conditioned him to the point of submission. He knew it was useless to argue. He was asked why he was an enemy of the Soviet Union, why he had come to Lida, what his further plans of espionage were, and so forth. Before he could answer any of these questions, the officer would shout to him, "Shut up!" Then he would hit Kuba with his fist. Finally, the prisoner was returned to his cell and it was now his cellmate's turn. They were subjected to this kind of interrogation almost daily for three months.

One night when his companion came back to the cell very near death, he whispered, "I shall not be able to stand it much longer. Please tell my wife and friends. Tell them how I died."

All during this time, Kuba worried about his wife. He knew she was expecting their child very soon, and knowing the bestiality of some of the NKVD officers, he prayed that no harm would come to her. If he could only receive some word of her but he had no chance to ask anything during his periods of interrogation by the officers. The guards only sneered when he begged for paper and pencil to write a note to her.

He found out later that she had been held in the same prison as he almost up to the last few hours before the baby's arrival. A last minute release enabled her to give birth to their son in more suitable, but still extremely uncomfortable surroundings. She was later allowed to go to their home but was kept under surveillance at all times.

One morning after Kuba had given up all hope, instead of another interrogation, he was taken before a commanding officer. He was told that despite his crimes, he was needed at his former job and that his employer had asked for a special release for his railroad worker. Kuba was told to sign a paper which acknowledged that he had received good and fair treatment while held as a prisoner. He could think only of his wife and child and snatched frantically at this opportunity to live again like a human being. He was assigned to work at the railroad depot in Baranovichi and was given his release along with other papers which made him a citizen of Soviet Russia, whether or not he liked it.

That is how one becomes a citizen of Russia. One doesn't ask, one doesn't sign a pledge of allegiance, nor wait a required length of time, as in other countries. One isn't required to learn the Constitution and Bill of Rights as in the United States. One is told to sign the papers filled out for him and he is then given a work permit, ration card and a passport and told that now, "You belong to Russia!" There are many kinds of Soviet passports. Each kind has certain limiting paragraphs, depending upon the individual's occupation, importance to the government, former political association, and so forth.

However, one is glad merely to remain alive as Kuba was that day when he walked out of the prison into the blinding light of day. At first he did not see his wife, as she was pressed against the wall and partially hidden by a bundle she was carrying. It was the sound of a baby crying which drew his eyes to where she was standing. He rushed to her, tears of relief in his eyes. Their embrace was interrupted by another cry from the bundle; and this was his introduction to his son.

Before they left for Baranovichi, Kuba received a few letters from his mother in Warsaw, her messages full of terrifying stories about happenings in the Polish capital. The Germans had set up a ghetto where all the Jews were to be kept as virtual prisoners, she wrote, and they had started raiding the Jewish quarters and shooting at random, just for the sport of it. She also wrote that many young men had been castrated and had died. There was no mention of his father in her tragic notes.

When he went to the NKVD office to get his traveling papers, he told the official about the castrations. "But that's impossible," he said. "Well-trained surgeons are undoubtedly in charge of such operations, and death is out of the question."

After his release from jail, Kuba learned that his wife's mother, father and brothers had been transported to Siberia. A mutual friend had received mail from them, so they were able to establish contact. The parents' letters told of appalling treatment and conditions. They had been placed in a labor camp and were treated like slaves. They begged for food and clothes to be sent to them. Later when Kuba returned to work, he and Franca sent them packages of food as often as they could, never knowing whether or not they were received.

With a heavy heart, they left for their new assignment. Their own troubles, coupled with tales of persecution of their loved ones and all their countrymen, gave them nothing to hope for, regardless of where they were sent. However, their spirits revived when they found the working conditions in Baranovichi to be much better than in Homel or Lida. Kuba earned much more money, and gradually they began to get settled.

Three new friends, Chaim Baker, his wife Bronka, and Symcha Zuckerkorn lived in the same apartment house. In the future, the fate of this group was to lead them through some terrifying experiences together.

Chaim Baker was about five feet seven, chubby and an accountant by profession. His wife, Bronka, was about the same size, dark complexion with dark hair and very attractive. They were both in their middle twenties. Symcha Zuckerkorn was a young man of about twenty with dark hair and a small mustache. He was an electrician by trade and very capable. Kuba had a hunch that Bronka was secretly in love with him. They were all members of the Polish Communist youth organization. The only problem that Kuba had with those people was the fact that they knew who his father was. However, as they recognized what the real

Soviet state represented, their beliefs began to change rapidly. Kuba was no longer in danger of betrayal by them.

Chapter Four

It was Sunday, June 22, 1941 and Kuba and Franca were having lunch in their apartment with their friends Chaim, Bronka and Symcha. They were listening to the latest news coming through the loudspeaker. Civilians were not allowed to own radio receivers, so everyone had a loudspeaker in their homes which was connected to a central radio station. Suddenly, the program was interrupted and the speaker announced that the People's Commissar of Foreign Affairs, Molotov, would give an important message to the people. Then the words arrived in the Russian language, which they had heard once before, when the Germans attacked Poland. "Last night, without declaring war, the German air force attacked our cities: Kiev, Odessa, Lvov, Brest-Litovsk, Bialystok, Vilno and Kaunas. At the same time, the German army crossed the Soviet borders and invaded Soviet Lithuania, Soviet White Russia and Soviet Ukraine."

After an emotional speech, Molotov concluded with the following sentence, "Our cause is just! The enemy will be defeated. Victory will be with us." The voice faded as military music filled the air.

They looked at one another in stunned silence as they realized that the strange pact between Nazi Germany and Soviet Russia was broken, and now as Russian citizens, they would once again be facing the ordeal of attack and invasion by the German Army. It was less than two years since they had gone through the same experience and they had not yet relaxed from the shock of the attack on Poland.

Military music filled the air. Kuba could almost read the thoughts of the others from the looks on their faces. Finally, Symcha broke the silence with a wry gesture toward humor. "Well, here it is again!" he said. "I guess we will have to start packing our knapsacks again and head for the marshes."

Chaim jumped up excitedly and said, "Don't be a fool, Symcha. You can't compare this situation with what happened before. You know the Red Army is far stronger than our pitiful Polish Army was. They will be stopped at our front gates. All that the Germans can do is to bomb our cities for awhile and then the Red Army will sweep through Poland and push the Germans clear back to Berlin." He paused as a thought crossed his mind. "Now, we'll be back in Warsaw in no time."

Symcha shrugged, but on his lips was a knowing smile. While listening to them, a thousand thoughts crossed Kuba's mind; he, too, knew that Chaim was wrong. Then he said, "I wish we had bicycles or something because it will be hard to travel on foot with little Victor."

Symcha crossed the room and laid his hand on Kuba's shoulder and said, "I'll help you carry the child, Kuba. Don't worry about it. Let's go for a walk and see what is going on in town."

An hour had passed since hearing Molotov's message and already the city looked like one in the middle of war. Most stores and markets were blocked up and the few remaining ones open had long lines of people waiting to buy whatever was available. They were desperately trying to stock some food for the siege they knew was coming.

Already the NKVD (interior security) troops were taking up their posts at designated points to keep order and to be on the lookout for sabotage. The place where the legal "black market" operated was vacant. Nothing was left but the bare tables and shelves. Building walls were covered with posters stating new regulations about blackouts, curfew, and giving notice that martial law was in effect immediately. All movie theaters and auditoriums were locked up. Some of the people were becoming panic-stricken and hurriedly threw a few belongings into cars, thinking only of getting out of town before the bombs started to fall.

The next day, when Kuba returned to his job on the railroad, he found even greater panic than in town. Trains loaded with retreating Soviet troops passed their stations with great speed.

In the afternoon, his foreman, came over to Kuba and said, "Well, Kuba, the city is to be evacuated and our railroad unit has been allotted a train to move all our workers eastward. That train will be the last to leave the city." The foreman looked him straight in the eye and asked, "Are you going with us or do you prefer to stay here?"

"Of course I'm going," Kuba quickly answered.

"Then," the foreman continued, "we are leaving at four o'clock in the morning, sharp! Be here, on time, with your family!"

Kuba hurried home to tell Franca the news. She started packing immediately. Victor, sensing the excitement, thought they were going to go to the park which he enjoyed very much. Kuba noticed that his wife was crying. He didn't know why, but at that moment a thought crossed his mind that they would not be together much longer.

They got to the railroad station at one o'clock in the morning, and there a painful surprise awaited them. The last train had already left the station at midnight. They went back home and as soon as they entered their apartment, the air raid sirens began wailing. They ran outside in a hurry, meeting Chaim, Bronka and Symcha on the staircase. There were no bomb shelters so they went out into the back yard, and hardly had time to throw themselves beneath a tree, when the bombs started exploding around them. It was a vicious air raid. The German planes dropped thousands of bombs all around the city. There were no military objectives in that city. The only object of any importance was the railroad station and a few plants surrounding it, but the Nazis mercilessly bombed innocent people. Kuba, Franca and their friends were overcome with hysteria. A frightened woman near them said, "Tell my husband I was killed under this tree," not realizing that if she was killed, all of them would be dead.

When the attack was over, Kuba and his friends left the city. They took turns carrying Victor and headed for Minsk, the capital of Belarus. Once again the roads and highways were crowded with refugees and again death took its share of innocent people. Millions died while attempting to escape to safety. According to Soviet statistics, three million soldiers and civilians were killed in the first four days of the German invasion.

When the group reached the city of Mir, some eighteen miles to the east, the strangest sight was a traffic policeman in the center of the city. Thousands of retreating Soviet troops marched through the streets and hundreds of vehicles rushed through the city at great speed, passing the vacated houses. Kuba and the others entered a large house to rest for a while but they couldn't find any food in the house and they were very hungry after the long march. Little Victor was crying because he was hungry. Kuba and Symcha went into the back yard and noticed, next to the door, a tree stump used for chopping wood with an axe leaning against it. At the far end of the yard, there was a chicken coop containing a half a dozen chickens. Kuba looked at Symcha and said, "Let's get one and kill it, then we will have some food."

Symcha opened the coop and went inside and the chickens began running around, making a terrific racket. Some of them ran out of the coop. Symcha succeeded in grabbing one chicken by a wing and then Kuba took hold of the chicken's neck. He was looking around for something to tie its legs. Then he said, "Symcha, take off your belt and tie the chicken's legs."

After the chicken was tied, they took it over to the tree stump. Symcha put the chicken's head down on the stump, and Kuba chopped it off with the axe. Symcha hung the chicken upside down on a nail that was sticking out from a post on the porch and Franca and Bronka started cleaning the chicken while Symcha started a fire in the stove. In a room adjacent to the kitchen, they found a metal bathtub. Water was heated and they took turns bathing.

Suddenly heavy shooting began on the streets. They could hear machine guns roaring and the explosion of hand grenades. They ran outside and saw that all the houses around them were on fire. Even a part of the house they were in was aflame. They made their way out of the city through the flames, narrowly escaping. Kuba carried Victor, and Symcha held onto the half-cooked chicken. They managed to get to a wooded hill which overlooked the town and there they stopped under a big oak tree. Symcha built a fire and began roasting the chicken which they ate and then stretched out on the ground, knowing that the Germans never ventured off the main highways. They felt safe for the time being even while in the city the German artillery and tanks kept moving.

THE ODYSSEY OF A PARTISAN

How long they had slept, they did not know, but it was still daylight when they awoke calm and quiet. Looking around, they could see the highway to Minsk in the east and it was loaded with German troops advancing into Russia, so that route was closed to them. They felt then that they would never escape the Nazis. There was but one road left for them -- back to Baranovichi. They cautiously went back to the city of Mir and found that more than half of the city had burned to the ground. It didn't take long for the frame houses to be swallowed by the flames. On the main street there were hundreds of burned and destroyed Soviet Army vehicles. Corpses were scattered all over the streets. Most of them were torn to bits and burned. The refugees picked their way through the rubble and eventually left the holocaust behind them.

About eight miles from Mir, the road was dusty and the foliage was turned yellowish brown, and on both sides of the road, in an open ditch, were piles of dead Russian soldiers and civilians. In order to avoid the horrible sight, they kept their eyes on their shoes, looking ahead only one step at a time. Bronka and Symcha were leading the group when suddenly they stopped and looked at something on the road. As Kuba reached them, Bronka fell to the ground in a faint and Symcha and Kuba picked her up and laid her in the shade of a nearby bush. Then Kuba saw it. Nearby there was a human leg lying grotesquely in the middle of the road. It was clad in a high boot of soft leather, such as the Soviet soldiers wore. Several yards further on was the limbless torso, flattened as though run over by trucks. To one side of the road was the head. Everything was covered by a heavy layer of dust and sand. Franca became hysterical and had to be carried away from the scene. They walked on in silence and Kuba was unable to get the picture of that scene out of his mind. He could not stop thinking of the soldier. He was probably a young boy whose parents at the time would be anxiously awaiting news of him. There he was: in pieces, unrecognizable, one of millions of victims of the German "Super" race.

Several miles further, they came upon a damaged Soviet Army vehicle containing the driver's body on the seat and two more bodies on the road. By that time, corpses, in any state, no longer bothered them. Chaim, Symcha and Kuba looked over the vehicle and found it was an armored car. Inside, they found a package of cigarettes in a box, helped themselves to a few supplies and proceeded on their journey.

The road led through open country. They saw farm houses and some sparsely wooded areas in the distance. Ahead of them, there was a bend in the road, with a few trees in a clump at the edge of the road. They could not see what lay beyond them until they came around the bend and there they came face to face with a German tank column at rest. Almost paralyzed with fright, they instinctively knew they must continue walking with no outward sign of emotion. No one paid any attention to them so they kept walking, looking straight ahead without glancing to either side. They were almost half way through the column when a German officer jumped down from a tank fender and stopped them by shouting, "Halt!" Three more soldiers joined him with their rifles drawn in readiness.

"Who are you and where are you going?" the officer asked in German.

Kuba stepped forward and answered in German, "We are refugees from the city of Stolbtsy and we are heading for Baranovichi to join our relatives there."

The German officer spoke again, "Have you met any Russian soldiers?"

"Only dead ones," Kuba replied.

"Open your knapsacks," ordered the officer. They obeyed and watched the soldiers rummage through their few belongings. They took what things caught their fancy, including Kuba's fine razor. When they finished, the officers ordered them to be on their way without delay. They expected to be shot in the back as they walked away, but fate was with them as the Germans were more concerned with what lay ahead for them.

Several miles farther, they were looking for a place to rest when they heard a faint groan coming from somewhere amidst the debris of dead soldiers. They found to their left, a wounded Russian soldier half lying, half sitting, supporting himself on his elbow with the aid of a bayonet stuck in the ground at his side. He was as pale as death itself and spoke in Russian, so weakly that they had to bend down to hear him. "Please shoot me," he said. "I can't bear it any longer." Kuba knelt down at the soldier's side and bent closer in order to hear him and the soldier saw then that Kuba was not a soldier and he spoke again. "I tried to kill myself with this bayonet, but I did not have the strength. Please take the bayonet and put me out of this misery and pain."

From where Kuba stood, there was no sign of injury and he could not understand why the soldier was so grim, but Symcha, who had walked behind the soldier, called to him, "Come here, Kuba."

Symcha pointed to the soldier's back. It was ripped open, a bloody, gory sight; a mixture of flesh and bones covered with dirt and dried blood. It was incredible that the soldier was alive and conscious. He was cut almost in half with his back broken and his legs paralyzed. The loss of blood alone had left him too weak to destroy himself, had he been able to move. He had been hit by a German dum-dum bullet, a flat-nosed bullet which explodes after entering the body, thereby ripping everything open on its way out and leaving a gaping hole.

Symcha put a cube of sugar in the soldier's mouth, trying in that poor way to comfort him, for none of them had the courage to fulfill the soldier's wish. They could only hurry away and leave him for someone else to find, who, perhaps could put him out of his misery. Not more than a mile down the road, they met three Russian soldiers and a lieutenant who were walking along with drawn guns in their hands. The Russians stopped them and the Lieutenant asked for cigarettes.

"Have you met any Germans?" asked the Lieutenant.

"Yes, about one hour ago, a German tank column," Kuba told him.

The Lieutenant thanked them and started to go, but Kuba spoke to the officer, softly, telling him about the wounded soldier they had just left. Perhaps he could take care of the matter? The Lieutenant cursed the Germans under his breath, again thanked them, and went on his way. In about ten minutes, they heard a shot ring out from the direction of the wounded soldier. They knew the soldier's wish had at last been granted.

The group continued walking the rest of the day and night, stopping only once to rest for a few hours at the river's edge. It was dawn when they saw ahead of them the bridge which was the gateway to Baranovichi. With relief in their hearts they hurried their steps. They did not know what lay ahead of them. They were almost at the bridge when they noticed sentries grouped in front of it and they could see the skull and cross-bones insignia of the German SS troops. From their previous experiences, they knew they would have to keep going without hesitation. The Germans were firing a machine gun towards the river, into the bushes and a clump of weeds. Kuba figured that the Germans were searching for hidden Russian soldiers but their path led directly in front of the machine gun. They heard a hoarse command, "Halt!" An SS officer stepped out of the shadows and looked them over, suspiciously. His eyes stopped at Franca's face. She had true Semitic features. Then the officer spoke again, "So, you are Jews?"

"No," Kuba answered immediately, without hesitation. "We are Polish."

"And what about her?" the officer asked, pointing at Franca.

"She is French," he lied.

The officer looked puzzled and said, "Show your passports." Kuba felt a numbing terror mount within him as he fumbled for his wallet containing his papers. The blood drained from his face, but with all the courage he could master, he handed the soldier the papers. Somewhere inside him a voice whispered, *this is it!* The soldier didn't even bother to look at Kuba's papers but turned to the one with Franca's picture. Franca gripped his arm and he felt her nails dig into his flesh. He thought she would faint. He didn't take his eyes off the Nazi. The soldier was taking his time and turning the document around in his hand. It was then that Kuba realized that this man could not read the Russian in which their passports were printed.

The officer said, finally, "Where does it state that she is French?"

Kuba pointed to the place where nationality was stated. In Russian it was written "Yevrey," which means Jew. "There it is," he said. "That is French in the Russian language."

"Jawohl," the officer said. "That is correct. You may continue on your way to town." They almost ran across the bridge, expecting at any moment to get a bullet from behind, but miraculously, it didn't happen. So they entered the city without further incident, but were still unable to believe that they had really fooled the Nazis.

Chapter Five

A great part of the city of Baranovichi had been destroyed, but fortunately, the house in which Kuba once lived wasn't touched. They had a place to live. For the first two weeks, the city was under control of the Wehrmacht and one morning Kuba was stopped on the street by a German officer. Then the officer found out that Kuba spoke German, and he ordered him to work for him as an interpreter. The officer paid him for his work with food. At that time Kuba's group lived together in his apartment. Symcha and Chaim found employment also, so they were better off than most. This didn't last long, however. After two weeks, the Gestapo arrived and gave an order for all Jews to move into a certain part of the city which was fenced in with barbed wire. Heavily armed guards were stationed around the fence. The guards were not only Germans. There were Belarusian and Ukrainian police in black uniforms as well as Lithuanian and Latvian SS troops. This was the ghetto. All Jews were prisoners. The next day they were ordered to put yellow stars on the chest and back of their clothing. In the morning, the Nazis came into the ghetto, selected workers and took them out for slave labor. Kuba was assigned to a machine shop which was managed by the German Army Ordinance Corps. The first few weeks, the Nazis paid wages in German money so they were able to buy food and other necessities on the black market.

Everybody worked, even the women. A neighbor took care of Kuba's son, Victor. They had rationing cards with which to buy food, but only enough to keep them from starvation. He made friends with a German Gendarmerie Officer who assured him many times that, in his heart, he really wasn't a Nazi. The officer asked Kuba to make rings for him and his comrades out of the brass from the shell casings and paid him well with food packages. His name was Alfred Gibke, from Heidelberg.

Alfred Gibke was in charge of the ghetto guards and occasionally he escorted columns of Jewish workers to their assigned jobs; that is how Kuba met him. Gibke was impressed with Kuba's perfect German speech and his skills as a machinist. He took an interest in Kuba and his family and visited them at home. He always brought candy and toys for Victor.

One night, in the first part of July 1941, a man came over from the nearby city of Nesvizh. He was wounded in the arm and told them a terrifying story. The day before, the ghetto in his city was surrounded by SS troops and Gestapo. All inhabitants, women and children included, were ordered to line up and march out of the ghetto. The Nazis led them to a special place behind the city. There the Jews were made to stand in front of long trenches and then the Nazis machine-gunned all of them. Only the last few Jews leaving the ghetto gave resistance when they heard the machine gun fire. They set fire to the houses and began fighting the Nazis with whatever weapons they could find. Several Nazis were killed. Eventually, everyone in the ghetto perished in that fight. Only a few wounded Jews, left as dead, managed to escape from the trenches.

The story told by one of those who had escaped, caused panic and commotion in the Baranovichi ghetto. Now, they knew what the Nazis planned to do with them. That same night, there was a meeting at Kuba's house. About eighteen young men and women were present. They decided to organize a resistance movement and began to collect money and valuables to buy weapons. Also, they ordered everyone involved in German defense work to steal weapons from the Germans and bring them into the ghetto. The following week they had several hundred members, but only a few rifles and guns.

Unexpectedly, one day in the first part of August, the ghetto was surrounded by SS troops. In the morning, the people were led out to work as usual. After that, the Gestapo entered the ghetto and selected three thousand old men and women and executed them outside the city. Kuba and the others could do nothing to help them because they were being heavily guarded. Kuba thought of his son, who was safe with the lady that was caring for him, hidden in a shelter built especially for them under the house.

The resistance organization now grew rapidly. More weapons were smuggled into the ghetto and some people even managed to smuggle in parts of machine guns and sub-machine guns. It became necessary to find hiding places for the weapons. Kuba and his squad, consisting of sixteen men and women, became engaged in digging a tunnel beneath the cellar of the house in which they lived. Some members of the group provided lumber, taken from abandoned houses in the ghetto, for shoring up the tunnel. In two weeks, they succeeded in building a forty foot-long tunnel which extended from the house to a concrete-ringed well. A hole was knocked out of one of the concrete rings, providing air to the tunnel. The tunnel was divided into sections for the storage of weapons, ammunition and food, as well as a shop area for the assembling and maintenance of the equipment. A long section of the tunnel was used as a target range and lighted candles were used as targets.

One day at work in the machine shop, a young Polish machinist came to Kuba's lathe and said quietly, "Let's have lunch together in the tool crib."

"All right", Kuba replied.

They were sitting on some boxes in the small tool crib and the Polish machinist kept looking around to make certain that there was no one nearby.

"A few friends and I watched the execution of your people behind the railroad tracks. There was a German newsreel crew taking motion pictures of the entire macabre procedure. Several Poles were also executed."

"I know about it," said Kuba. "A few people managed to escape and return to the ghetto."

The young Pole continued talking, after a short pause. "From our hiding place, we observed three or four Jews who were chummy with the Nazis. They were not executed, but returned to town with the Germans.

Kuba looked up, startled by this information. "Did you recognize any of them?" he asked.

"One of them looked very much like that old man that owned a grocery near Pilsudski Street." Kuba was thinking hard. There were rumors in the ghetto about some informers, and the name Steinbeck was often mentioned. Steinbeck was Kuba's landlord. "There is some talk in town that you people have organized an underground," the Pole continued. "I belong to the PPS, Polish Socialist Party, and we are organized." Kuba did not reply, but looked sharply into the young Pole's eyes. "You must trust me, Kuba, I know who your father is," the young Pole said, with a warm smile on his face.

The Pole, whose name was Stasiek, put his arm around Kuba's shoulder and gave him a friendly squeeze. The bell rang and they went back to work. Stasiek was a short man, about twenty-one years of age with blonde hair and blue eyes. He was an excellent machinist and a true Polish patriot. He eventually traveled to Warsaw to join his grandparents, and in the course of events, perished in the Warsaw ghetto uprising of April 1943, along with a group of Polish Socialists who joined the heroic Jewish defenders of the ghetto.

That evening, as he was leaving the shop with the rest of the workers, Kuba could feel that someone behind him was pushing a parcel into his coat pocket. He did not turn around, but went directly to the outhouse in the back yard. There, he discovered that the parcel contained a small caliber automatic pistol, two loaded clips and a pack of cigarettes. He examined the pistol to see if the firing pin was in place. It was, and he now knew that Stasiek was a true friend. He succeeded in smuggling the gun into the ghetto, and after passing through the gate, he turned to the right, across the empty lot, toward the house which he, his wife and son shared with forty-five other people in addition to the landlord and his family. The house consisted of three bedrooms, a kitchen and two outhouses in the back yard which were used by all the people in the house. The landlord, Chaim Steinbeck, and his family lived in the kitchen, which had partitions separating the actual kitchen from their living quarters. The other rooms were occupied by the rest of the assigned people. The walls of these rooms were lined with three tiers of bunks for sleeping, and from the center of the ceiling, a contraption extended that resembled an anchor. This was used for hanging their clothing at night because there was no room anywhere else.

Chaim Steinbeck was a tall man with a bald head who was nearsighted. He had on steel-rimmed glasses, which enlarged his eyes in a grotesque way. His eyes were shifty and he never looked into other people's eyes when talking to them. He always carried a short pencil behind his left ear like a typical small town grocer. He had long sideburns, which he twisted between his fingers when talking.

Steinbeck retrieved a huge amount of saccharine and candy from his store, and was doing a thriving business among the people of the ghetto with those items. He accepted only jewelry, gold or American dollars as payment which he sealed in tin cans and buried in the cellar.

Kuba met with the leaders of the ghetto underground that evening in the courtyard behind his house. He reported on the events at the machine shop.

"And so, the Polish underground made contact with us and here is their calling card," he said as he produced the pistol given to him by Stasiek.

"That is encouraging," said Stolovitski, "but we must be very careful." Stolovitski was a young man, about 23. He had black, curly hair and a small mustache. He was about five feet eight inches tall, lean and muscular. His dark eyes were penetrating and demonstrated continuous alertness. He had a good sense of humor and was very decisive, a born leader.

At that moment, there was a noise coming from the open doorway of the house. For a moment Kuba got a glimpse of Steinbeck's face, and then it was quiet. Kuba, pistol in hand, ran through the doorway followed by two other members of the group. They noticed Steinbeck descending the stairs into the cellar. "Do you suppose that he overheard our conversation?" Stolovitski asked.

"He may have. By the way, there is some talk in town that Steinbeck might be one of a number of informers in the ghetto."

"We must take some measures to discourage anyone from informing the Germans about our activities," said Stolovitski, and the meeting broke up.

During the following week, two informers were mysteriously shot to death as they were meeting with their Gestapo contact. In reprisal, the Germans executed twenty young men and women near the ghetto gate. The guards were doubled around the ghetto and everyone was searched when passing through the gate.

And so came the day of October 9, 1941.

They had practiced shooting in their bunker the night before. The men who were in charge of hiding the weapons overlooked three rifles which were leaning against the wall of the bunker. When Kuba went to work in the morning in the machine shop, as usual, it was raining. At the shop he took off his overcoat with the yellow stars on it and hung it up on the wall and began to do his work on the lathe. It was about nine-thirty in the morning when the door suddenly opened and Alfred Gibke, Gendarmerie Officer, came running toward him. "Kuba, follow me immediately." He looked at Gibke with surprise for a moment, and then reached for his coat, but Gibke stopped him. "There is no time! Hurry up!"

Kuba became frightened and followed Gibke to his car where Gibke's dog, a huge German shepherd, was in the back seat. They drove away immediately and when they came to the next corner Gibke cried out, "Look behind!"

Kuba turned his head. In front of the machine shop they had just left, four SS trucks loaded with troops had stopped. Some of them were jumping from the trucks and running to the entrance. Gibke speeded up the car and after awhile said, "They were after you, Kuba."

"Why?" asked Kuba.

"I'll tell you later— be patient." After half an hour of driving, Gibke stopped in front of his residence. It was an old, Polish estate, hidden by an abundance of trees. He took Kuba into a room and locked the door behind them. Kuba's heart was pounding violently while he awaited Gibke's explanation. Thousands of thoughts crossed his mind. Finally, Gibke began to talk.

"Last night, your landlord Steinbeck brought over three rifles to the ghetto guard and told them that he had found them in the bunker built under his cellar. He said that they belonged to you. The guards searched the bunker but could not find anything else. After that, the officer in charge of the guards came to my office and reported everything to me. It was my duty to inform the Gestapo immediately, but I held it up until half an hour ago when I left my office. Now you are safe here, I'll bring you some food, and you are to stay here all day. In the meantime, I'll think of a way to save you."

"But what about my wife and Victor? Will they be all right?" Gibke did not answer. He looked away from Kuba, but could not hide the anguish on his face. Without an answer, Gibke left the room and locked the door behind him, leaving Kuba alone with his thoughts and the dog, named Printz. In his imagination he saw the worst and paced the floor all day.

At about eight o'clock in the evening, Gibke returned and asked him to sit down, and began to speak. "Kuba, this will probably be the darkest day in your life. There is only one thing I can do for you and that is to help you escape. According to the reports I am receiving, there are Polish partisans in a forest about fifty kilometers south of Baranovichi. I know that you have more weapons hidden in your bunker. If I can get you to the ghetto, you can organize a group for the number of rifles you have, and I'll help you to get out. Then, you'll be on your own to try to join those partisans in the woods."

Gibke left the room for awhile and when he returned he was carrying a heavy knapsack.

"Here is some food and clothing for you." Kuba looked at the items placed before him and could not believe what he saw. Gibke took out of his pocket a nine millimeter automatic pistol and three boxes of ammunition. "This is for you. Remember, you are not to be caught alive, that is why I am giving you this gun, and remember, you have never heard the name of Alfred Gibke. Now, let's go."

Alfred Gibke was a middle-aged German chemist, graduated from Heidelberg University. His father was a member of the Communist Party since the Weimar Republic in the early twenties.

Alfred was married, but he lost his wife and two children at the hands of some Nazi hoodlums, who claimed that he was Jewish.[1] He was drafted into the Wermacht in 1939 and participated in the campaign against Poland and Russia. When he met Kuba at the machine shop in Baranovichi, he immediately became very friendly and said to Kuba, "I want you to know that in spite of the fact that you are Jewish, I wish that I could help you, because in spite of the fact that I am a German, I am not a Nazi. I hope that you will believe me and I shall prove that to you."

"I believe you, Feldwebel, and I am inclined to trust you," Kuba replied. And thus a friendship developed between the two opposite victims of the Nazi regime.

It was a stormy night and the streets were flooded and muddy from the rain. The car stopped in front of the ghetto and Gibke and Kuba went inside. When they turned at the next corner, Gibke told him to go after his comrades and that he would wait for him here. Kuba located sixteen of his comrades, including two women, and told them where to meet him within the next half hour and then he returned to where he had left Gibke and together they went to the house where he had left his wife and son.

All around them, a man-hunt was going on in the dark streets of the ghetto. They could hear the sound of machine-gun fire and of running in heavy boots. They kept to the shadows and the dark doorways on the way to Kuba's house.

How can one explain, sanely, what they found there? In reporting the incident to the Free World, one would have called it a German atrocity; a houseful of innocents, including a baby — shot in reprisal. For Kuba, it meant the parting of darkness to look into the profoundest depths of hell, beyond all pain. The bitter anger, the blind hatred and hopeless revulsion he felt when he saw the small body of his son lying on the ground amidst the dead bodies of every tenant of the house, can no longer be put into words to express what he felt. He carried his son, Victor, to a small clearing and dug a shallow grave for him. Gibke helped then he carved a

---

[1] In the original text, a few pages after this remark, there is reference to Gibke's family as if they were still living. It was unclear if Gibke was married a second time and had a new family or if the text was referring to the family that he lost. –ED.

crude wooden marker, as he spoke softly to Kuba: "You'll come back and find it after the war."[2]

Searchlights began crossing their bright scissor-like beams over their heads. Kuba turned and walked rapidly back to his house, with Gibke at his heels. A single light was burning in the kitchen when he burst into the room through the back door. Steinbeck was seated at a table, calmly eating his supper. Kuba would have shot him on the spot, but, Gibke grabbed his arms from behind and said into his ear, "Kuba, Kuba don't be a fool! Not now!"

Seeing him in the company of a German officer, Steinbeck thought that Kuba was a prisoner and stood up, shouting, "That's the Jew who concealed the weapons!"

In Polish, grinding the words out between his teeth, Kuba told Steinbeck, "Some day I will return and everything will be paid. You will die a miserable death."

Gibke was still squeezing Kuba's arm when they were outside in the rain. They walked for a while and then Gibke said, "I would really hate to be in Steinbeck's shoes whenever you catch up with him." All that time Gibke was holding Kuba's right wrist in his grip. Finally he let go and produced from his pocket a pair of wire cutters. "I will remove the guard from the southern part of the fence for a period of twenty minutes. I hope that you will be out of the ghetto by then. I also hope that if we survive this madness you will contact me at my home in Heidelberg.

Kuba found his comrades and he told them to wait for him. There were sixteen of them, two women and fourteen men. They had removed sixteen rifles and a number of hand grenades as well as ammunition from the cellar. "Let's go!" he said, and they moved toward the southern fence of the ghetto. Kuba looked around and then said, "Here, Rotman, cut the wires!"

Rotman returned after awhile and said, "I cut a big hole in the fence. It's funny, there are no guards outside!" It was quiet except for the pounding rain. They left the ghetto, following a narrow

---

[2] The details of Franca's death are unknown. There are references to her being hanged throughout the text, but the author never reveals in the text how he learned of this or if he has imagined it because he doesn't know what happened to her. The family reports that Gibke told him she was hanged. –ED.

road which led south towards a thick forest. When they passed the city limits, Kuba looked back and became overwhelmed with grief.

"My life and everything I loved is buried there. Some day I will return and take revenge!"

The rain increased and lightning crashed with its pointed arrows all around them, an ominous mirror of his own thoughts.

Part II:
Into the Forest

Chapter Six

Sun rays filtered by low-hanging branches of willow and birch trees illuminated a large clearing among the expanse of the Polesye marshes of eastern Poland. A narrow trail crossed the clearing from north to south. Deer were grazing to one side of the trail and several rabbits were hopping around. A pack of wolves was hiding behind the trees on the north, observing the deer intensely. The leader of the pack, a large, gray wolf, began to move towards the deer. The others followed quietly, their heads low and eyes riveted to the prey. Sensing the danger, the deer raised their heads and sniffed the air. The sound of breaking twigs startled the deer and they sprinted off into the surrounding trees, closely followed by the wolves.

Kuba and his group of resistance fighters entered the clearing. Weary from their long journey, they looked around cautiously, yearning for some rest. "Let's rest here," Kuba said, his eyes scanning the surrounding trees. He removed his rucksack, put it on the ground and then checked his rifle. His companions sat or stretched on the grass. Kuba looked at the sky. The sun was up in the eastern sky. It was midmorning. He turned to the group and said, "We will rest here for a few hours. Noah and Jacob take up guard positions at the ends of the trail. You, Rotman, come with me. We will scout around the area."

Kuba and Rotman followed the trail to the south for about fifteen minutes. Except for the sounds of birds and occasionally animals, nothing disturbed the quiet of the marshes. The trail turned slightly west and led up to a small hill. In the center of the hill stood a topographical wooden marker, about twenty five feet high. It was a tower with a platform on the top. "We can climb up there and see the whole surrounding area," Rotman said.

"Good idea," Kuba replied. Standing on the platform the two men studied the panorama of the Polesye marshland. It was a sea of green, shimmering water covered by thick foliage and trees and stretching for miles and miles in all directions. Kuba unfolded his map and with the help of his compass he began to orient himself.

"Where are we?" Rotman asked.

"Look over there, to the south, that long line of pine trees. There is a village. I can see a church steeple glittering in the sun. That must be the village of Luki, according to this map. It is actually a large island on the swamp."

"Look over there, to the left, there is another island," Rotman said.

The Polesye marshes cover several hundred square miles, extending from the area of Pinsk in Poland into Belarus and the Ukraine. Seen from a distance, the type of terrain could be determined. Pine, spruce and poplars indicated a higher elevation, dry forests and possibly villages and farms. Birch, maple, willows and other leafy trees indicated the presence of water and swamps. The two men returned to the clearing and joined the rest of the group for a meal of bread and cheese. Their food supply was very low and Sonia, one of the girls, mentioned that during the meal. Kuba thought about it and said, "We can do some hunting for food quietly and safely here." There was a rich abundance of animals, birds and fish in the forests and meadows. Herds of elk, deer and packs of wolves and wild boar were roaming freely through out the area. Occasionally, brown bears and more rarely bison, called zhubr in Polish, appeared. The bison were dislodged from their natural habitat in the not too distant Belovezh wilderness by numerous German hunting parties. Of course, there were rodents, from squirrels and rabbits to field mice and swamp rats. There were also a variety of snakes, but only one, the zhmiya, was poisonous.

It was to this dangerous and primitive area that Kuba's small group headed. They moved silently through the woods, with Kuba in front. He had a map and compass and with these items they found their way south. After three days and nights of walking, they crossed the Brest-Moscow highway without detection or serious incidents. They avoided the villages and towns on their way, because, at that time, the Germans were still very sure of themselves. There were attachments of pro-Nazi Belarusians patrolling the villages. That is why Kuba's group avoided meeting people.

Several miles south of the highway, there was a village by the name of Tuchoviche. At that village one of the largest swampy forests of Polesye began. Kuba's group circled around the village and entered the forest. Their journey became more difficult with each step, as their feet sank several inches into the swampy ground. Thus they traveled until dawn.

Completely exhausted, they stopped to rest in a pine forest. Two men were posted as guards, while Israel Laxin took up a position about a half mile from the camp in the direction of the village and Lazar Shuster, a forty-five year-old, heavy set man, took up a position in the other direction. The two women, Sonia Laxin, sister of Israel, and Esther Miller, began to prepare a meal.

In contrast with brother Israel, Sonia Laxin was a chubby girl, about eighteen with a pleasant, freckled face which always seemed to be smiling. Esther Miller was somewhat older with blonde hair and a prominent nose. The two women kept to themselves most of the time. Now they all faced a serious problem. They had very little food with them. Kuba worried about what they would eat tomorrow. He decided to talk it over with the group. They built a small fire and sat around it. Kuba could see the anxiety, apprehension and uncertainty of their destiny in their eyes. They were sitting silently, looking at Kuba, and he felt the burden of being responsible for all of them. Their fate lay in his hands. He looked into the face of each one sitting there by the fire, the red reflections of the fire's flames dancing on their faces. The youngest was sixteen-year-old Jacob Geler. The oldest was Isaack Banchick, about fifty, and then there was Noah Rotman, Osherovski, Henry Lato, Elie Miller and his wife Esther, Sonia and the rest of them, whose names have been forgotten. They discussed their critical food situation and the most logical plan was suggested by Rotman, "I think that we will have to try to buy food from the peasants tonight."

"And what if the police are there?" asked Lazar.

"We'll have to investigate first," Rotman answered.

THE ODYSSEY OF A PARTISAN

Kuba was listening to them, and all of a sudden it became clear to him what they must do. "We'll have to wait until daylight. Then, three of us will reconnoiter the village and vicinity so that we will be able to determine how to handle the situation," Kuba said.

At dawn Noah and Jacob went with Kuba to investigate the area. They moved quietly through the woods. The soft ground was covered with moss and leaves from the trees. They often crossed foot paths, and several times they saw peasants herding cattle off in the distance. West of the village, the Shchara River cut through the forest and on both sides of the river there were single farms several miles apart. Some of those farms were located deep in the forest and were called chutors in Russian. The men did not see anyone on the roads leading to the farms and Kuba decided to post a lookout until sunset in a strategic position so that the chutors and the roads leading to them could be observed. Jacob climbed a tall tree and hid in the branches where he could see the entire area.

Nothing changed during the day. Neither civilians nor police appeared. About nine o'clock that evening, the entire group left their hiding place and went to the first chutor. A light was shining through the window and occasionally a dog barked. They divided into three units, each unit to approach the house from a different direction. Kuba's unit went there by way of the road and the dog began barking. The men held their rifles at the ready and approached the gate in the white picket fence which surrounded the house. When Kuba opened the gate, the door of the house opened and the light from the open door fell upon them. A tall peasant was standing in the doorway.

"Who is it?" the peasant asked.

"Friends!" Kuba answered. The peasant hesitated for a few seconds and then began walking toward them. When he came close, they noticed that he was hiding something behind him. "Drop your weapon," Kuba commanded. The peasant stopped, Kuba raised his rifle. The peasant dropped an ax to the ground. "Don't be frightened. Come closer," Kuba said. The peasant moved a little closer. Kuba asked him, "Are there any strangers in your house?"

"No," the peasant replied.

"We would like to buy some bread and bacon from you."

After a few seconds, the peasant turned meekly and answered, "All right. Come inside." Osherovski and Kuba followed the peasant inside, where his frightened wife was standing near a brick oven. Three children, in long nightgowns, were sitting on a big bunk, in a corner, on which the whole family slept. The peasant's wife looked at them with distrust. The peasant looked at Osherovski awhile then asked suddenly, "Are you Jews?"

"That's none of your business," Osherovski answered.

The peasant looked angrily toward his wife and shouted, "Why are you standing there? Give them a loaf of bread and a chunk of bacon."

The woman left for the other room and when she returned she had a large loaf of bread and a large chunk of bacon. "Please take it, good people, but don't harm us," she said.

Kuba took fifty rubles out of his pocket and put it on the table as Elie, who had entered the house in the meantime, took the bread and bacon. Kuba went over to the peasant and offered him his hand in a friendly shake. "Don't be angry and don't condemn us," said Kuba.

"I am not," the peasant answered.

"Are there any Germans or police in the village?"

"They come in sometimes, but only in the daytime."

"And partisans, do they ever visit you?"

"They have never been in our village yet, but a little farther south, near Lake Wygon, they often visit the villages."

Kuba looked into the peasant's eyes and gave him a friendly smile, then said in a low voice, "We are partisans, but don't tell it to anyone because you'll be sorry."

The peasant squeezed Kuba's hand in a friendly manner and replied, "I'll be quiet."

They left feeling that their hungry days were over. Their spirit was revived with the food and the thought that at least a part of the population, and perhaps a large part was not anti-Semitic. They would not have to starve now. With renewed energy, they began their march south as the dog was still barking back at the chutor.

Chapter Seven

The partisans marched through the forest at a fast pace. Now that they had a definite destination, Lake Wygon, where, according to the peasants, partisans were hiding. They were moving along the bank of the Shchara River without going into any villages or towns or even chutors. Kuba understood that they were far away from the places where Germans or police were present.

The country was very beautiful. On both sides of the river there were massive walls of trees. The ground was covered with high-growing moss and the open places between the river and the forest were covered with wild flowers. In the early morning, hundreds of birds were flying from one group of trees to another and their singing was like a prayer of thanks for the beautiful morning. That day the partisans walked about twenty-five miles and stopped only twice to rest and eat. At night, they found shelter under a thick canopy of tree branches.

The next morning, the terrain was changed as they again entered swamps. It was foggy and they couldn't walk as fast as the day before. There were no more roads, so they continued along the river bank but it was getting harder to walk, due to the swamps. According to their map, the river ran into the lake. Their clothes became wet from the water and fog, but cold and weary as they were, they continued on until about four o'clock in the afternoon. The fog became denser and they could hardly see two hundred feet ahead of them.

It was very cold that day, as winter was approaching. The group traveled all day through the forest, again stopping only twice for food and rest. They were miles away from any human settlement. Late in the afternoon, while they were resting and some of them were napping, there was a rustling sound in the bushes to their left. Kuba grabbed his rifle and got to his feet and motioned to the rest of the group to keep quiet. He then began moving cautiously in the direction of the noise. He soon discovered the source of the noise; a large buck was standing in the bushes and rubbing his antlers against the bark of a pine tree.

Kuba was about thirty yards away from the deer, but must have been in a down-wind direction because the buck never stopped his activity. Kuba remembered their low food supply and came to a quick decision. He raised his rifle, took aim and fired and the buck jumped and fell to the ground. At the sound of the gunshot, Rotman came running toward Kuba. "What happened?" he yelled as he approached Kuba.

"I just got us some food," said Kuba and began walking toward the buck.

"That's great!" said Rotman, taking off his belt and tying the animal's hind legs together. He then hung the deer upside down from a tree branch and pulled out a butcher's knife, which he kept strapped to the inside of his boot. He began draining and skinning the buck while Kuba looked at him in amazement.

Rotman smiled, and said, "I used to work for a butcher some time ago." Rotman was a very healthy-looking fellow, heavy set with black curly hair and prominent muscles. Whenever he was assigned a job or mission, he did not ponder about it, he just did it. This is why Kuba liked to work with him during any situation. Kuba noticed a soft spot in Rotman's nature during their early travels through Polesye swamps. Both Kuba and Rotman had lost their families recently and they both grieved for them in a similar manner.

"I sure miss my wife Ettel and the children. I hope that we will be able to catch that son-of-a-bitch Nazi that did them in," Rotman said at one of their missions when they were alone.

"We shall get him!" Kuba said, tears in his eyes. "He is the same man that killed my son and arrested my wife." Suddenly Rotman put his arms around Kuba's neck and began to cry. Kuba was also crying and he said, "My dear brother, if we live long enough we shall take revenge of our tormentors. From now on it is to kill Nazis wherever we find them. That is our destiny!"

After that Kuba went into a stage of desperation, thinking about his dead son Victor and his wife Franca who was later executed by hanging by the Nazis. And so at one of their informative meetings Kuba designated the purpose of that particular partisan group, "From now on we shall be known as the People's Revengers. We do not want to survive this war just for the sake of staying alive. We want to take revenge on all enemies that participated in the killing of our loved ones!"

All sixteen newly escaped prisoners of the Baranovichi Nazi ghetto clenched their fists and said in unison, "SO HELP US GOD!"

The carcass was cut up into several sections and then Rotman wrapped each section into some clothing and several people carried them away. There was no water available at the place where they rested so they moved to the southeast toward the River Shchara.

A half hour later, they came into a large meadow, with a huge lake in the center. To their left was the River Shchara which deposited its waters into the lake. Kuba consulted his map and said, "This is the Wygon Lake." About five miles to the south, the Oginski Canal crosses the lake perpendicular to the river. It is only five o'clock. Let's go to the canal."

They moved along the outskirts of the forest following the shoreline until dark, when they reached the canal. There was a building with a lookout tower on the opposite side, so Kuba motioned to his people to lie down. Cautiously, he moved toward the canal, running from tree to tree until he came within a few feet of the canal. There he dropped to the ground behind a tree and began looking for some sign of activity at the building. The canal was about thirty yards wide and there was a drawbridge in front of the building, retracted or inoperative and several boats were tied up at the opposite shore. Kuba looked at his map and realized that he was at the pre-war border between Poland and the Soviet Union and that the building was most likely an old border guard outpost. No lights were showing through the windows so Kuba got to his feet and called to his comrades to join him.

"What do you think?" asked Osherovski.

"This is an old border guard outpost and it looks deserted," said Kuba.

"How can you be sure that there are no Germans waiting for us there?" Rotman asked.

Kuba looked at the building across the canal and saw that except for the sound of the strong current in the canal, it was very quiet. Suddenly Kuba raised his rifle and said, "There is only one way to find out. Get ready to run into the forest!" He fired a shot into the window next to the main door. The shot sounded very loud and reverberated across the forest and marshes. Nothing happened; there were no replies from the other side. They waited about a half hour and then came out of the forest to the shore of the canal. The water was very cold and there were pieces of ice floating by. Kuba was wondering how to get the group across to the building. He turned to them and said, "One of us will have to swim across and bring back one of those boats. Who would like to volunteer?"

There were no volunteers. Kuba looked at the group of frightened people and handed his gun to Rotman, then stripped down to his underpants, took the rifle and jumped into the canal. The water was ice cold. Kuba held his rifle above the water and began to swim for the opposite shore, but the current carried him downstream and he finally reached the other side at some distance from the building. He was shivering from the cold when he got out of the water and began running toward the building, with his rifle at the ready. He circled the building and found no sign of life, so again at the shore, next to the drawbridge, he jumped into the first boat. There were no oars either in the boat or on the ground. Kuba ran toward the building, which was surrounded by a wooden fence and succeeded in ripping out a long board and took it back to the boat. He untied the boat and using the board as an oar. He made his way back to his group.

Sonia Laxin handed him a towel and a pair of her brother's underpants. He dried himself, got dressed and then, with Rotman's help, took eight people across the canal and Rotman returned for the rest of the group. Everything was accomplished in almost complete silence. With their weapons ready, the group entered the building. There was a large room with a huge fireplace, two tables and benches. Against the walls were four beds with bedding neatly folded in military fashion, giving the appearance that the post had been abandoned in an orderly manner. Two more rooms contained four more beds, some tools, sacks of flour, salt and sugar and other miscellaneous items. A stack of firewood was next to the fireplace, as well as a number of cooking utensils and a cast-iron cooking rack inside the fireplace. A sink with a water pump was in the corner of the room next to the fireplace.

Osherovski built a fire and it soon became quite warm in the room. Kuba worked out a schedule for guard duty and sent out three men to the assigned posts on the perimeter of their camp. The girls gathered the pieces of venison and placed them on a spit in the fireplace and then dug out some potatoes and cabbage, which were half frozen, from a cabbage and potato patch near the house. They began to clean the vegetables and prepare dinner.

Some soap was found in the house and the men took turns heating water in the fireplace and taking a bath outdoors. Rotman found a sheet metal tub in a tool shed in the back of the house and cleaned it and filled it with hot water for the girls to use to take a bath.

They spent two days in that house. The meat was excellent and the group rested well after their long journey. From the tower above the house, they had an excellent view of the surrounding area and Kuba spent several hours studying the lake, forest and marshes. To the east there was a road which curved toward the north and at a distance Kuba could see a village with an embankment behind it, probably railroad tracks. Kuba decided to stay clear of that village and continue the journey south along the shores of the canal.

It was a Friday morning when the group began packing their belongings and preparing for the continuation of their journey to find partisans. The food, which consisted of some cooked meat, canned sardines and flat bread which looked like matzoh, baked by the girls, was divided equally among all. From the tool supply at the house, they took three short-handle axes and several military-type shovels with folding handles.

They traveled single file just within the forest, following the canal to the south. The ground was firm and walking was easy so the group was able to cover about fifteen miles without any problem. At dusk, they found a dry place in a thick pine forest near the canal and set up camp for the night. Kuba stationed guards near the canal and in the forest. They had not encountered any trace of humans during the entire day, causing everyone to feel very secure, as if there were no war at all.

The next morning, the group got underway at about six o'clock as a wet snow began falling and visibility was poor. When they stopped for some rest and food, they heard a strange noise, like a waterfall, coming from upstream of the canal. Kuba and Osherovski went to investigate the source of the noise and walked some distance to where the canal turned to the left and came out onto a large meadow surrounding the canal. Ahead of them, a massive bridge crossed the canal and the sound of falling water came from that direction. Kuba then sent Osherovski back to bring the entire group and when everyone was assembled, Kuba pointed to the bridge.

"Osherovski, Rotman and I will investigate the bridge. The rest of you take up positions under trees and give us cover, if necessary," he said.

The three men moved toward the bridge. Kuba could see smoke rising from near the bridge and noticed that the grass on the opposite side of the canal was burning. He felt uneasy. Everything looked very strange. Not far from where he stood, a small boat was tied to a post on the bank. "Let's investigate," Kuba told the other two. The rest of the group remained hidden. They sat down and watched as Kuba crossed the canal in the boat with Noah and Osherovski beside him. Kuba worked the board as an oar, and soon the three men reached the other side and tied down the boat. Kuba looked around, wondering what lay ahead. The three men began to carefully walk forward, with their rifles ready. They saw more burning grass and trees near the bridge and noticed that several boats had been destroyed and overturned.

"Maybe there are Germans here," Noah said.

"We'll find out very soon," replied Kuba. They approached the bridge cautiously and on the other side of the bridge they could see the ruins of a building which was still smoking, and lying near the bank were the remains of three charred boats.

The sound of falling water was much louder here. They couldn't see anyone moving about so they started slowly across the bridge. Osherovski was first. He was about twenty feet ahead of Kuba and Noah was some twenty feet to the rear. Suddenly Osherovski stopped. "Look, dead bodies!" he shouted to them.

Kuba and Noah ran toward him. Kuba felt surprise when he saw that there were two dead bodies, both dressed in German uniforms, both shot through the head. "They are Nazis," said Noah, staring at the corpses.

"Yes, now we can cross the bridge without fear. There isn't a living soul around," Kuba replied. On the other side of the bridge there were more bodies of German soldiers and all kinds of German documents and photographs were scattered on the ground. They discovered that this was not a regular bridge. It was a dam. The strange noise was caused by the water running through the floodgates.

They found a large number of dead bodies on a lower platform of the dam, all Nazis except for one in peasant clothing. There were more bodies near the ruins of the building. The rest of their group then joined them and looked in awe as they crossed the channel. According to the map, the Wygon Lake was only a few miles away so they sat down to rest behind the ruins of the building.

Kuba looked at the mysterious battlefield; he knew that a terrible fight had taken place here between the partisans and the Nazis. Later, he learned what had actually happened from some peasants. The dam was known as "Desiaty Shluz." One week earlier, more than fifty Germans in six boats had sailed through the canal as an attachment of about thirty partisans were heading in the direction of the dam. Armed with Army rifles and three machine guns, the partisans came out of the woods near the town of Slonim. The best machine gunner in the group was an eighteen-year-old Jewish girl from Slonim, Raya Schwartz. The partisans were fired upon by the Germans near the dam, and returned fire immediately. They were in a better position than the Germans, taking cover behind trees while the Germans were still in their boats. Only two boats reached the shore and the Germans were able to take cover during the hour and a half of fighting.

While everyone was busy shooting, Raya Schwartz crossed the bridge to the German side and opened fire on the Germans with her machine gun. She was hit three times by Nazi bullets, but before she died, the last of the Nazis was dead. They had been on their way to pacify a village which refused to support them. The dead bodies of the Germans were not buried because the Nazi high command was afraid to send out new troops to the area.

Kuba's group did not meet any partisans near the Wygon Lake because the unit who had been there had left a short time earlier. Wygon Lake is one of the largest lakes in the former Republic of Poland. It is about eight kilometers long and six kilometers wide, located in the middle of a virgin forest with its endless marshes. The forest of birch trees stands in almost three feet of water but there are islands of dry land throughout the forest and peasants had built their villages on some of the islands and on other islands they had their crop fields. In the summertime, it is impossible to reach the fields, except by boat, because everything is flooded.

Kuba and his group stopped in a village named Svecice where the inhabitants had never seen any Germans. There were no motor roads leading to the village so only in the winter were the peasants able to visit other villages. The people were very friendly and eager to help.

Kuba decided to settle down in the area on one of the dry islands and, with the guidance of two carpenters in the group, they built two huts in the ground, which the Russians call ziemlanki.

The "ziemlanka" or earth hut is a simple and very effective shelter. An area of ground measuring about fifteen by twenty-five feet is cleared and leveled. Then a trench about two feet deep and three feet wide by twenty-five feet long is dug out along the center of the longer side. Finally, an A-frame is built over the entire area by using logs and tree branches. The roof was made water-tight by the use of leaves and foliage. This method sealed the roof as well as camouflaged it. The two side walls were made from logs, with doors at both ends and inside the hut, a thick layer of leaves were spread on the ground along both sides of the trench. Later, Kuba's group obtained straw and spread it over the leaves. This was to be their new home.

They made friends with some of the peasants who were very helpful to them. They learned how to walk over the marshes and how to find invisible paths in the swamps. The peasants also helped the group obtain enough food supplies from the nearby villages to last at least two months.

Now that they were a real partisan group, they sent out scouts to investigate the local vicinity. One day, Kuba led a reconnaissance group to explore a more distant area about ten miles from camp when they discovered a road cutting through the forest, a gravel road with telegraph poles alongside. The map showed this to be the road between Hanceviche and Deniskoviche.

It was about noon when they reached the road. They noticed fresh car tracks and examined them closely when suddenly they heard the sound of trucks coming in their direction. They took cover immediately in the nearby bushes and waited. A few minutes later several motorcycles and a truckload of Nazis sped by. They remained concealed in the bushes for the next half hour while more cars and motorcycles passed in both directions. On their way home, Kuba said to his comrades, "We were only a few feet away from our bloody enemies and they couldn't do anything to us."

"But why didn't we open fire on them?" asked Jacob.

"Because we haven't enough ammunition to begin a fight with them," Kuba answered.

They walked in silence for the next several minutes and as they entered the first swamp on their way to camp, Osherovski said, "I have an idea how to fight the Germans without ammunition!"

"How?" Kuba asked.

"With a wire."

"How will you fight Germans with a wire?"

"Let's come back here tomorrow and I will show you," answered Osherovski. Silently they returned to their camp and that evening they discussed Osherovski's plans and decided to return to the highway in two days.

It was about nine o'clock in the evening when they reached the highway. There were four of them: Osherovski, Jacob, Lazar and Kuba. They succeeded in cutting off about fifty feet of telegraph wire, which they then hid in the bushes. That was enough for that evening. They then went deeper into the woods to spend the night. Everyone was excited and lying on the soft moss. Kuba was thinking about tomorrow's undertaking. All kinds of thoughts went through his head. What would happen if they were unsuccessful? Maybe they wouldn't have time to escape. He recalled everything they had gone through until now. After all, what had they to lose?

Kuba put his fingers into his shirt pocket, fishing for a cigarette, when he came across a hard metal object. He took it out and looked at it in amazement. It was a small padlock which his mother had given him when he bought a bicycle before the war started. He looked at it and began to cry suddenly with real tears. He could plainly see his mother's face as she was talking to him during their final parting. "Kuba, you are not just my son. You will be our avenger regardless of whether we are still alive when the end of this Holocaust comes!" From that moment on, the little padlock became an omen to Kuba. Before each dangerous mission, he touched it and felt assured that no harm would come to him because his mother's spirit was watching over him. Finally he fell asleep.

The next morning, while eating some cold meat for their breakfast, they began to put their plan into effect. They found two trees standing opposite each other on both sides of the road and from these Osherovski stretched the wire between the trees about four feet from the ground. After this was done, they took cover in the bushes about twenty feet from the highway, got their weapons ready and lay quietly there, waiting to see what would happen. Kuba gave his comrades a final order, "Remember, if there is a car or truck coming, we escape immediately."

Several hours passed and they began to doubt that anything would happen that day. "Maybe the Germans will not drive by today," Jacob said. It was noon when Kuba began thinking of calling off the plan and arose to his feet, but before he had time to say a word, his ear caught the racing sound of a motorcycle. He lay down immediately.

"Get ready," he whispered to his friends. They raised their rifles. The sound of the motorcycle grew louder and Kuba could feel his heart beating faster and tension mounting in every muscle in his body. He pressed his forehead against the barrel of his gun, to relax a little. The motorcycle was approaching along the road, carrying an SS officer on his way to Deniskoviche. The officer neared the trees where the wire was strung. Sixty feet more, thirty feet more, ten feet more, then it happened. The roar of the motorcycle became faint so Kuba rose to his feet, his comrades following and carefully they went to the road. Reaching it they stopped startled at the sight. Lying in the middle of the road was the Nazi's body, his head nearly cut off by the wire and several feet away lay the overturned motorcycle. For several minutes, they watched their dead enemy quietly.

Jacob whispered, "We actually killed a Nazi. They can die too."

"That was our first revenge!" said Lazar.

"For my child, and others murdered by the Nazis, we will take revenge whenever we have a chance," remarked Kuba. The wire remained in place. Kuba looked at it and felt proud. Now they were real partisans, fighters for freedom and justice.

Osherovski picked up the German's weapons, a sub-machine gun and an automatic pistol and handed them to Kuba. He then went back to the dead Nazi and pulled off his boots.

Chapter Eight

It was the end of October of 1941 and Kuba's group was settled in their permanent partisan camp near the Wygon Lake. It consisted of four earth huts, built in a semi-circle amongst the trees. At the center of the semi-circle there was a firepit for cooking and a table and benches made out of split logs, held together by wooden pegs. The camp was located about two miles from the lake and five miles from the village of Svecice to the north. The forest extended for many miles to the south and east. A large stream flowed toward the lake at the south of the camp. They used this stream for drinking water, washing and other needs. The site of the camp was a picture of pure serenity; no signs of war or destruction anywhere. Kuba's people went about their chores, keeping house, fixing clothes, storing supplies, trying to keep themselves clean and planning future actions.

One day when the girls returned from the stream where they had bathed, the Laxin girl found Kuba and said, "You know, there is a trail leading eastward from the opposite side of the stream. There are some hoof tracks which don't look too old."

Kuba and Rotman went to investigate the trail and followed the tracks for a few miles and then Kuba decided to lead a party up the stream to find out where the trail led. After about twenty minutes, Kuba accompanied by Osherovski and Lazar, began following the trail upstream. It led deeply into the forest and they found evidence of armed camps and at least twenty horses. At one point, about five miles from their camp, they came across a secondary trail on the right which also led into the forest. It was smaller and seemed to have been made at a much later date than the main trail. The men had learned to move very quietly among the trees and after about fifteen minutes, they came to the end of the trail where they found a few mounds of dirt to the left and footprints everywhere. Someone must have left in a hurry.

Kuba kicked one of the dirt mounds and found it to be very soft, so he began digging. Soon all three of them were digging, using a shovel which Osherovski always carried with him in his belt. They uncovered a large hole containing parcels wrapped in clothing and leaves. They unwrapped them and found that the parcels contained ammunition, rifles, pistols and four machine guns, all made by the Soviets. Kuba selected the most suitable weapons for his group and a sufficient amount of ammunition and then told Osherovski to bury the remainder.

They returned to their camp that evening and raised the morale of his people with their news. Kuba realized that their find was not a partisan ammunition and weapons dump, but, rather a Red Army hiding place for weapons, before retreating.

While they were eating dinner, the group discussed the possibility of finding other partisans. They had learned from some inhabitants of the Svecice village that a group of mixed Jewish and Russian partisans had been active in that area for a few weeks and then moved to the east. The group had participated in the battle of "Desiaty Shluz." The people of Svecice were particularly friendly to Kuba and his group; especially the two brothers named Wasilewski who were Polish and members of the Polish Socialist Party. The two brothers provided Kuba with information about the activities and movements of the Germans and police in the area. The older one, Stefan, knew of Kuba's father. "Are you in any way related to Comrade Arthur of the Jewish Bund in Warsaw? You have the same last name."

Kuba looked at Stefan and said, "Yes. That is my father. How do you know about him?"

"Oh, his is the only voice that comes through on our little crystal radio that my brother and I have hidden in our barn. We saw him once in the city of Slonim before the war at a Polish Socialist Party meeting and he was the most honest and most powerful speaker that visited this part of Poland."

Kuba shook hands with the two brothers and they in turn embraced him and kissed him on both cheeks in the old Polish way.

After that they introduced him to the others. There was the farmer, Ivan Kurilovich, in his sixties and an old partisan in World War I. He taught Kuba how to cross a swamp, how to recognize especially deep swamps by the type of water lilies on the surface and how to walk quietly, without leaving tracks behind.

Kuba studied the faces of his comrades for awhile and then said, "Obviously, we are the only active partisan group in the area. Eventually, more people will escape from the ghettos and join us and we now have enough weapons for fifty people. However, in view of our find today, we must consider another factor. It is certain that groups of escaped Soviet soldiers are hiding in the area and eventually, we will encounter them. Because of the deep anti-Semitism among some of the Ukrainian, Polish, Lithuanian and even Russian groups, such an encounter might prove to be extremely dangerous. We must be very careful."

"How will we know if there are such groups near us?" asked Rotman.

There was no ready answer to that question. They continued eating in silence, thinking about the problem. After awhile Kuba said, "We must contact the Wasilewski brothers. Rotman and I will go to Svecice before sunrise. Osherovski will be in charge of the camp." It was still dark when Kuba and Rotman reached Stefan Wasilewski's house. Kuba tapped out a signal on the door, waited about a minute, the door opened and Stefan motioned them to enter. Kuba told Stefan about their discovery of an abandoned camp, without saying too much about the weapons. Then he asked if Stefan knew anything about escaped Soviet soldiers.

Stefan looked at Kuba with a smile on his face and said, "Yes, we know about several bands of soldiers who turned into bandits. They raided villages for the purpose of stealing, raping and killing. Many farmers and peasants are terrorized by these groups, who claim some villages as their territory. They have never come to Svecice, however, we found three abandoned horses in the meadow outside the village. They are Red Army horses with saddles. If you ever come across such a band, be ready to fight. By the way, why don't you get horses for your group? You can take those three horses right now and we heard that in a meadow near Novosielski there are more than a dozen horses loose."

Stefan's wife came into the room with a pot of tea. The three men sipped the tea and conversed quietly while Stefan told them about many villages that were burned to the ground by the Germans who killed many villagers, and dispersing the rest to the nearby forests and marshes. Kuba looked at Stefan and asked, "What would you and your brother do if this should happen to your village? Have you made any plans?"

"Yes, we prepared a hideout for our families in the forest. My brother and I would join your group." Shortly afterwards, Stefan took them to the meadow, where they picked up the three horses. Kuba and Rotman returned to camp on horseback.

Two days later, Kuba, accompanied by Henryk, Noah, Elie, Lazar and Laxin, left for the Babin chutors to pick up some supplies. They planned to go by way of Novosielski and pick up the horses that Stefan had mentioned. It was a warm day when Kuba and his men crossed ten miles of swamps and marshes, taking a short cut to Novosielski. Part of the way, they had to walk over logs, laid out end to end. It was like walking a tightrope. Near the village, there was a stretch of road made of logs called "grobla", a pontoon-type road over the swamps, built by Germans during World War I. To reach the "grobla" they had to take hidden paths over a swamp, marked only by plants sticking out of the water. They reached Novosielski in the evening, but did not enter the village because they didn't trust the inhabitants. Many of their sons were serving with the German police and Gestapo. Instead, they circled around the village until they reached the "grobla" and then sat down to rest.

It was a clear night. Millions of stars were sparkling in the sky. Kuba found the Big Dipper and the North Star, which reminded him of his boyhood when he was a Boy Scout camping in the summertime. Their leader told them how to recognize stars and how to find the North Star. For the moment, the present was all but forgotten, while in his imagination he was once again in his boyhood. It was Henryk who brought him back to the present.

"Somebody's coming on the grobla," he said excitedly. They held their breaths. From a distance they could hear voices; a large group of people were headed in their direction. Kuba rose to his feet. Their strategic situation wasn't very favorable. There was water on both sides of the grobla and behind them was the unfriendly Novosielski. There was no place to hide.

The voices came closer and they could recognize the Russian language. "Police!" Laxin said, frightened. There was not much time for thinking, but Kuba made a quick decision. Three of them were to take up a position on one side of the road and three on the other. They then fell to the ground and got their rifles ready. Someone's rifle bolt was stuck and he had to repeat the action, breaking the stillness around them with the characteristic sound of the rifle.

The group approaching them stopped. They had noticed Kuba's men by now and Kuba could see them clearly. The group was somewhat frightened and stood in a huddle.

"Who is it?" asked Kuba, in Russian. There was no answer. He noticed a movement amongst them. He didn't like it. "Answer or we will shoot," Kuba shouted to them.

"We are Russians," a voice answered.

"What kind of Russians?" Kuba asked. Kuba knew they were not police. They would not have waited so long.

The same voice from the group continued, "One of you come forward for negotiations."

Kuba was the nearest to them. Rising to his feet, he whispered to his comrades, "Careful. Keep watch and be ready to fire." He walked forward a few steps and someone from the group approached him, and when he came closer Kuba could see that it was a Soviet soldier in a torn uniform. He had not shaved in weeks and he held a rifle in his hand.

Kuba looked at the miserable state of the men and thought, *Is this all that is left of the once famous Red Army? What will happen in the months ahead? How are partisans like himself going to survive? Or maybe this is a repetition of Napoleon's march on Moscow in 1812.* Suddenly Kuba looked at the escaped prisoners with a new perspective. A new thought struck him. *Of course! We, the haggard, persecuted people of this land will defeat the Nazi intruders in time and become part of the history of Europe. Win the right to live for Jewish people.*

"We are partisans and who are you?" Kuba began the conversation.

"We are prisoners of war, just escaped from a German camp."

"Where is your camp?"

"Near the city of Pinsk."

"What have you decided to do now?"

"We would like to join the partisans."

"How are you armed?" Kuba asked.

"One machine gun and three army rifles."

"Where did you get them?"

"We worked at a railroad station near Pinsk, loading German war trophies on trains and a lot of Soviet arms and ammunition. We succeeded in stealing what we have and escaping."

Kuba's comrades had joined him by this time and the other war prisoners also came closer. Kuba observed them and saw that they were all young people, twenty altogether, and that one of them had his arm bandaged in a dirty rag.

"Wounded?" Kuba asked.

"Yes," answered the wounded one.

It was clear to Kuba that the prisoners spoke the truth. They were glad that they had met partisans. "Is there an officer among you?" Kuba asked.

The man who had first spoken replied, "I am a first lieutenant of the infantry."

"What is your name?"

"George Kartuchin," the lieutenant replied.

"And we are a group of Jewish partisans," said Kuba. They shook hands and Kuba told George about the horses in the meadow. They found the horses without difficulty. There was no one near the meadow, and they had succeeded in rounding up about two dozen horses. Kuba decided to postpone the trip to the Babin chutors and to return to camp instead.

There were not enough weapons for the new group in Kuba's camp and he was not ready to disclose to George the fact about the hidden weapons in the forest, so he decided to test the new group by sending them on a mission to obtain some weapons. As they were now a group of thirty-six, they built two more earthen huts. According to Kartuchin's advice, they divided their partisan attachment into four groups; eight men in each. The two girls, George and Kuba were not included in the groups. Two of the groups, under the leadership of George, left the camp to get some weapons. They returned four days later with fourteen rifles and a machine gun, taken from the Nazis in a fight. A third group, led by Osherovski, left the camp to get more food supplies and returned with a small amount of food several days later. He told Kuba that his group had met another group of partisans in one of the villages and that they did not allow him to collect any food from the peasants, but ordered him to give up their weapons. When Osherovski refused, they opened fire. Osherovski's group answered with fire and left the village. Fortunately, there were no casualties.

Incidents such as these began to occur frequently. Friendly peasants informed Kuba that there were many loose partisan groups who did all their fighting in the villages when the Germans weren't around. They would rob the peasants of cattle and private belongings, beat the peasants and rape their wives and daughters. Their leader called himself "Ataman," the title of the leaders of Cossack hordes in the Ukraine. There were other partisan groups which did some fighting against the Nazis, but they were not properly organized and each group did the fighting on their own. Several times, Kuba met the commanders of other groups and at those meetings they discussed the serious situation that had developed. Frequent quarrels among the various partisan groups resulted in numerous fatal casualties of partisans, as well as civilians. The leader of one group proposed to bring together the leaders of all partisan groups in the Polesye area for a meeting. His name was Gregory Koshevoy. He was a Cossack and his group consisted of eighteen Cossacks from a special Red Army unit of Don River Cossacks. Gregory was a heavy set man, with a round head, blue eyes, dark hair and a drooping mustache. He was about six feet tall. He and his group were still wearing their Cossack uniform: black tunics and pantaloons, the bottoms of which were tucked into black boots. Black fur hats and a string of bullets that fastened at an angle to the center of their chests completed their uniform. They were armed with rifles, revolvers and long swords.

With the help of friendly peasants the call for a "summit" meeting reached most of the partisan groups. The selected date was in September of 1941, the place was the Cerkva (Russian Orthodox Church) in the village Luki.

Gregory's Cossacks along with several score of other partisans arrived at the village two days prior to the meeting, to assure full security. Kuba and George represented their partisan unit. All together thirty five partisan leaders participated. Because of his first initiative, Gregory Koshevoy was elected Commander of all Polesye partisans and George Kartuchin— deputy Commander. The individual leaders reported the state of their ordnance, food acquisition and the various anti-German actions that they had initiated. It was noisy in the church. Everyone tried to talk and emphasize their own particular problems. Finally Gregory raised his arms to quiet them down and said: "Comrades...We have taken the first step towards a united resistance fight against the German intruders. We have most of the ingredients for such an effort. First of all we have our strong will to live and fight. Based on our experience we know that we can obtain food from the land and weapons from our enemy. But we urgently need much more! We must establish contact with the Allied military forces, in our case, the Soviet High Command. Unfortunately we do not have a single radio transceiver. In our entire gathering of fighters there exists only on old radio receiver, over which we hear news reports occasionally. The only way to solve this problem is to find among us two men with the guts and determination to travel east, cross the front-line, which is now between Smolensk and Viazma, and contact the proper people in Moscow. I am requesting two such comrades."

They all fell silent. They bowed their heads and got lost in their own deepest thoughts. Kuba closed his eyes and his thoughts returned to that dusty stretch of road where he last watched his father trying to get to the edge of the forest. He saw the faces of his mother and sister with desperate tears running down their cheeks as he was leaving with Franca. Finally he saw the tortured body of his little son, Victor and a fleeting vision of Franca's limp body hanging from a lamp post. A knot formed in his stomach, a heavy pressure in his chest and a lump formed in his throat. He got to his feet.

"Comrades! I will go! I hope that my companion will be familiar with the terrain beyond Minsk and Smolensk." He sat down and wiped the perspiration from his forehead. There was silence in the church for a while, and then everybody applauded.

Suddenly, from the back of the church, a young voice spoke. "Comrades! My name is Ivan Kolesnikov, corporal of infantry of the Red Army. I was born in Smolensk. My father is a railroad man there. I know all the hidden trails through our forests and swamps. I will go with Comrade Kuba."

Ivan was nineteen years old, a little under six feet tall, blonde hair, blue eyes with a very friendly, smiling face. He was a member of a partisan group in the vicinity of Telechany, a town east of Brest. Kuba was glad to have him as a companion on this dangerous undertaking. They were to leave from Luki for their mission in three days.

Kuba and George joined the Cossack leader Gregory Koshevoy after the meeting and, over a bottle of vodka, they discussed some details of the mission. In his deep, baritone voice Koshevoy said, "One very important item, Comrade Kuba, that you must remember is that when you approach the front line, get rid of any German weapons in your possession. Soviet soldiers might take you for Germans and that would be the end."

"Thank you. Kuba replied. "What about the territory east, towards Minsk? Do you know of any partisans in that area?"

"Oh, to the southeast of Stolbtsy the General Komarov brigade is roaming around. You will hear about them from the local population. Again, be very careful."

In the evening Kuba and George mounted their horses and returned to their camp. They rode in silence following narrow trails and swamp crossings. Halfway to their camp George stopped his horse near a cluster of trees and said, "Zakurim, let's stop for a smoke." The two rolled up cigarettes and lit up. Kuba looked up to the sky. The stars were very bright and he soon found the Big

Dipper. George followed his gaze and said with a smile, "Beautiful".

Kuba smiled and after a while he said, "George, tomorrow morning we will get our men together and talk about the meeting. I saw you take notes back in Luki, so you will give them all details."

"Of course, Kuba, and another thing we have to discuss is with you leaving in three days, we have to select a new leader for the group."

"Oh, there is not much of a discussion necessary for that. You, George, are an officer of the Red Army and more qualified for the position than I. Our two groups blended together very well and our common interface during the various actions against the Nazis was excellent. I have a feeling that if I succeed in crossing the front line and telling the proper people the story of our existence and particularly your escape from German captivity and following deeds, you might be promoted in rank and perhaps even receive a medal for bravery."

With a solemn expression on his face and somewhat misty eyes, George put his hand on Kuba's shoulder and said, "Thank you, Kuba. You will probably be a high officer in the Army some day. I hope we will meet again. Don't be too hard then on lieutenant Kartuchin."

Next morning Kuba and George reported to their comrades the outcome of the meeting. George recounted the details of the discussions and decisions agreed upon. In conclusion he said, "Your commander, Kuba and another partisan, Ivan Kolesnikov, volunteered to try to cross the front line and contact the Soviet High Command. If they succeed our situation here will change drastically. Our fight against the Nazis will take on a new form. We will have purpose and specific assignments. We will be in continuous radio contact with Moscow. We wish them success and good luck. We hope that they will return to us soon. Hooray for Kuba and Ivan!"

Kuba got to his feet, raised his arms and said: "Comrades, thank you for your good wishes and now back to important business. You people who escaped with me from the Baranovichi ghetto became my family. I am certain that you will continue our sacred mission of revenge under your new commander, Lieutenant George Kartuchin. He is the best and most suitable person to replace me. He promised me to help you and any other lucky escapees from ghettos and concentration camps to survive this war with honor and dignity. Our cause is just! The enemy will be destroyed! Final victory will be ours!"

The girls and a few men brought some food and even a few bottles of vodka were found for the occasion. A huge bonfire was built and everybody joined in the singing of Russian and Jewish songs. The few guards on the perimeters of the camp guarded the partisans from any uninvited intruders.

Chapter Nine

The two partisans had to travel four-hundred-fifty miles to reach the front lines. They had to cross all of White Russia and a large part of European Russia. They traveled only at night in order to avoid the enemy and dared to travel during the day only through the forests. It was a hard journey, crossing through unknown marshes. They circled around villages and towns and avoided highways and other kinds of improved roads. Their food supply lasted only three days, at which time they were in the vicinity of a town called Smilovich, near Minsk, the capital of White Russia. They arrived on a dark night with cloudy skies. The forest path they took led them through a small meadow and near a peasant's house where a light was burning on the inside. This was strange for that late hour. After observing the area for awhile, they went to the house and as they came closer it became obvious that the house belonged to very poor peasants. There was no barn and the livestock were located in a separate room in the same house with the peasants.

Looking through the window, they noticed a man sitting near a table repairing a pair of shoes and in the corner of the room, on a large bunk, several people were asleep. They couldn't recognize whether they were men or women. The room was lighted by small wood torches that were sticking into the wall between the logs. Ivan knocked on the window. The peasant put away the shoe he was repairing and slowly came to the window.

"Who is it?" he asked.

"Partisans. Open the door." The peasant went to the door and unbolted it and Kuba and Ivan went inside. The living quarters consisted of only one room with the kitchen in one corner, a house similar to all other houses in White Russia.

"Good evening," Kuba said.

The peasant answered their greeting and looked at them curiosity. In a moment he said, "You are hungry. Sit at the table." They seated themselves at the table while the peasant pulled some baked potatoes from the oven and placed them before Kuba and Ivan. "Excuse us, but we can't give you anything better to eat, that's all we have and we have eaten like this for months."

They were hungry and the potatoes tasted very good. Placing two glasses of milk in front of them, the peasant said, "We are living a dog's life. No meat, no bacon, eggs or butter. We'll probably starve to death before long."

"How many cows do you have?" Ivan asked.

"We had three and a big pig too, but now we have only one cow and two goats left. The Nazis took away the rest."

Kuba studied the room and saw that the peasant's wife and two children were sleeping on the bunk and that the room was very dirty. Ivan asked the peasant, "Did partisans ever come to you?"

"Oh yes, very often." For several minutes they ate in silence. When they had finished, they arose from the table and the peasant then treated them to tobacco and an old newspaper.

"Roll yourselves some cigarettes, friends." He tore off a square piece of paper, put some tobacco in it and rolled a cigarette. After lighting it, the peasant asked, "Are you going far?"

"Very far," answered Kuba.

"To the front line, maybe?" the peasant asked. Kuba and Ivan looked at the peasant suspiciously. Maybe he worked for the Nazis. Maybe he was in the Gestapo. The peasant understood their thoughts and smiled in discomfort. "I didn't mean anything wrong. Maybe I can even help you get there." Ivan and Kuba exchanged glances. The peasant put on his coat. "I will lead you out." They went outside. It was raining. The peasant led them to a forest path. "I have a friend. He lives on a chutor that is on your way. He can help you find your way farther."

"Do you know him well?"

"Very well. He belongs to the same religious sect of Old Believers that I do." They walked silently, leading their horses. The peasant was barefooted and must have been cold, but didn't show it. When they came to a crossroad, the peasant stopped. "Over that road many partisans and soldiers have gone to the front line. You will make better time and be safer on foot rather than on horseback." They looked at each other for a moment. The peasant was about forty years old, but his mustache made him look much older. He made certain there was no one around, then came closer to them and almost whispered, "Take the road to the left. You have to go about ten miles. There will be several chutors in Sokolov. You will cross a small bridge and on the other side you will enter the first house to the left. You will recognize the house by the well in front of it. It is a Russian well, a zhurav. Knock on the window three times and ask for Ostap. He has a red beard. Tell him that Konstantin Chvoik sent you." He gave them more instructions on how not to lose their path and, particularly, not to turn to the right because there was a German garrison in the town of Zhabna. After a short conversation, Kuba and Ivan decided to leave the horses with Konstantin.

It was raining hard as they walked along the path pointed out by Konstantin. Their feet slipped in the mud, making it very hard to walk. This path crossed many other paths, often dividing into two, but they followed Konstantin's instructions and reached the end of the forest at dawn. They noticed silhouettes of houses from a distance, the Sokolov chutors. They crossed a small bridge and on the other side, there was a path on their left which led to the house. They took the path and saw the zhurav well at the front of the gate. It was wooden water well. Near the well stood a pole with the upper end divided into a "V" and another pole resting in the "V". One end was heavier than the other and the shorter end had a chain which held a bucket on the end.

They opened the gate and approached the house, Kuba knocked on the window and the door opened immediately. A peasant with a long red beard stepped from the house, looked at them, smiled and said, "What can I do for you?"

"Are you Ostap?"

"I am," he answered.

"Konstantin Chvoik sent us to you," they answered.

"Come on inside," he said. The house was very clean as compared to Chvoik's. Ostap had two grown sons, one of whom was married and had a child and lived in a village near Zhabna, but the Nazis were after him for helping partisans, so he stayed at his father's house. Ostap served them a fine breakfast of bacon, eggs and vodka and while eating, they discussed the war situation in the country.

"How about your house here? Is it secure? Didn't the Germans come over here?" Kuba asked.

"No, they don't come here, and if they do, we will know it beforehand and have time to escape," replied Ostap. Saying that, Ostap filled the glasses again with vodka and then after breakfast led them into another room and told them to get some rest. They asked Ostap if one of them might guard the house while the others rested. Smiling, he answered, "We are like partisans here. This house is guarded day and night and you don't have to be afraid of anything. In that way, and with our help and the help of others who are with us, many partisans and soldiers have crossed the front line."

"Are you connected with the Red Army?"

"No. We are an organization of Old Believers and have nothing to do with politics." He stroked his long red beard for a moment. "The main thing for us is our Holy Earth, Mother Russia," he said slowly. "No matter who is ruling in the Kremlin, if a foreign power attacks our country, we defend her. This is one of our means of defense. Our grandfathers used to lead Russian soldiers through the front lines when the armies of Napoleon were near Moscow, and we are doing it now when the armies of Hitler are near Moscow. We have nothing to do with the communists. They are our bitter enemies, but we are Russians and we love Russia."

Kuba and Ivan immediately fell asleep.

It was dark outside when they awoke. In the other room, they found Ostap cleaning a rifle, an old rifle from the First World War which the Russians called "berdanka." "I've had this rifle hidden since the last world war and I think I'll still have some use for it," Ostap said, smiling.

After they ate, they left the chutor, led by Ostap in his wagon. It was still very cloudy but it wasn't raining so the horses trotted rapidly. Ostap told them that they were going to meet the old Moysey who lived in the Beresino Forest, a pitch-burner and also an Old Believer. "He will lead you further to the front," Ostap told them.

They rode almost the whole night and on the way, Ostap treated them with sandwiches and vodka, and sang some Russian folk songs. As the sky began to clear, they could see stars shining through. They reached the forest, thick with fir trees, and after several hours of driving through the forest, they came to a small house and stopped. A large dog ran out barking. A tall chimney and two cisterns were visible behind the house. This was the pitch-burning shop. Moysey came out of the house, a completely gray man, very tall and broad. Though he was very old, he looked strong and healthy. He had spent many years burning pitch there, with his dog as his only friend. Moysey was not a very talkative man. He only spoke a few sentences in all the time they spent with him.

Ostap brought a large box of food from the wagon including food supply for the old man. Since the war, he had not burned any pitch and had it not been for the help of his friends, he would probably have starved to death. In answer to their question of why he remained in the forest and didn't live with some of his friends in the villages, Moysey replied, "My presence here is necessary for our cause."

That was all he said to them until they left his house. After breakfast, Ostap bade them farewell and returned to his home. During the day, they slept in Moysey's house and in the evening Moysey led them to a chutor about fifteen miles away where a peasant by the name of Stepan Chramoy took charge and a wonderful journey began for them: from one peasant to another, from one chutor to another, from forest to forest. By foot and by horseback, they came closer to the front, closer to the Red Army and their destination. They were led by a dedicated organization which was born ages ago in defense of the Russian earth. Kuba had seen the patriotism of the Russian people and knew that such people could not be defeated, not even by Stalin.

Kuba and Ivan traveled in this manner for ten days, handed over from one Old Believer to the next. It was a real underground railroad. They reached an area east of Smolensk and travel began getting difficult. The front was very close and German and Italian troops were everywhere.

One of the last guides was a farmer named David Astrakhanov, with whom they spent a day and a night. At his house they were guarded by his ten children. The following evening, David said to Kuba, "We go now. Your next guide will take you to the front line." They got into David's wagon and headed toward a distant forest.

They reached the front after a two week journey. To Kuba, the terrible explosions of artillery shells sounded like an enormous thunder storm and at night the sky was lighted by the glare of fires. Every day, the glares became closer and brighter. Cities were burning. Thousands of airplanes flew over their heads and often, they witnessed air battles. On one particular night, they came so close to the front that they could see anti-aircraft search lights and artillery shells tracing streaks like lightning in the sky. Anti-aircraft shells rose from the ground, much slower, leaving a red violet trail behind them. Machine guns of all calibers were firing millions of bullets into the sky. They looked like falling stars and the entire sky resembled a fairyland. Kuba didn't think, at that moment, that all those falling stars carried death with them. This was the front! They had arrived at the last leg of their journey.

That evening their guide was a one-eyed peasant, with a painful expression on his face, who talked more with his hands than with his mouth. Kiril was his name. Several weeks earlier, he had escaped a German concentration camp, and his entire family had been burned alive in his house by the Nazis. Kiril was burning with revenge. He led them for several miles, parallel with the front line and again they entered swampy country, through a meadow and to a forest. In the beginning, the forest was very dry, but as they proceeded deeper, the swamps reappeared and at one place the trees were standing deep in water. A log path began there. Kiril left them for awhile and returned with four long sticks, divided on the ends like forks so that they could be stuck into the mud and not sink into the swamp as the men supported themselves on them while walking over the logs. After Kiril gave them the sticks, he looked at them and said, "From here on you will travel by yourselves."

He told them that the log path would lead them to a village that was on the other side of the front, but they would have to be very careful and investigate the vicinity before they entered the village. "There are only nine miles left to travel," he added. They shook hands with Kiril, and with a sad voice, he said, "Tell the comrades about our sufferings." With that, he departed.

It was a hard trip. They had to stop and rest very often. It was not easy to walk over round logs. After several hours of this, the road broke away and there were no more logs in front of them, only water. The logs had likely sunk into the mud. They sat down and ate the rest of their food supply and after an hour of rest, they got into the water, which reached their chests, and held their rifles and ammunition over their heads. Once again they found a log path and walked all day until late into the night. Now and then, artillery shells exploded around them.

It was about three o'clock in the morning when they came out of the forest. The night was clear and the moon was shining brightly. Ahead of them was a village and because they were very tired and hungry, they knocked on the door of the first house they at which they arrived. A peasant came to the door, and the first thing they could say way, "Give us something to eat!"

Inside, the house was very warm, the shades were pulled down, and they ate like wolves.

"Is the front line far from here?"

"From which direction are you coming?" asked the peasant.

"From the west."

"If so, you crossed the front line three miles back."

"And who is occupying that village?" they asked.

"The Red Army. The third house from here is the headquarters of a Soviet division." They jumped to their feet and were so excited that they couldn't say anything. The peasant looked at them, smiling. Finally, they had reached their destination. Several miles away heavy shooting was taking place.

Part III:
Fighting Back

Chapter Ten

The road, which turned into a street, was deserted and muddy. Some pieces of furniture were scattered on the front yards of the houses. Those were really log cabins with thatched roofs, built about a hundred feet apart and most likely about a hundred years old. They lined the right side of the road. On the left side were empty fields with signs of earlier cultivation, stretching far into the country to a dense line of pine trees. It looked as if the villagers left their homes in a hurry to escape advancing German Armies. A lonely dog was barking in the middle of the road. A red, hammer-and-sickle-adorned flag was hanging from a pole at the third house. A group of Soviet soldiers in full combat gear were standing in the front yard of the house behind a picket fence. One soldier was rolling a cigarette when he spotted the two approaching men. He dropped the cigarette, raised his rifle and yelled: "Stop, who goes there?" The other soldiers pointed their weapons at the two strangers.

Kuba and Ivan raised their arms, their rifles strapped to their shoulders. The Soviet soldiers surrounded them and all marched into the house. Kuba tried to tell them who he and Ivan were, but the leader of the group, a sergeant, threatened him with his gun and said sharply, "Keep your mouth shut."

They were led into a room where a dozen soldiers were sitting on benches along the walls. At the far end a Soviet lieutenant was sitting behind a table. The sergeant saluted and said excitedly, "Comrade Lieutenant, we captured two spies!"

"Take their weapons!" The lieutenant ordered. Kuba and Ivan were rudely disarmed and then ordered to empty their pockets and place everything on the table. The two partisans followed the order.

Kuba put his little bag of tobacco and matches on the table and said: "We are partisans from the Polesye marshes and we were sent here to establish contact with the Red Army." The lieutenant, a young man in his twenties with flax-colored hair and mustache, came out from behind the table, picked up a roll of maps and approached the partisans.

"Now, let's have the truth! Which German SS unit sent you here, and where did you get the Soviet weapons?"

"That is not so. We are partisans and those are our weapons. We..." The lieutenant hit Kuba hard across the face with the roll of maps. The other soldiers joined in delivering blow after blow to the Kuba and Ivan's sides, backs and heads. Kuba was bleeding from his mouth and nose. Ivan's left eye was blood-shot and turning purple. His forehead was bleeding.

"Tie their hands," the lieutenant barked harshly. "Tomkin, take them out to the truck!" As they were led out of the room, the officer picked up a field telephone and began talking loudly to someone. Several tanks were parked behind the house. There were also a few trucks. The lieutenant came out through a back door, accompanied by a major, who they had not noticed before.

"Take them to the Military Headquarters," the major ordered. The lieutenant motioned the two partisans into the back of a truck. Four soldiers jumped in after them and forced them to lie down on the floor. The truck started moving along the road in an easterly direction. The one called Tomkin was driving and the lieutenant was sitting next to him. It was a painful journey for Kuba and Ivan. They were laying face down on the wet and dirty bed of the truck, with their hands tied behind their backs. The road was full of potholes and bumps that caused the two partisans a lot of pain every time the truck passed over one of these. Two hours passed before the truck slowed down and finally came to a stop. Kuba could hear voices, the sounds of passing motor vehicles, horses and a child calling its mother.

"Arise!" a soldier yelled and Kuba was pulled up to his feet. They were in a town. Two and three story buildings lined both sides of the street. Civilians, mostly women and children, were standing on the sidewalk, watching the truck. They were in front of some military headquarters. Kuba was ordered off the truck.

He jumped off. A soldier behind him held his arm tightly. He looked back at Ivan and felt pain at his side. Two soldiers were dragging Ivan. His face and the left side of his chest, showing through a rip in his shirt, were bloody. His head was hanging down limp.

They were brought into a small room and made to sit on the floor near the wall. A number of officers and soldiers were standing in front of them. A captain was sitting behind a desk, writing on a sheet of paper.

Kuba, still in shock, began to comprehend the gravity of the situation in which he and Ivan found themselves. The NKVD officers were determined to prosecute them as German spies. That meant torture and death. The Russians never asked him about his name or nationality. The bestial murder of his family by Nazis and his long participation in the partisan war against them meant nothing to the NKVD. He was contemplating his tragic life when somebody kicked him in the ribs and said, "Get up and go stand before the Captain at the table!"

Kuba struggled to his feet and walked up to the table. The soldier that kicked him untied his hands. The Captain did not look at Kuba's face. He placed a sheet of paper in front of Kuba and told him to sign it. Kuba read the top line on the paper and his blood rushed to his head. He read the words again: "I hereby confess that I am a Nazi spy and enemy of the Soviet People."

His heart was pounding and he yelled out in anguish, "No! I am not a spy! We are partisans fighting against the Nazis! Comrade Stalin referred to us on the radio as Avengers of the Soviet People! You cannot..." A blow to the head knocked Kuba down. He tried to get up, but another soldier hit him with a chair on the side of the head. He lost consciousness.

He tried to see through the darkness. Someone was talking to him in a very loud voice. Why can he not see them? Now there is a gray light on the left. A woman is coming nearer. It's Franca with little Victor in her arms. No, it's a man, a Cossack. It's Gregory Koshevoy handing him a letter of recommendation to the Soviet military authorities. The letter... where is the letter? Someone shook him violently. He screamed out loud, "Where is the letter?" He opened his eyes.

Ivan was shaking his shoulder. "Wake up Kuba, please." He looked at Ivan's face. One eye was blood-shot and the skin around it dark blue. His head was wrapped in a bloody rag.

"What happened, Vania?" Kuba asked.[3] There was a bittersweet taste in his mouth. He touched his tongue with a finger. It was blood.

Ivan looked at him with tears in his eyes. "Oh Kuba, they beat you so much. Every day. Five, six days. At times I thought you were dead."

Kuba looked around the room. There were gray brick walls and no windows. Only two old blankets lay on the floor. It was a prison cell, about six by ten feet. There were blood smudges on the wall. There was a heavy steel door in one wall. It had a little square cut out, with three vertical bars in it. "Where are we?" Kuba asked.

"In Moscow, the Butyrki prison. They brought us here over a week ago. You were semiconscious most of the time, even when they took you out for interrogations. I fed you some bread when they gave it to us. I think that they decided something for us, because today there were no interrogations."

Kuba looked up at the ceiling. A single light bulb hung from the center. In one corner of the cell stood a small bucket with water in it and a metal cup attached. In the opposite corner was a larger bucket which served as a toilet. A grinding noise caused Kuba to sit up. His head was throbbing. The door was being unlocked. Three guards entered the cell. One stopped near the door while the other two approached Kuba, picked him up by the arms and led him outside. The door was locked behind them. They followed a long corridor. There were several doors on both sides. They came to a staircase and went up two flights. There was another long, unfamiliar corridor. The two guards were silent. With frozen, dark expressions on their faces, they looked straight ahead. Kuba suddenly had a feeling that they were leading him to his execution. There was an open door on the right side. The guards

---

[3] Vania is the familiar name for Ivan in Russian. –ED.

led Kuba inside. They stopped before a desk. A heavy set lieutenant was sitting behind it. A large picture of Lavrenti Beria, head of the KGB, occupied one wall. On the opposite wall there hung a picture of Joseph Stalin. There was a door in the wall behind the desk. On the center of the door was a plate with a name on it: "Commissar M.A. Kagan."

"Sit down." The Commissar handed Kuba a cigarette, which he lit, but his stomach had been empty for so long that he became violently dizzy at once. "What is your name, your nationality?" asked the Commissar.

"I am a Jew from Poland," Kuba answered in a voice no louder than a sigh. The Commissar's face underwent an immediate and remarkable change. He jumped to his feet and leaned across the table, peering at Kuba through the thick lenses of his spectacles.

"You are Jewish?" he asked.

"Yes," Kuba replied.

"Can you speak Yiddish?" Kuba began to talk Yiddish as fast as he could, explaining how he had come to Moscow. The Commissar handed him a paper. "Write something in Yiddish." He wrote a sentence. Still a little suspicious, the Commissar told Kuba to remove his pants and show that he was circumcised. Convinced now that Kuba spoke the truth the Commissar nodded gravely and sat down.

Kuba had no strength. The past few days of hunger, beatings and desperation seemed to weigh heavily and all at once he was ready to collapse. The Commissar called a guard and ordered him to bring Kuba some tea and "suchary", a kind of hard toast. While Kuba ate, the Commissar stood looking out the window. "Come here," the Commissar said. "I want to show you something."

Kuba looked out the window into a large courtyard below, surrounded on three sides by blank, windowless walls. Opposite one of the walls, six soldiers were standing with rifles. "Those are your executioners. They are waiting to shoot you presently." But instead of being shot, Kuba and Ivan were given a bath and breakfast and sent to a doctor. Kuba was certain that all these things happened because the Commissar was of Jewish origin and he recognized Kuba as a fellow Jew and the Soviets knew that it was unlikely for a Jew to be a Nazi spy.

Looking into the bathroom mirror, Kuba was amazed at the haggard, bearded, swollen face it reflected. It bore no resemblance to the face he knew. Later, they were issued new uniforms and made members of the Special Forces of the Red Army. Ivan was put on a plane that very night and returned to their partisan group behind the lines, where he was dropped by parachute, along with radio equipment and supplies enabling him to stay in contact with Moscow and Kuba was sent to a special military school of the armed forces to be trained for activities and reconnaissance work behind enemy lines.

Most of the instruction and studies at Diversionnaya Shkola, as the school was called, were concerned with recognition and interrogation of spies, demolition and sabotage, executions and, of course, the psychology of various nationalities. They were taught, for example, that Germans were part of a machine. The machinist operates everything efficiently, except when there is no officer or boss to give orders, then the machine just stops. The Germans will believe anyone who speaks German well and with a tone of authority. About Americans, they were taught that money is the keystone to all cultural life, economy and politics in the United States; all U.S. power is centered on Wall Street. The lend-lease which Russia was then receiving was explained by saying that American security was threatened, and the Soviet Union was the only power that could save the United States from Hitler.

Only a small number of the students at the school were Russian. Most of them were Poles, Germans, Spaniards, Greeks, Italians, Yugoslavs, Czechs and English. There may have been some Americans, but Kuba did not know an American from an Englishman. To him they were all English. At Diversionnaya Shkola they were also trained in parachute jumping. Towards the end of the course, the students were divided into partisan groups, and Kuba was given the rank of second lieutenant and assigned to the special partisan group number 258, under the command of Colonel Kiril Orlovsky, a Russian with seven years experience in guerrilla fighting, decorated with the Order of Lenin, the highest Soviet medal. He had led partisan groups in Poland until 1924. Those groups were known to the world as the hordes of Mucha Michalski. After 1924, Orlovsky was active in China and later in Spain.

The school was located on Dzerzhinsky Street, next to a series of military barracks which housed Air Force officers and Orlovsky's group. They were given three rooms, four men to a room. Kuba shared his room with Volodiya, a Croat, Otto, a German, and Nikolay, a Ukrainian Cossack. The group consisted of twelve men, including Colonel Orlovsky and his adjutant, Loris, a Spaniard.

It was December and the city was covered with a white blanket of snow making the sidewalks icy and slippery. Kuba and the others were issued winter uniforms consisting of fur hats, white camouflage coats and a so called "plashch palatka," a large, rectangular piece of waterproof cloth in khaki color which was worn like a poncho but could also be made into a pup tent.

On December 14, Kuba was having dinner at the officer's dining room with the others in his group. Loris came in and told them that the Colonel had called a special meeting in his room of the entire Partisan Group for seven o'clock that evening.

The meeting was very brief. As soon as everyone was present, Orlovsky read a special order: "On the December 15, 1941, the Special Partisan Group No.258 will depart for the Arctic regions of the Soviet Union for special training. Your commander will issue final instructions."

At six o'clock the next morning, the group boarded a twin engine Soviet Air Force plane and took off for Murmansk, near the Barents Sea. Kuba looked out the window and observed the snowbound countryside, north of Moscow. The plane flew over extensive forests, glittering in the snow and ice and Kuba thought about the forests near the Wygon Lake and wondered how Ivan got back and what had happened to his people since he had left them. The plane landed at Petrozavodsk, on the shores of the huge Lake Onega. After refueling, they took off for Murmansk. The forests changed to the tundra of the Arctic as the plane flew over sparsely populated areas until they reached the White Sea, and landed in Murmansk in the afternoon. There were few motorized vehicles at the airport and the most common means of transportation were sleighs pulled by reindeer.

THE ODYSSEY OF A PARTISAN

The group spent the following ten days in the area of Murmansk, participating in maneuvers that involved activities behind imaginary enemy lines. During their free time, Kuba and his closest friend, Otto, explored the city, visiting the Arctic museum, several so-called restaurants and cinemas. On one occasion, they were invited to a party which took place at the apartment of a girl who worked for the Air Force.

There were three girls in the apartment, all tall, blonde, well-developed and Finnish. They almost looked like sisters. Kuba, Otto and another officer, were greeted warmly by the girls and were offered glasses of vodka. The girls' apartment consisted of two small rooms, an alcove and kitchenette. A large, round table was in the front room, covered with food and drinks and on a small bench near the window, an old gramophone was playing tangos, waltzes and Russian dance music. "I am so glad that you could come," said the girl from the Air Force office, as she approached Kuba with two glasses in her hands. She was the shortest of the three, and her blue eyes regarded Kuba with interest.

"Thank you for inviting us," Kuba replied. He took the glass which she extended to him, and followed as she led him to a bench where she sat next to him.

"To your health!" They toasted each other. There was a cast iron stove in one corner of the room, into which the girls dropped large pieces of wood from time to time. It was getting quite warm in the apartment and Kuba asked if he could remove his jacket.

"Of course," the girl said, as she began to remove the heavy sweater she was wearing over a light green blouse with short sleeves that was very tight on her, emphasizing her prominent bosom. Kuba suddenly remembered that he had not been with a woman for quite some time. The girl noticed his stare and she blushed slightly with a coquettish smile on her face.

"Let's eat, my friends," she said, moving to the table. They all joined her and began to fill their plates with food. There was a mountain of meat, cheese and other foods on the table. The meat tasted good, but it was very dark and there was a musky odor to it. After they ate, Kuba learned from the girl that this was a combination of bear and moose meat. The three couples drank more vodka and began to dance to the music of the gramophone. "You dance very well," the girl said to Kuba. "Do you like to tango?"

"Very much, especially with someone who dances as well as you."

They danced around the table, bumping into the other couples. The girl stopped dancing and went to the table, picked up two glasses of vodka and motioned to Kuba to follow her. "Let's go into the other room, where we can dance without bumping into anyone." Kuba smiled at her and followed her into the other room which was somewhat larger than the front room and was furnished with two beds along opposite walls and a large dresser. An open door led into the alcove and Kuba noticed a bed in there. The girl sat down on one of the beds and motioned to Kuba to join her. They sipped the vodka and he put his arm around her. She looked up at him, smiled and moved closer.

"Is that where you sleep?" Kuba asked.

"No, I sleep in there," the girl answered, pointing to the alcove.

"May I see it?"

"Maybe later. Now I want to dance some more." The gramophone was playing a tango again and they danced silently, listening to the conversation and laughter in the other room. Otto and his girl danced into the room and they both appeared to be unsteady on their feet. They headed straight for the other bed, and still embracing, fell on it, laughing. Kuba watched them, amused, when he felt his girl pulling him toward the alcove. "Let's hide in here." They sat on her bed with their arms around each other, sipping from their glasses. After finishing their drinks and placing the empty glasses on the floor, she came into Kuba's arms and they kissed. "Do you want me?" the girl asked in a husky voice.

"Oh, yes." She got up and closed the door. It was dark in the little room and when she returned to the bed and Kuba noticed that she had begun to remove her blouse. She stretched out on the bed, pulling Kuba towards her. In their passion, they could not hear the noise from the other room.

There was quite a New Year's party at the officers club in Murmansk, with plenty of drinks and ladies for the occasion. During the two weeks the group remained in Murmansk. In the first week of January 1942, the Partisan Group No.258 received orders to proceed across the border into Finland. Orlovsky's group was assigned a guide who happened to be the shaman of a village in Lapland. He was about sixty years old and spoke only a few words of Russian. However, he had the rank of major in the old Czarist Army of Russia.

In the morning, they left by sleigh pulled by reindeer, and in about a half hour, the shaman announced, in his best Russian, that they were in Finland. It was difficult for Kuba to get used to the unchanging light of the polar night. The ten partisans, plus Orlovsky and Loris, suffered a bad case of "snow blindness" so the shaman provided them with wooden goggles which had narrow slits in them, and they helped very much.

During the following weeks, Kuba traveled with Orlovsky's group in one of the three sleighs pulled by reindeer. They made their way to the northwest until they reached the Barents Sea and there they turned west toward the town of Petsamo. Kuba sat next to Otto in the sleigh. They were dressed in fur coats with parkas and fur-lined boots, but it was very cold. Otto, a medium-sized blonde man in his thirties was telling Kuba about his life in Germany before Hitler came into power. Kuba asked him about his education.

Otto said, "Oh, I was a student at Heidelberg University and a member of the Communist Party. I never graduated because in 1934 I had to leave Germany before the Nazis could get me."

"What did you do then?" Kuba asked.

"I lived in France for a few years, and when the civil war started in Spain, I joined the Loyalists. In 1938 my entire brigade was evacuated to the Soviet Union."

"What did your father do for a living?" Kuba asked.

"He was a professor of chemistry at the university," Otto replied.

Suddenly Nikolay, who was sitting behind Kuba, pointed to the left and yelled, "Look at that fox go!" Crossing their path, running at high speed, was a polar fox with a bluish coat.

"I wonder what is chasing him," Kuba said. Then they heard a deep growl coming from the ocean side where a huge polar bear was chasing the fox. The bear stopped suddenly, stood erect and looked at the fast-moving sleighs, then turned and went toward the seashore.

A continuous rumbling noise came from the ocean, covered with moving ice fields. Everything was grayish white, no color changes, except when the Aurora Borealis began its colorful display, stretching across the entire horizon. It was neither day nor night, as Kuba knew it.

Occasionally, they stopped at temporary villages of the nomadic Lapps. Orlovsky's group spent several days resting in each village. In their honor, the villagers usually organized a feast of roasted reindeer meat and fish, a very friendly and hospitable people. There was always a large herd of reindeer near the villages and, to the Lapps, the reindeer were the source of everything, food, clothing and even building materials as in their "yourtas" which were constructed of reindeer hides.

The group did not meet any military units during their journey until they came close to Petsamo. They had just cleared a small hill, when the shaman stopped suddenly and motioned to everyone to be quiet. He got off the sleigh, walked ahead several feet and began studying something further ahead. He turned and motioned to the rest of the group to join him. They all lay down on the snow and the shaman pointed to a wisp of smoke a few dozen yards away that was rising from the snow-covered mound. As they watched, a hatch opened and a German soldier appeared. Only the upper part of his body was visible. Using binoculars, he looked around, dropped his binoculars and fired his gun several times in the direction of the north, where something must have attracted his attention, then descended into the mound and closed the hatch. It was obvious that the mound was actually a German bunker, one of many in the area, which guarded a German submarine base in Petsamo.

Orlovsky turned to Kuba and said, "Kuba, take Pasha and Nikolay with you and crawl up to the hatch on the bunker. Now observe the two pipes sticking out of the mound. The larger one is a chimney and the other one is a periscope. You can see it rotating occasionally. You are to move only when it is pointing away from you and the next time the hatch opens, call out in German to the guard and grab him, then use your hand grenades and destroy the bunker."

The three partisans crawled up the mound, watching the movement of the periscope, then tied together six hand grenades and waited. About fifteen minutes later, the hatch opened and the guard started ascending from the bunker.

"Hey, comrade," Kuba said with authority.

"Who is that?" the guard asked and came out of the bunker. Nikolay grabbed him and covered his mouth with his huge palms. Kuba pulled the pin from one of the grenades and hurled the bundle into the bunker. They quickly rolled down from the mound, Nikolay holding the German. It was a muffled explosion, but the top of the bunker caved in and there was no noise or movement coming from within. Nikolay tied the hands of the German, behind his back, and they marched him back to Orlovsky. Later, Kuba learned that this was their objective; to capture a German for interrogation about the base in Petsamo.

They got into their sleighs and headed in a southeast direction. Now Orlovsky was sitting next to Kuba and the German was in the back between Nikolay and Otto. They were interrogating the prisoner, with Kuba serving as interpreter. Otto's Russian vocabulary was still very limited. They learned that the base in Petsamo was the home for a special group of U-boats which were blocking the Arctic Sea's approach to the major Soviet port of Archangelsk.

After two days of travel, a group of Lapps appeared from nowhere. They talked to the shaman and he in turn motioned to Orlovsky to join the conversation. It turned out that a large force of mixed German and Finnish troops were blocking their road to Murmansk. Orlovsky returned to his group, pulled out some maps and began to study them while talking. He said, "We don't want any encounters with Finnish forces. Let's see what we can do. Oh, yes. We can travel directly southeast and get to Kandalaksha on the White Sea. That is the way!" Orlovsky turned to the shaman and conversed with him as best he could. The group headed southeast. It took them five days to reach Kandalaksha. The German prisoner was transferred to the National Security people and Orlovsky's group was granted a three-day furlough.

When the Orlovsky group arrived in Moscow, it was bad. German forces were in the town of Mozhaysk, half way between Vyazma and Moscow. So the group was immediately ordered into service for the defense of Moscow. His unit was incorporated into a Red Army brigade that was preparing to march to the front. The city was almost deserted. Most of the government offices, the Cabinet and the Politburo were evacuated to Kuybyshev in the east. There were almost no military personnel visible in the center of the city, only Stalin and a number of lower officials remained in Moscow.

Special Partisan Group No.258 was on a reconnaissance mission about two miles ahead of the Soviet troops. The weather was bitterly cold and it was painful to breathe. They were dressed in their white camouflage coats and advancing across a snowfield toward a forest. Pasha, who was out in front of the group, suddenly dropped to the ground and motioned to the rest of them to do likewise. A reflection of metal or glass was coming from the forest. Orlovsky crawled up to Pasha and the others followed. Then he looked through his binoculars and said, "Germans!"

Kuba looked through his binoculars and was amazed. The troops in the forest were pointing machine guns and cannons in their direction but did not fire at the partisans who were only about seventy yards away from the forest, and in an open field. Twenty minutes passed and nothing happened.

Orlovsky gave an order. "Pasha, you circle the field to the left and enter the forest. Kuba, you do the same to the right and yell in German at the troops. I have an idea as to what you will find in the forest, but it is too early to be sure. If everything is all right, fire three shots from your pistol."

It took Kuba ten minutes to reach the forest. He got to his feet and began to move amongst the trees, then stopped cold as he came face to face with an enemy soldier. The soldier was leaning against a tree and held a rifle in his left hand. He looked straight at Kuba but made no move. Kuba raised his sub-machine gun, but the soldier did not move. Carefully, Kuba began to move toward the soldier until he was only a few feet away. It was not a German, but an Italian soldier and his helmet was covered with a layer of snow. Kuba touched the Italian and jumped back. The soldier fell backwards to the ground, but his limbs remained in the same position. He was frozen to death with clothing too light for a Russian winter. There must have been a battalion of Italian troops in that forest.

Pasha fired his pistol three times. The rest of the group came running into the forest. Volodiya radioed the commanding officer of the Soviet troops and reported the situation.

Two days later, the No.258 group was in the trenches of a Soviet brigade, facing a German division who had been lobbing artillery shells at them for three hours and there was nothing the Russians could do. Kuba and the others were sitting in the trenches with their backs toward the enemy, so as not to get hit by shrapnel. About noon the German artillery barrage slowed down, Pasha stood up and peeked out but he could not see anything. As he turned, he saw something on the Russian side of the trenches. He pointed and everybody got up and looked. About two dozen trucks were coming towards them. Each truck had four large-diameter tubes mounted over the cab. The trucks stopped in a parallel line behind the trenches and Soviet soldiers got off and went to the rear of the trucks. The front ends of the tubes were elevated, and then it happened!

There was no sound of shooting, just the sound of a huge locomotive letting out steam. Small rockets, in a stream, began pouring from the tubes toward the Germans. Kuba looked in the direction where the rockets went. The German trenches were there and now instead of snow, Kuba could see a thick wall of smoke. The Germans were silent. After awhile, Soviet tanks passed the trenches and were ordered to attack. Soviet troops followed the tanks. Hundreds and hundreds of soldiers were moving through the snow fields. When they came closer to the German lines, a terrifying cry arose from the thousands of troops. It was the yell of a Russian soldier in attack, "Hurra!"

The soldiers held their rifles with fixed bayonets and when they reached the German lines, they saw a terrible sight, everything was burned black, human bodies, artillery, tanks and everything else. The Germans were already in retreat at the farther lines.

Later, they learned about the mysterious trucks, the famous new weapon developed in Russia and called "Katyusha." The Russians chased the retreating Germany Army toward Vyazma. Group No. 258 was called back to Moscow where they were to return to school for more training in preparation for their first mission behind the German lines.

Chapter Eleven

It was clear to Kuba that the citizens of Moscow were accustomed to hard times. They had gone through wars and revolutions, hunger and death, but this was probably the worst of all times. Curfew hours were from six at night to six in the morning. He saw hundreds of people standing in lines, all day long, near the stores, waiting for their rations, but most of them returned home in the evening without receiving anything. In other ways, life in Moscow was similar to any other major city during a war. Women, who were willing to go with the military anyplace, in return for even a few pounds of sugar, were everywhere. This was particularly true in the railroad and subway stations.

There were German bombing raids on the city without any spectacular results showing very little damage, which was odd for Moscow was almost unprotected with no combat troops in the city. As a matter of fact, aside from a number of balloons and a handful of anti-aircraft guns, the city had no protection and could have been taken by the Germans at any time during that period. However, Hitler wanted to take the city intact and he was afraid that the Russians would destroy it if the Germans made a move. He wanted another Paris. In a way, this was a war of nerves, and both the Germans and Russians paid dearly for it. The economic and psychological state of the Soviet citizens before the war was bad enough, but now it was worse, much worse. They were clothed in rags and even their feet were wrapped in rags and their eyes had a frightened and desperate look. The children were skinny and undernourished in appearance and ran through the streets, begging passersby for money and food. Many began to steal whenever they had an opportunity. The games the children played reflected the war. Instead of cops and bandits, they played Nazis and Red Army soldiers, and were aware of spies. The Mos-

THE ODYSSEY OF A PARTISAN

cow radio had warned the citizens about German spies and paratroopers and the entire city was carried away in a frenzy of spy chasing. The children only modeled the grown ups. Every day Kuba saw a group of children chasing a man or woman and crying "Spy!" The effect of this was terrible and resulted in the police or NKVD troops arresting suspects. They rode the street cars, buses and subways and listened to the conversations of the passengers and when they heard a word which they didn't understand, they immediately shouted "Spy!" Always there was a policeman nearby to make the arrest.

The air force troops stationed in Moscow at that time were better off than any other troops. Their rations were the highest and they were issued the best food. Most of it was imported from the United States, but the partisan group obtained their food supplies from the army commissary, located in a distant part of the city. Every week, two of the men went to pick up the food supplies for the entire group. One day it was Otto's and Kuba's turn. They boarded a bus heading for their destination. It stopped at a subway station, which was identified by a large neon sign and a balustrade in the middle of the sidewalk. There were several raggedly clothed teenagers with fishing poles in hand, standing around the escalator-well of the station. Kuba and Otto watched one of the boys lower his fishing pole and come up with someone's fur hat. Actually they were stealing, and then they ran toward the nearest black market place to sell their loot.

As they were watching the spectacle, Otto began to laugh and said, "This is a real theater play!" They were standing on the back platform, dressed in their officer's uniforms and observing the people around them. Occasionally they exchanged some remarks about the city and the people, especially the young girls on the bus. They conversed in German because it was still difficult for Otto to speak in Russian.

"Now that's a beautiful girl," Otto said in German, pointing at a girl who had just boarded the bus, and before Kuba could answer, a young boy of about twelve, who had been watching them intensely for some time, let out a yell, "Spies!"

Otto and Kuba found themselves pinned to the floor, and everyone was yelling. A policeman appeared from the front of the bus and they were handcuffed. The policeman marched them to the nearest station and the NKVD was called. After their documents were checked and a few telephone calls made, Kuba and Otto were released to Colonel Orlovsky, who arrived in a military staff car.

The various partisan groups were assigned some very obscure missions, such as the relocation of over two million Volga Germans, who had settled in Russia during the reign of the German-born Tsarina, Catherine the Great. The Soviet rulers worried that these descendants of Germany might turn out to be collaborators of Nazi Germany. They were removed from their Autonomous Republic on the Volga River, with its two major cities of Marx and Engles, in twenty-four hours and moved to Siberia, near the city of Verkhoyansk, the coldest place on earth.

In his new position as lieutenant first class, Kuba was thinking about a trip to the east to visit his uncle and aunt, Avram and Tema, in the city of Gorki. However, he soon found out that no one was allowed to leave Moscow.

Early in March of 1942, Orlovsky's group was ordered to prepare for a special mission in line with their training. The original Orlovsky group was assembled at the Pushkino military airport at nine o'clock that evening. They were each equipped with special parachutes, submachine guns, sidearms and about forty pounds of special equipment. It was snowing and cold and the partisans were huddled together at one end of the terminal, talking amongst themselves about the forthcoming mission. Kuba, Otto and Nikolay were standing together, smoking and wondering what lay ahead of them, when the order came to board the plane. It was an American plane, a Douglas 26, with no seats so the partisans sat on the floor against the walls of the plane. The plane took off as soon as the door closed.

Kuba looked out through the window, but it was too dark to see anything. They flew over Belarus, Poland, Romania and Hungary. They had been told not to talk during the trip, but Kuba turned to Otto and said, "Where do you suppose we are going?"

"The Adriatic coast," Otto replied, quietly.

It was almost midnight when the plane began its descent. Kuba could distinguish a forest and lake below. The plane made a large circle and Kuba spotted five bonfires burning below set in a rectangle with the fifth fire burning in the center, a pre-arranged signal. Orlovsky got to his feet and ordered the partisans to line up in front the door. The door was opened. The plane circled the area once and the pilot gave the signal to begin the jump. Kuba was fifth in line. He checked his parachute straps, making sure that the ripcord was in the right place. One after another, the partisans disappeared through the door. Kuba never quite got used to the idea of jumping out of a plane and his stomach knotted up. He was very tense. When it was his turn to jump, he closed his eyes and just ran out of the plane, without thinking. Otherwise, he would have frozen at the door, as he did during his first practice jump.

He was falling head first, and he kept his lips pressed tightly together against the onrush of air. Then he opened his eyes and counted, one-twenty-one, one-twenty-two, one-twenty-three, and pulled the ripcord. The chute opened and stopped his free fall with a violent jerk. He looked around and saw the parachutes of his comrades all around him, and noticed that the bonfires were to his left. It was windy and the parachutes were heading in the direction of a river.

Kuba realized then that something was wrong. Machine gun fire was coming towards them from the ground. As he came closer to the ground, Kuba saw many uniformed soldiers near the bonfires. It became clear to him that the Germans, with advance notice of their arrival, had set up a landing pattern of their own.

Suddenly Kuba felt that his parachute was dragging, jerkily, and that he was falling more quickly. He looked up and saw that his chute had several bullet holes in it. He could hear the bullets whizzing by. Directly below him, he spotted three Germans firing at him with sub-machine guns. Kuba grabbed his machine gun and began shooting at the enemy, but to no effect. He was swinging back and forth, hanging from the nylon cords. In desperation, Kuba unfastened a hand grenade and pulled out the pin, raised his knees and with his hand, held the grenade between them. As soon as he could see the three figures on the ground between his knees, he dropped the grenade. He was about seventy-five yards from the ground. The shock of the exploding hand grenade moved him faster toward a tree-covered hill. He noticed that several parachutes were on the ground in that area.

Kuba's parachute got caught in some tree branches in a forest on a hillside and he was hanging about twelve feet from the ground. He could not detect any movement on the ground below him. He was about to cut the nylon straps of his chute, when he heard someone approaching. Kuba raised his sub-machine gun, feeling very helpless with that big, white parachute above him. A man dressed in a khaki coverall like his own, came into view. The man looked up at Kuba and whistled the signal tune of the Orlovsky group. Kuba replied and the man came into the open. It was Toliya. Kuba again pulled out his knife and cut the nylon straps, then slid down the tree trunk to the ground.

"There are Germans everywhere!" Toliya said quietly.

"Yes. Looks like we have been betrayed," Kuba replied.

"Let's go find the others," said Toliya. They did not attempt to pull down Kuba's parachute. Toliya headed in an easterly direction toward the river and the field where the bonfires were set up. They found several other members of their partisan group, including Colonel Orlovsky, hanging from a treetop. After awhile they realized that the area was a plateau above the coastal region of the city of Split in Yugoslavia.

They reached the outskirts of the landing area in about twenty minutes. No one was missing from the original group. As they looked on, German troops combed the area, trying to locate the paratroopers. On the banks of the river, Orlovsky set up a defense line against the German troops as heavy shooting broke out on the western side. The partisans headed in that direction, circling the open area of the bonfires and taking advantage of the forest for cover. The fighting increased in intensity and the Germans seemed to be retreating towards the coast. Then a new army appeared in the clearing. They were not uniformed soldiers and they were chasing the Germans. They were a unit of the Yugoslav partisan army under the command of Josip Broz, whom the Yugoslavs called Tito. Tito, a former auto mechanic from the Porsche Auto Werke in Austria, was a heavy set man with blonde hair and had a German shepherd dog at his feet at all times. He had a broad, friendly face and green eyes and his officers and soldiers liked him very much; this was apparent in their behavior when Tito was around. A reception was held for the paratroopers in a mountain chalet, fireplace and all. There was a tremendous amount of food, drink, music and dancing. Tito greeted everybody and proposed a toast to the invincible brotherhood among people.

Kuba was assigned to a group which was about to take off for the interior. The group consisted of thirty men under Lieutenant Milovan. Milovan was a young Croatian with brown hair and brown eyes. Kuba liked him immediately and they became friends.

The group traveled on horseback over a narrow trail into the mountain range toward the city of Sarajevo. The horses were moving quite fast, in spite of the steepness of the terrain. It was dark when the group reached a large, level clearing. In the center of the clearing was erected some kind of a shrine, surrounded by a wrought-iron fence. All the men dismounted and kneeled in silent prayer near the fence.

Milovan told Kuba that the shrine was the grave of an ancient regional hero named Milosh Miloshevish, who led an uprising against the Turkish rulers of their country. Miloshevish had belonged to a Slavic tribe known as the Uskoki. They were Slavs who lived in the vicinity of Split. They were trained from childhood for military service, similar to the Russian Cossacks. The legend tells of the heroism of the Uskoki in their fight against the Turks. When they stormed the Sultan's palace, Milosh met the Sultan's daughter and they fell in love. The two lovers attempted to escape into the mountains, but were captured by the Sultan's Yanichars, special troops. Milosh was executed in a horrible manner. The Turks wrapped him tightly in cloth, in a sitting position. He was impaled on a needle-sharp, greased pole which penetrated his anus. Special ropes and weights secured his upright position. The pole penetrated his body. It took him three days to die.

When the sound of approaching horses reached them from the opposite side of the clearing, Milovan ordered his soldiers to mount up and execute a defense line. One partisan took up a forward position and challenged the approaching horseman. "Who is coming?" he asked in a loud voice.

"Chetniks!" came the answer. "And who are you?"

"Partisans!" A large group of riders entered the clearing and dismounted and kneeled near the shrine. Their leader was dressed in a black semi-uniform with a sword at his left side and a large fur hat like a Cossack papakha on his head. He walked over to Milovan and the two talked quietly. The leader was about fifty years old. Kuba noticed that there was tension between the two groups. Then the Chetniks mounted their horses and their leader saluted the partisans by raising his sword and crying out, "Long live Yugoslavia."

When the two groups departed, in opposite directions, Kuba asked Milovan about the leader of the Chetniks. "Oh, that was Drago Mikhailovich," replied Milovan. He then explained to Kuba the situation in Yugoslavia. There were two major forces of resistance, the Chetniks under Mikhailovich and the partisans under Josip Broz or Tito. The partisans with Tito suspected the Chetniks of collaborating with the Italians occasionally and that caused a lot of friction and some armed conflict between the two groups. Both had a common enemy, the Ustashi, which were organized by the Germans. The Ustashi were not unlike the SS. They were outright traitors who helped the Germans in their attempt to pacify the people of Yugoslavia.

Later, Kuba was to recall the period in Yugoslavia as in a dream. It had been a busy period. He had met many people and one of them was Marshal Tito, a Communist of the old school. Tito and the officers of his staff shared the same food and the same equipment with their men. He was at all times certain of himself, unswervingly dedicated to his cause and resolute in having his own way. Tito was the kind of man who cannot endure having a master, especially the kind he found in the Kremlin.

Kuba had come to know him as well as any soldier ever got to know him. For a period of more than eight months, Orlovsky's group trained the partisans under Tito. Then, during the second week of May 1943, Kuba took part in the great partisan offensive which ended in the taking of the city of Zagreb.

One afternoon, after a day of hard fighting, their detachment took the small town of Gornji Vakuf. Accompanied by two other officers, Kuba entered the house that had been the German headquarters. As they opened the door, a barrage of bullets came from a Nazi with two pistols. He wounded one partisan before they could silence him with a burst from their sub-machine guns. In a corner, near the window of a large room, was a desk with some papers on it. Kuba picked out the German documents that were of some value to them and a copy of the official German newspaper, VOELKISCHER BEOBACHTER dated May 15, 1943. Kuba had not seen a newspaper for a long time so he put it into his pocket and returned to camp.

Several partisans had made camp in the surrounding forest. Cooks prepared meals over a large bonfire. Kuba sat down on a rock near the fire and took out the newspaper. Suddenly there was a commotion among the soldiers. He rose to his feet to see what was going on. Two partisans were helping a very old, blind man. They sat him near the fire. He had a long, gray beard and held some kind of instrument in his bony hands, a single string gusli. The old man talked to the partisans for awhile. Then he began to play a very monotone melody. He was telling an old tale about the heroism of the Uskoki in their fight against the Turks. It took the old man more than half an hour to finish his tale and in all that time the partisans listened attentively. It was very exciting and romantic. It reminded Kuba of the old Guslars in Polish history.

Late in the night, when everyone was asleep, Kuba finally took out the newspaper and began to read by the light of the bonfire. On the second page, his eyes came upon a very familiar name, his father's. In a very crude form, the Nazi paper told of his father's suicide. He couldn't believe it. He read it over and over. What had happened? The last news heard was that his father was in New York. The paper said that his father, a member of the Polish Government in exile, had committed suicide in London.

Kuba could not sleep that night. Before his eyes, he saw his father's image. It was the image from that highway between Warsaw and Lodz before they lost each other. Other scenes appeared through the night. There were visions from his childhood—his father leading him to school for the first time, the graduation ceremony when he got his diploma from high school. He was awakened to the image of his father the whole night.

A few weeks later, the Orlovsky unit returned to Moscow.

Chapter Twelve

The unit received their first furlough upon returning from Yugoslavia. All of Kuba's comrades had friends or some relatives in Russia and they left immediately, but Kuba had a three-week furlough and no place to go. He spent a couple of days visiting theatres and the Moscow Opera House. He saw the opera "Carmen" by George Bizet. That reminded him of the Warsaw Opera House where he had seen the same opera some years ago. All of a sudden he remembered that he did have some relatives not too far from Moscow, his aunt and uncle, in the city of Gorki. He even remembered their address. There was no time to lose.

The trains going east were crowded with thousands of people. Some had waited for weeks and months in the railroad stations to get onto a train. As an officer, it took Kuba only a few minutes to get into a special compartment for officers. The journey lasted two days, passing many towns and villages which had been partially bombed out by German planes. The populace had gotten used to it and went about their business without any thought of the enemy.

In that area, there were many plants and factories producing war equipment and several forced-labor camps. The prisoners were used for road work. At the railroad stations where they stopped for short periods, there were restaurants and cafeterias, but civilian passengers couldn't buy anything. Everything was for high army officers or party officials.

Finally, they arrived in Gorki, a very large, gray city on the Volga River. Kuba's uncle lived in the Lenin district of the city, just opposite the largest auto plant in Russia, the Stalin auto plant. It took him three hours to find Tambowska Street. He succeeded and knocked on the door of the house.

A middle-aged woman opened the door, looked at him and started calling for her daughter. "Sonia, come here quickly. Some army officer is here to see you." Kuba started laughing and explained that he did not want to see her daughter. He wanted to see his Aunt Tema. She looked at him in surprise and said, "I didn't know that Tema had a nephew in the army. Why, she's only a refugee from Poland."

"I too am a refugee from Poland. Now where is Tema?" he asked with some worry.

"Well," she said, "Tema and her husband left for Tashkent in Central Asia, back in 1941."

"Do you have their address?" he asked.

"No, they didn't write to us."

Disappointed, he said, "I came here from Moscow to see them. I guess I will have to return."

She looked at him and said, "Why rush off like that? You can go out with my daughter and have a good time. She knows a lot of nice places in town."

"No, thank you," he said, "I will return to Moscow." He spent that night at the railroad station and early the next morning boarded a freight train for Moscow. Again, he was wandering around the streets of Moscow. By the end of the second week of his furlough, he was in the vicinity of Kolkhoznaya Square. He joined a group of people standing around a newspaper stand. Almost all official Soviet papers were on display and, he noticed a Polish language paper, the WOLNA POLSKA. The headline struck him: "The last fighters of the Warsaw ghetto are still fighting the Nazis."

He bought a paper and sat down to read it on the steps of a nearby store. There was a story of the last heroic struggle of the Warsaw ghetto fighters. He closed his eyes and once again saw Warsaw; the street where he was born and raised, his friends in school and now pictured whoever was left of them as soldiers fighting such an uneven battle.

His father's name was mentioned in the paper in connection with the uprising. He looked at the editorial page and found the name of the editor, Wanda Wasilewska. He knew her. She was one of the leaders in the Polish Socialist Party, an educator and author by trade. He decided to go to see her and find out some more facts about Warsaw. He knew this could be very dangerous. It might end tragically for him, but he couldn't stop.

The offices of the FREE POLAND were located in an old brick building on Mala Bronnaya Street. The girl at the reception desk looked at him, a little frightened, and asked what she could do for him. "I would like to speak with the editor, Wanda Wasilewska."

"Just a minute, please," the girl said, not asking his name or the reason for his visit. She was too frightened.

After a while, she returned and led him to another room, a large room, two desks, one opposite the other...and there she was, Wanda Wasilewska. She still looked young and attractive in spite of the fact that she had a daughter who was about to be married. She looked at him, surprised, and asked, "What can I do for you, Lieutenant?"

Kuba wanted to speak to her in Polish but now, facing her, he forgot the language, so he spoke to her in Russian. "I know you from Warsaw. I am the son of Arthur."

She looked up at him and smiling, she said, "Why didn't I guess it! You look exactly like him!" Then she started talking about Kuba's father. She spoke of his journey from the Warsaw ghetto to Belgium, across Germany to France. Then, after the Nazis occupied France, she told of his travels through Portugal to the United States. Finally she told of his appointment in 1942, as a member of the Polish National Council. She related that Arthur did everything that was possible to help the Polish underground, especially the underground in the Warsaw ghetto. She spoke gravely about his suicide. Arthur took his life when he realized that despite his efforts, there was no effective help from the Allies to prevent the Jewish population of Warsaw from being murdered by the Nazis. He committed suicide as a protest, hoping to shake the world apathy in the face of the unprecedented mass slaughter of a people.

She then told him the story of the Warsaw ghetto uprising. While she talked, he was carried away by her words and saw himself fighting, together with his nearest friends, their last battle. He could see the tall, twelve-foot ghetto wall with the slogan of the ghetto fighters painted upon it: FOR YOURS AND OUR FREEDOM! Wanda Wasilewska pressed a button on her desk. A girl entered the room and Wanda ordered tea. While they were eating lunch in her room, she told Kuba that there was a Polish Army being organized in Russia and that she was one of the organizers. The army was named after one of the most famous Polish heroes, an associate of George Washington, Tadeus Kosciuszko. She urged Kuba to get a transfer to that army. "All you have to do," she said, "is talk to your political commissar and he will grant you a transfer." Kuba promised her he would and left the office.

The following day he stood before his political commissar, the same man who had saved him once before when Kuba had crossed the front lines in 1941. Kuba handed him his request for a transfer to the Polish Army. The commissar looked at Kuba with much surprise. Slowly, he tore the request into tiny pieces and threw them into the wastebasket. "Now remember, Kuba, there is only one road out from our service and that road leads to the Solovecki Islands," a famous Soviet prison on the Arctic Sea. "You forget about this and I promise you that no one will ever hear about it from me. Now, go back to your base. An assignment is waiting for you."

Kuba left the commissar's office in a hurry. Leaving the Second Army Building he crossed Arbat Street. Arbat Street was guarded day and night. It was the street that leads from the Kremlin towards the country mansions of Stalin and his associates. It is also the road to the Solovecki Islands. Many high Communist leaders have traveled that road to the Islands. Kuba hoped that he would not get arrested because in that case his life would not be worth a penny.

Chapter Thirteen

It was October, 1943. The night before, they had been unexpectedly ordered to board a plane, and before they knew it, they were bailing out near the Wygon Lake. The Orlovsky group was once again on the swamps near the lake, resting in a tent made from a parachute. This was the same group which had been formed during the schooling in Moscow. All but two men in the group were asleep. Pasha was on guard and the Spaniard, Loris, was guarding their belongings. Suddenly, Kuba was awakened by Pasha. "Get up. It is your turn to go on guard duty," said Pasha.

"Who is it?" asked Kuba.

"What's the matter with you? Don't you recognize people?" Kuba had again been semiconsciously dreaming and when he heard the clear voice of his commander and saw the friendly eyes, he was jolted awake. "This is our last partisan mission," said Pasha.

"Why our last?" asked Kuba. He tried to remember why the commander had expressed himself in that way but something was disturbing his thoughts. It was the loudspeaker in the airport cafeteria giving another weather report. They had not slept for the last two nights.

An old waiter by the name of Matvay came over to them and said, "War, war, always war...for thousands of years, war. Men carry swords for centuries and never lay them down."

Their commander, Orlovsky, gave them the last instructions. "On this mission we have two alternatives: fight as never before or perish. If we succeed, we will stay over there until the Soviet Army joins us. We have to pave the road for the army. But, please, don't sleep. Keep your eyes open!"

It was raining. Kuba pressed his body close to the tree and looked into the darkness. Everyone was asleep and they who are in Moscow are also asleep. Only I am awake and there are other soldiers and partisans awake all over the world. There is a war going on and because we are awake and the enemy is afraid, he has had a rough time lately, losing one battle after another near Moscow and Stalingrad. Their theory about a Blitzkrieg had burst for the first time since 1939 and they had to retreat.

Kuba walked amongst the trees. For a few seconds he saw two gleaming eyes which disappeared after awhile and he wondered what it had been. It was getting colder by the minute, and he wanted to sleep. He stopped again and visualized pictures from the past. He heard a bell ringing while somebody was calling them for lunch at a summer camp near Warsaw. He was eleven years old and a girl's voice cried out, "Let's go eat lunch!" This was Hana Kastel, his girlfriend from his childhood and later a fighter in the uprising of the Warsaw ghetto. He could see very clearly, two boys playing croquet: Kuba and his teacher, Gilinski, playing volleyball and other boys also playing with them.

He lost a point and the teacher said to him, "Don't depend on others to do your job."

The rain was increasing and it broke the silence. Right after that a few shots rang out, very close. That wasn't a dream! He recognized a Soviet sub-machine gun sound and ran to the tent. Everyone was already on their feet. "What has happened?" Colonel Orlovsky asked.

"I don't know," answered Kuba. "The shots came from over there."

"Take your arms," ordered Orlovsky. They started to walk in the direction of the shots. "Loris is over there," the commander said. They crossed a road on the other side of a small forest where they had left their belongings after landing. Again shots rang out, a few bullets buzzed past them. They found Loris behind their belongings and from a distance someone was shouting at them, but they could hear only rifle shots. The partisans did not shoot. Suddenly they saw the enemy, lying near the road.

"Surrender!" Sanya ordered loudly. The enemies sprang to their feet and began to withdraw. "Fire!" Sanya ordered. The partisans fired their submachine guns and two of the enemy fell immediately. Two others escaped into the forest and the partisans tried to chase them into the open. The commander and the rest joined them. After some time, only two of the enemies were left. They came out into the open field and ran toward a farm, but bullets got to them first. The partisans ran toward them and found one of them was still alive and only slightly wounded in the leg. Both were clad in black uniforms of the Belarusian SS and were on their way to a nearby village when they met up with Loris. The commander asked them about some activities of the Belarusian police and the Germans.

"Do they prepare any special moves against the partisans?" The prisoner did not answer.

It was daybreak when the commander asked him the last question. "Did you take part in any fights against partisans or other Soviet citizens?"

"I didn't do any fighting against Soviet soldiers, but..." and the prisoner stopped suddenly.

"Go ahead," the commander said. "What do you want to tell us?" The commander took his gun from its holster and the prisoner continued.

"I took part in shooting the Jewish population."

"Where?" asked the commander.

"In the cities of Mir and Novogrudok." The commander raised his gun and pulled the trigger. They went deeper into the forest now that they knew where they were. It stopped raining and the dogs were barking on the farm.

Kuba thought of the enemy, and the words he had heard from old Matvay at the, airport cafeteria came to him again... "They that took the sword shall perish by the sword."

Chapter Fourteen

It was a warm fall night when Kuba's first time came up; until then, he had taken part in several missions to destroy transport trains, but his duty had been to guard the men who planted the mine. Now he had to plant the mine himself. The main assignment of the special partisan group No.258 was to slow down the delivery of military equipment to the German armies at the front. Night after night, three members of the group went on a mission with a large charge of explosives and night after night, a German transport train was blown up. Within a period of two weeks, every member of their group was assigned at least once to plant a mine on the railroad tracks.

Right after dinner the commander told Kuba to get ready. Vlodik and Otto were to go with him. All three got busy right away. They put twelve kilograms of explosives, called "tolulol," into a wooden box. Then the commander gave them instructions where to perform their operation and whom to contact in the villages.

Kuba left camp with Otto and Vlodik while it was still daylight, each taking a turn carrying the knapsack which contained the explosives. After an hour of marching, they arrived in the village of Lopatichi and stopped there to get a drink of water. It was getting dark and the peasants were driving their herds home.

The three partisans were sitting on a bench in the center of the village when from a nearby hut a girl came out with a pitcher in one hand and a tin cup in the other. Smiling, she came towards them. "Drink some fresh milk, my eagles," she said, and handed the cup to Kuba. Kuba drank the milk with great pleasure.

"Thank you," he said, and passed the tin cup to Otto.

"Don't mention it. You are our defenders," the girl said, refilling the cup. Other peasants came over to them and Otto, who could hardly speak a word of Russian, got up and went for a walk along the only street, watching for unexpected visitors. Meanwhile, Kuba and Vlodik had a conversation with the peasants. Perhaps they could gain some useful bits of information.

"Is the front line far from here?" Muzik, a middle-aged peasant asked. He looked grizzled and tired, his hand resting on the back of the bench where Kuba sat.

"Yes. The front is still pretty far away, but it won't take long and you will hear them," Kuba answered.

"It is about time that our armies came here," an old peasant said. The Nazis had again burned a village with all its inhabitants not far from Wygonowschina.

Muzik then began to talk. He kept on looking about him, as he was afraid of anyone shooting him in the back. "The Germans rounded up the people of Novosiele and placed them in the church and surrounding house—all of them—men, women and children. Then they poured gasoline all around the area and at the walls of the buildings and set them afire. The cries of those people were loud enough to wake up the Lord and his Son, our Savior Jesus Christ, but nothing happened. Those people just died a terrible death."

"What happened to the nearby villages?" Volodiya asked. "The same thing!" Muzik said. "My son was in Narovitche, and he saw the Germans doing the same thing. He almost did not make it out of there."

Kuba looked very sharply at Muzik and then asked, "What are you people going to do about it?"

"Oh, Comrade Captain, we decided to join up with you, who are our real defenders, and fight the enemy. We thought that we might join the forces of the heroic partisans from Kletsk who represent the majority of the Jewish community there. To us, those people who are mentioned in our 'Pravoslavnyi' (Orthodox) books are the real People of the Lord! Holy people! We shall stick with them!"

The conversation continued for quite awhile and it was quite dark by the time they left the village. They called aside one peasant from the group, named Fedor, a skinny, mustached fellow with a wart on the tip of his chin, who was one of their informers from the village.

"Come with us for a walk," Kuba said to him. Fedor followed them, silently. When they were outside the village, Kuba asked him, "What's new?"

"Nothing special."

"Is the guard enforced on the railroad?" Kuba asked.

"No," he answered, "only, they put up a new bunker."

"Where is it?"

"One mile east of the Budi."

"How many men?"

"Seventeen," he answered. "One German and the rest Ukrainians."

"How far do they patrol the tracks?"

"About two and a half miles."

"All right," Kuba said. "Wait for us between one and two o'clock in the morning. We'll stop at your house."

"I wish you success," said Fedor as he looked at the knapsack on Vlodik's shoulders. It was a beautiful night. Millions of stars were in the sky and the men made good time through the forest, circling around villages.

When Kuba's turn came, he took the knapsack from Vlodik's shoulder who asked, "Are we going to the tower?"

"Yes." Kuba replied. A half mile from the railroad tracks they stopped for a cigarette, checked the mine and saw that everything was in order. Everyone was a little nervous but they didn't show it. The danger was not only from the Germans. The mine also was hazardous. They knew of many accidents to partisans caused by faulty mines. After a short rest, they proceeded through the darkness.

The three partisans came to the end of the forest. Farther out the Germans had cut the trees for a hundred feet on both sides of the tracks and machine guns were set up in the bunkers, enabling them to fire on the clearing. The men lay down in order to observe the surrounding area. On the other side of the tracks, a small tower made of logs could be seen. Such towers are topographical markers, and are erected at specific intervals throughout the countryside in Europe.

It was quiet all around except for the distant barking of dogs and peasants singing. The rails shone in the moonlight. "They are coming," Otto said suddenly. Now they could hear heavy footsteps on the ties of the tracks. After awhile, they saw five Germans coming, a railroad patrol. The Nazis were marching in a single file, steel helmets on their heads and their weapons on their shoulders. The partisans could hear the sound of gravel under their heavy boots. The Nazis passed the tower and stopped. One of them said something and the others burst into laughter. They were talking for several minutes, and then one of them took his rifle and fired a tracer bullet into the direction from which they had come. From a distance, a shot answered. The Nazis continued marching down the tracks.

The partisans waited five minutes, and they heard the whistle of a locomotive from afar. "Now," Kuba said. He took the mine and they left the forest.

"Take care of yourself," Otto said to him. They started running, Vlodik about ten feet or more at Kuba's left and Otto at his right. He tried to walk quickly but it was almost impossible as the gravel was slippery and he made a lot of noise. Kuba carried the mine on his left shoulder and his submachine gun in his right hand. Again the stillness was disturbed by the whistle, now much closer than before. His two comrades lay down near the tracks with their weapons ready to shoot. Kuba, laying flat on his belly, between the rails, put the mine under a rail between the ties and fastened the fuse to the top of one rail. He looked around and again everything was quiet. On his right, he could see two headlights coming down the tracks towards him, growing larger and larger. He got to his feet and whistled quietly, his comrades rose and started running toward the woods. He looked again toward the train. The headlights were very near, only two hundred feet away, looking like the eyes of some giant animal. He then ran towards the woods as fast as he could to get as far as possible from the dangerous spot and there he fell to the ground near his comrades. They held their weapons in readiness.

The train was now in full view, an army supply train heading for the front. "I think I did everything right," Kuba whispered. His comrades did not answer, looking intensely, instead, in the direction of the train as it was approaching the mine. They pressed their bodies hard to the ground and covered their heads with their arms. Then it happened—a sudden flash, and, immediately after that, a terrific explosion; pieces of steel flew over their heads. All was again quiet.

Kuba lifted his head and saw that almost the entire train lay in a ditch and only two cars remained on the tracks. They got to their feet and proudly looked at the destruction just completed when suddenly a machine gun was fired in the opposite direction from one of the cars on the track. They retreated deeper into the forest and stopped after several minutes. The shooting was far behind them now and the partisans lit cigarettes.

"Well, we did it, Vlodik said with his Serbian accent.

"Yes," said Kuba, "and now back to Lopatichi." They reached Fedor's farm, where he was waiting for them, about one o'clock in the morning.

"Congratulations," he said. "I heard everything." They went inside. Fedor's wife was wide awake and prepared some food for them. Fedor got out a bottle of moonshine vodka, called "Samogonka" by the Russians.

Pouring some whiskey into each of the glasses, Fedor picked up his glass and said, "Let's drink to victory." They emptied their glasses.

"It was a terrific explosion. We haven't heard one like it for a long time," said Nastia, Fedor's wife.

"Woman, be quiet. It's none of your business," Fedor told her. He was already a bit drunk. The partisans spent several hours with them and at sunrise they sent Fedor out to learn what had happened on the tracks. In the meantime, they took turns napping. Fedor returned about eight o'clock that same morning, then all of them left the house and went towards the woods. "You did a good job," Fedor said. He told them that it was an army train loaded mostly with soldiers and equipment and as a result of the explosion, most of the soldiers were killed. The Germans in the nearby garrison of Budi were furious. While Fedor was talking, they moved swiftly towards their camp and after a couple of kilometers, they shook hands and Fedor returned home.

It was a beautiful summer day, the sun was bright and the birds greeted them as they sang and flew from branch to branch, as though nature also was happy with the partisans.

Chapter Fifteen

Not far from the old Soviet-Polish boundary on the Brest-Moscow highway was a little town by the name of Shinyavkia. Before the war, this town had a population of nearly seven thousand, half of them Jews. By the end of 1941, all the Jews had been shot by the Nazis and buried in a ditch outside of town. Among the peasants of the nearby villages, it was said that long after the execution of the Jews, the ground over their graves moved and, when the first snow fell in 1941, the snow turned red immediately, as though it were soaked with the blood of the buried people. The Germans converted the town of Shinyavkia into a very important strategic point, fortifying it alongside the highway and putting up bunkers all around the town. In the vicinity of Shinyavkia, there were several large estates. The Germans set up food supply bases there and stationed a garrison of German and Belarusian military police. The largest of the estates was that of Tucha, located about three miles east of a town near the highway.

Two friendly peasants in a nearby village succeeded in setting up a contact with some of the Belarusian military police stationed at the estate and through them the partisans were able to contact the police and meet them on a farm belonging to an uncle of one of the policemen. All were sons of peasants from the nearby vicinity and were drafted by the Nazis to serve in the military police. To keep their appointment with the partisans, two of the policemen showed up, Sasha Kireichik, a sergeant, and Fedor Shalik, both policemen in their early twenties and natives of a nearby village. They wore black uniforms with a skull and crossbones sign on their hats.

Kuba's commander talked to the policemen for a long while and convinced them to work with the partisans. They agreed and gave the partisans very important information about the garrison and the Tucha estate and then stated that there were several more policemen who would like to escape and join the partisans. Commander Orlovsky explained that before they could be admitted to the group, they would have to perform a certain assignment. That assignment was to help the partisan group raid the estate where they were stationed. Sergeant Kireichik, especially, would have to take care of the guards around the estate so that when they entered there would be no resistance. After a two-hour conference, the policemen agreed to everything and promised that they would bring a plan of the estate and of the guard posts to the next meeting.

Before he left, the Colonel told them, "Remember one thing. If you try to betray us, you won't get away with it. Our bullets will reach anywhere."

"You don't have to worry about that, Colonel," the policeman answered. "We will do our job."

A week later everything was ready for the attack. The partisans left their camp in full force and entered the village at midnight. The Tucha estate, located a couple of hundred yards south of the highway in a very swampy area, was circled by a river giving it the appearance of an island. It was enclosed with a twelve-foot steel fence with only one gate to a bridge over the river, which was raised at sunset so that no one could enter. The whole island was covered with chestnut trees, a rarity in this part of the country. A cemetery lay between the river and the village.

The estate consisted of five buildings. A mansion built by a Polish count several hundred years ago was in the center of the island, surrounded by four long brick buildings, barns, warehouses and distilleries. The quarters of the Germans and the police were in the mansion.

All the peasants were asleep when the partisans entered the village and met the policeman, Shalik. "Everything is ready," he said. "Sasha is waiting for us at the cemetery." Armed more than usual that night, they left the village. Everybody had his assignment and knew the attack plan well. The commander had explained everything to them. Kuba had two extra hand grenades and a lot of ammunition with him. They met Sasha and the other policeman at the cemetery and sat down on the grass along the road for a short rest.

"No smoking," the commander said and he started to question Sasha who, with the other policeman, was armed with a rifle. "Is everything ready?" the commander asked.

"Yes, Colonel," answered Sasha. "We will have to wait another half hour because the German officers are just now going to sleep. They were playing cards until now."

"Who is on guard at the gate?" Orlovsky asked again.

"A policeman with a machine gun, but we got him drunk," Sasha answered. They were sitting quietly. From the river came the peculiar serenade of thousands of frogs. They did not stop for a second. Far away they heard a series of machine gun shots. "Must be on the railroad."

Kuba was sitting quietly and didn't move. It was chilly and the grass was damp and getting into his bones. He wanted very much to smoke. Sasha got up and took his rifle. "I'll go take a look," he said as he left for the bridge.

They waited another half hour, the commander constantly looking at his watch. Finally Sasha returned and said, "Let's go." They got up. The policemen went first, followed by Sanya, Toliya and Pasha. They let the others cross the bridge and then followed. Some noise, like a fist fight came from the other side when the rest of the partisans got on the bridge; and again like metal being dropped to the ground. A few seconds later they heard a groan, then quiet again. Toliya came towards them carrying a German machine gun. He was without his hat and his hands were covered with blood.

"One of them is already gone," he said, smiling, and gave the machine gun to Otto.

"You stay here," the commander said to Otto. The rest went through the gate and saw on the ground, to the right of the gate, the bloody body of a dead policeman. Toliya had used a pocket-knife on him.

"Everybody, take your posts!" the commander ordered. They ran toward their positions. Sanya, Vlodik, Pasha and Kuba went to the entrance of the mansion. Loris and his group went toward the windows of the soldier's sleeping quarters. One of the windows was open. Sasha took care of that. The German and Belarusian police were sound asleep in their bunks.

The commander and other officers of the partisan group stopped near the gate. Loris was to give the signal by throwing a big anti-tank grenade into the sleeping quarters. Then they were to attack the rooms from inside through the halls. They waited a few minutes. Meantime, Kuba checked his automatic pistol. Everyone did the same. Suddenly a terrific blast shook the whole area, almost knocking them to the ground. Sanya tapped Kuba on the shoulder. "Quick, go first!" he ordered.

Kuba pushed the door open and rushed in with his submachine gun ready to fire. There were four doors on both sides of the hall. He went to the first door on his right. The door opened suddenly and a German with a gun, in his underwear, ran straight into Kuba's gun. Kuba pulled the trigger immediately. He was so excited that he didn't hear the sound of his own gun. He jumped over the German's body and reached the door. The others were right behind him. By now someone had turned on a light in the hall.

It was a large room. The first thing Kuba noticed was a heavyset German in a long nightgown standing on his bed at the right, trying to pick up a submachine gun which was hanging on the wall. "Hands up!" Kuba shouted.

The fat Nazi stepped down from the bed, with his arms raised. A shot was fired in Kuba's direction, the bullet going close by his hat and hitting the frame of the door. Kuba turned half way and pulled the trigger again. This time his submachine gun sounded like a sewing machine. At the other end of the room there were two beds, one behind the other, and behind the last bed was a German officer with a Luger in his hand, his body hanging over the headboard. The third bed was empty and the fat Nazi was still standing with his hands up. "Get out!" Kuba ordered him. The German was shaking all over when he left the room. He was taken outside toward the gate to the commander. "I've got one alive," Kuba reported. Several more shots came from the house, and then everything was quiet. Sanya and Pasha got another live German officer. Vlodik was wounded in his forearm, but not very badly.

About five minutes later, the entire group was gathered around the commander near the gate. Three more policemen joined them. They had been on guard duty in other parts of the estate on Sasha's orders. They didn't know the result of the explosion. Anyway, it was quiet in that room where Loris threw the grenade. "And now let's get to work," the commander ordered. "Open up all the buildings." They went to the buildings and broke open the doors and gates. They let out sixteen horses and wagons and the policemen harnessed the horses to the wagons. There was a beautiful black stallion, about three years old. It took three men to harness this horse to a wagon.

"Come here quick somebody!" Pasha yelled from the other end. They all went. Pasha had the door open to a barn. Inside were stalls with several hundred pigs in them. The commander came along and said, "We'll take some of them. We can use them. Our supplies are low."

The former policemen drove some wagons toward the barn and loaded the wagons with pigs, three to each wagon. In the distillery they found several containers of alcohol and loaded those also. The partisans were all so busy that they didn't notice the time going by. An hour had gone by since they had attacked the estate. They got ready to leave, but suddenly the sound of motor vehicles came from the highway. Heavy equipment was rolling toward the estate. "Let's get out of here, quick!" the commander shouted.

The wagons rolled quickly over the bridge, driven by the policemen. They followed behind them. Later Kuba noticed that Pasha, Toliya and Sasha had stayed behind. Two partisans were on the other side of the village when those three caught up with them.

"It's done," Pasha reported to the commander. Kuba looked back and saw that the estate of Tucha was afire. The German vehicles on the highway came to a sudden stop and there was the sound of machine gun fire and several cannon shots. This was a unit of Germans with tanks, shooting at the estate. The partisans jumped on the wagons and whipped the horses to make them go faster. The two German prisoners in the wagon with Kuba were tied together, back to back. They were shaking. It was hard to say whether they were cold or scared.

"Are you cold?" Kuba asked the one nearest him. No answer. Kuba took a blanket and threw it over both of them. The wagon was bouncing over the rough road. Kuba was sitting on a dead pig, and his boots were bloody. They were riding west now, Sanya leading the way and changing directions very often to avoid miring in the swamp.

Kuba watched the two Nazis on his wagon and he had a peculiar feeling. He remembered what the Germans had done to his people. The one facing him looked at him from under the blanket and wanted to say something but was scared. This Nazi was about forty-five years old and his hair was turning gray. Kuba looked at him, not seeing him.

"Comrade," said the German.

"What do you want?" asked Kuba in German.

"Are you Russian or Polish?" he asked.

"I am a Jew," Kuba said very slowly. The German turned pale with an expression of a grimace on his face.

"What are you going to do with us now?" the German asked quietly.

"You are going to Berchtesgaden on furlough," Kuba answered, laughing very loudly and turning his back on him. On the other side of the wagon, Loris was sound asleep. The bumps and shaking of the wagon didn't bother him. It was a long journey. Many times they had to get out and help the horses pull the wagons out of the swamp. At about eleven o'clock in the morning, they reached the first farms of the village of Lopatichi, near the forest in which they had made their camp and stopped to rest. The six former policemen started cleaning up the pigs. They singed the hair with burning straw and then butchered them.

The partisans did not have a jail or guardhouse in their camp so they locked the prisoners in the bathhouse. Their fate was to be decided the next day.

Otto, who knew something about medicine, put a dressing on Vlodik's arm. He wasn't badly wounded— the bullet had gone through the flesh. All the others went to sleep except Kuba. He couldn't get to sleep for a long time. He was thinking about the raid on the estate. It had gone smoothly. And they captured two Nazis. Tomorrow would be their last day, a short trial and then execution. Finally, the sound of the wind through the trees lulled him to sleep.

Chapter Sixteen

Grisha the commissar awakened Kuba. It was dark outside. "Come on, you will serve as interpreter." Putting on his belt and gun, Kuba went with the commissar to the Colonel's hut. Inside, behind a table, their commander, Colonel Orlovsky, was sitting with the chief of staff, Volodiya and Sanya. On a bunk to the left sat the two prisoners.

Answering Kuba's greeting, the commander said, "It's good that you came. We cannot converse with them because of the language." Kuba took a seat next to Sanya. After finishing what he was writing, the commander said to Kuba, "Tell them who I am and ask them who they are."

Turning to the prisoners, Kuba said in German, "This is Colonel Orlovsky. You were taken prisoners by the partisan group No.258." The Nazis were silent. They were very pale and had a frightened look on their faces.

"What's your name and rank?" Kuba asked one of them.

"Oberlieutenant der Gendarmerie, Herman Eibner," the prisoner answered. The commander immediately put it down on paper. Kuba continued.

"How long have you been a member of the Nazi party?" The prisoner remained silent, Kuba repeated his question several times.

When the prisoner still didn't answer, he treated him with the same kindness as the Nazis had treated their prisoners. He pulled out his gun from its holster.

The prisoner answered immediately, very quietly, "Since 1936."

"How long have you been in the service?"

"Since 1939 when the war began," the prisoner answered. After that he answered all of the questions. They learned that he had taken part in the military campaign in Western Europe and was decorated with the Iron Cross. The other prisoner also answered all the questions immediately. When Kuba spoke to him, he stood at attention and after each answer he added in German, "at your service."

"What is your name?" Kuba asked.

"Wachmeinster der Gendarmerie, Walter Neuwirt, zum befehl," he answered. The commander made notes of everything and asked some more questions which the prisoners answered.

"Ask them if they are hungry," said the commander. The answer was "yes." Sanya went out and got them a half-loaf of bread and two pieces of bacon. The commander took a bottle of vodka from his bunk and poured two glasses, and handing it to them he said, "Drink. That's your alcohol. You made it on your estate."

Kuba immediately translated. They were eating slowly. They were not given any knives so they had to take bites off the loaf of bread. By now they didn't look so scared. When they had finished eating, the questioning resumed. They answered all questions quickly. They had been in Belarus for more than a year. And so the investigation continued for a time until the commander asked them, "What special assignments did you take part in?"

Special assignments for the Gendarmerie, Gestapo and the German military police forces were to kill the Jewish population of towns and villages, to burn and liquidate the population of unfriendly villages, and to raid partisan camps. The prisoners didn't answer this question. It didn't help when all of them pulled out their guns. They had to use physical force to make them talk. It took a long time. Volodiya beat them with his belt. The German lieutenant finally cried out, "It's a crime to beat an officer. It's against military ethics to beat prisoners!"

After Kuba translated it into Russian, their commander angrily jumped from his seat. "And how does the noble German Army handle THEIR prisoners?"

"We only obey orders," the lieutenant said. He wanted to say something more but Orlovsky would not let him. He hit the German in the face with his fist so hard that the Nazi fell backwards.

"Shut up when you are not spoken to!" Orlovsky said. The German lieutenant got to his feet and wiped his bleeding nose with his sleeve. "Now, answer my question," the commander said, very sternly. The prisoners began to talk. They said that in 1942 and 1943 they had taken part in the mass slaughter of the Jewish population of Baranovichi and other towns and villages in the vicinity and that one had taken part in killing the population of many villages. Furthermore, they said, the SS was preparing a raid on this forest as special military attachments had arrived for that purpose in the area. The interrogation continued until after midnight. When it concluded, the commander asked the Nazis, "What do you think of the murder and destruction you have committed?"

"We only obeyed orders," the German lieutenant answered.

"Don't you have a human heart in your body?" Orlovsky said, again very angrily. "Didn't your conscience ever talk to you?" He was walking back and forth in front of the Nazis. They didn't say a word. Suddenly he stopped and said, "Tomorrow morning you will be shot." Orlovsky was looking at the German lieutenant. Then he added, "You'll be shot by one of your victims, a Jew who was in the ghetto of the city of Baranovichi." Slowly Kuba translated it to German. "Take them out," the commander ordered.

Volodiya, Sanya and Kuba took the prisoners back to their hut. Otto was there on guard. The next day, after breakfast, the commander ordered everyone to the prisoners' hut. They were told to stand in front of the hut in two lines, fully armed. The two prisoners were brought out, their hands tied behind their backs. Commissar Grisha read the charges against the prisoners and pronounced sentence. Loris and Kuba were to be the executioners. Putting silencers on their guns, they took the prisoners into the forest where Pasha and Shalik had already prepared two graves. The entire group was standing in the background, watching, while Loris and Kuba executed the two Nazis.

When all this was happening Kuba was thinking: *Is that really the revenge that I wanted for my family? Even if I shoot him, what will that do? But he cannot go free in this world after what he did to my son and wife. And even according to the Bible we are right. An eye for an eye! But this is more than just an eye! I WANT THOSE NAZIS DEAD!*

When they returned to the camp, Sanya their radio operator talked to headquarters in Moscow. The conversation lasted about an hour and a half, during which time Sanya reported their achievements in the last few days. Moscow informed them that at midnight they were to expect an air drop of supplies, some armaments and new men for their group.

After dinner they began readying their little "airport" on an island in the swamp. It wasn't exactly an airport. There were no planes. But it was where their supplies were being dropped. In a special hut built from logs, there was a large supply of dry firewood and behind the hut there was a small stream and a barn which they had built for the horses.

About nine o'clock in the evening, the entire partisan group went to the airport. They harnessed the horses to wagons and kept them ready then they divided into four groups, each group having a certain part of the clearing to trace the falling parachutes. A special group prepared the signal fires for the supply planes, one in each corner and a fifth in the center, five of them. At eleven-forty p.m. the partisans lit the signal fires. It was a very dark night and the reflection from the fires made trees look like ghosts. The four groups took up their positions: Otto, Toliya, the commissar, Sasha and Kuba were in one group. The moonless sky was clear and full of stars. They sat on a log and waited. Kuba checked the time, two minutes to twelve. They lighted cigarettes and everyone waited impatiently. Then they heard the roar of an airplane from a distance.

"There they come!" Sanya shouted. The partisans got to their feet. The roar of the plane became louder. Finally the plane was overhead, flying very low and without lights. They could see its dark body against the sky. After making a full circle over the signal fires, the plane flashed his tail and wing lights several times, his greeting to the partisans. They saw large, dark objects dropping toward them from the plane; their supplies, falling one after another. The plane circled the airport four times and then flashed his lights and disappeared into the darkness of the sky.

"This is a Douglas plane," Pasha said. It was really a transport plane, part of Lend-Lease, built by Douglas. There were many of these in Russia during the war. There were fourteen parachutes in the sky above. The partisans watched them intently so as not to lose sight. There was not much wind but one parachute drifted away from the clearing. They ran after it.

Toliya and Kuba were looking up and a parachute was coming straight at them containing a man instead of a package. They waved their hands at him and when he was only a few hundred feet overhead, they could hear him shout, "Regards from Moscow." He landed and was helped to free himself from the straps. Altogether their supplies consisted of seven bags of armaments, clothing, drugs, literature and seven men, all old friends from Moscow. Their leader was Major Nikolsky, who later became the commander of their group after Colonel Orlovsky was wounded.

They got all the supplies together, taking two hours to find one of the bags (weighing about three-hundred pounds) lost in the swamp. It was quite a job to pull it out of the swamp. Finally, all the supplies were high and dry and they started back to camp.

Kuba was sitting on a wagon with Otto and Kolia, one of the newcomers. On the wagon was a supply bag made of green canvas and printed on it was "M-42, 258" and served as a reminder to Kuba of the time when he was in Moscow. "How is it here?" Kolia asked.

"Not bad. We don't just sit around," he answered.

"Do the Germans attack you often?" asked Kolia.

"So far there have been no attacks on us," Kuba answered.

"But we pulled a trick on them yesterday." He told about the attack on the estate Tucha.

As they rode quietly, Otto began to sing a German song, "Mein Vater ist Tishler, sein son das bin ich."

"Is it frightful here?" Kolia asked.

"When you live through what we have been through, nothing will be frightful to you," Otto answered.

Kolia took out a pack of "Belomor Kanal" cigarettes and passed them around. "On the front it is different," Kuba said. "There you have the enemy always in front of you. Behind, you have friends. Here, you have enemies all around and they are much stronger than we are." It was already sunrise and everything came to life. The birds began to sing and from a distance they could hear the noise of cattle and barking dogs.

"We are like fleas," Otto said. "The flea bites in one place and jumps over to some other place immediately. We do exactly the same. Today, we blow up a train in one place and the next day we attack a German garrison in another place. It's hard for the enemy to track us down because they never know where we come from and where we go, and how many men we have."

In camp, Vlodik was waiting for them. His left arm was bandaged. "How are you?" He greeted the new comrades in the Serbian language.

"How are you, yourself?" Nikolsky greeted him.

"Where did you get that?" Yasha, one of the newcomers said, pointing at his arm.

"A bee stung him," said Pasha, laughing. Everyone was laughing, including Vlodik.

"You are always joking," Vlodik said to Pasha, with his Serbian accent.

"Oh, he got it last night," said Colonel Orlovsky, smiling at the major. Among the newcomers, there was a young woman by the name of Anna Aksakova, about twenty-five and small, a medical doctor, just out of school. Her face was heavily pockmarked, a result of a small pox epidemic of two decades earlier. She had blonde hair and a warm smile and was quite attractive, a Cossack girl from the city of Tikhoretsk in the Kuban River in the eastern Ukraine. This area was known as Cossack Land, stretching from the Kuban River to the Don River on the east. The entire area is covered by huge plains which are called steppes, and there the grass grows so tall that it can hide a rider on horseback.

When Nikolay, who was also a Kuban Cossack, found out about Anna, he came up behind her, grabbed her in his enormous arms and lifted her off the ground. "Hey neighbor!" he yelled.

Everyone laughed and clapped their hands. Anna was also laughing, but she started pounding on Nikolay's head with her hands and shouting, "Let me down, you brute!" Nikolay put her down on the ground, gingerly, and ran into his hut. He soon returned with his accordion and began to play and dance a Cossack dance, then stopped in front of Anna and the partisans formed a circle around him.

"Dance with me, Cossachka!" he begged.

Anna went into the circle, put her hands on her hips and began to dance and everyone clapped their hands to the music. It was almost noon when the commander stopped them. "It's time to rest now. We'll dance some other time. There is a lot to be done and we must be ready for it. We will rest for two hours and then we shall start building more earth huts." They ate bread and bacon and, after posting guards, they went to their huts, not knowing that they would not be able to work around the camp for a few days because several German SS brigades had arrived in their vicinity. One occupied the village of Lopatichi, only three miles from the partisan camp. The Germans were there to clean out the partisans from the area.

Chapter Seventeen

Two days had passed. The partisans had built two new huts for the newcomers and another for Anna, their doctor. She took good care of Vlodik's wounded arm and he was getting along fine. It was late in the fall. The mercury had fallen and it was cold, especially at night. They couldn't move around in the area too much, due to the large number of Germans stationed there. One particular evening they had been sitting around the camp fire to relax and rest. It was very cold and the fire kept their faces and chests warm, but they had to turn around in order to warm their backs. Colonel Orlovsky rolled a cigarette and lit it. They were quiet except for Anna, who was singing very quietly while mending their clothes.

The commander looked at her for awhile and then he touched her hair with his hand, saying, "I left a daughter your age in Moscow." Anna smiled at him, put down the trousers which she had been mending and fixed her hair. Nikolay came out to the campground with his accordion and Anna picked up a guitar that had been leaning against a tree and played several chords. Then she began to sing. It was a partisan song which all of them knew, but it sounded so different when she sang it. It was a very touching song about a partisan who was far behind enemy lines and yearned to be with his girl whom he had left at home. The song was so close to everyone's heart, actually describing their fate, for anyone of them could easily have been the hero of that song:

You are now far away, far away,

Between us there are forests and steppes,

I can't possibly reach you today,

But, death awaits me at the very next step.

Play harmonica, in spite of snow storms,

And untangle our unhappy luck,

I do feel warm in this earthen hut,

From your warm and unquenchable love.

It was so true, they were much closer to death than to staying alive, not suspecting how close to death they would be by the morning. Anna finished her song. They sat around quietly, thinking about their fate, when the commander broke the silence. "Remember, Loris, the times in Spain?"

"I'll never forget it," replied Loris. The commander began to talk about the Spanish Civil War in the years between 1935 and 1938. He had been the leader of a special NKVD group sent from the Soviet Union and Loris, a Spaniard, joined his group over there. The commander told the partisans about their work, how they used to kill the Socialist and Republican troops that were not friendly or sympathetic to the Communist rule and the Kremlin. He did not talk only about Spain. He told them about his childhood in a village in Belarus. He was the son of a peasant. When he was seventeen years old, the revolution of 1917 broke out. His father and older brother had been killed in World War I. The young Orlovsky joined the revolutionary movement and then the Red Guard, today's Red Army, believing only one thing: that they were going to overthrow the Czar. He was a very brave boy and distinguished himself in the fights against different Czarists generals and became a first lieutenant. He fought against the Cossack, Ataman Kilchak, while in the ranks of the famous Russian revolutionary Chapayev, in the Ural Mountains. From there, he was sent to fight the Polish troops in 1920, and so the years passed. Orlovsky befriended Felix Dzerzhinsky, the first head of the famous GPU (secret police) and became a member of that organization. He talked until late into the night and several of the partisans fell asleep. Finally, all the partisans went to their huts.

Kuba didn't know how long he had been asleep when he was awakened by a terrific noise in the camp. Someone had stepped on his foot and he jumped up. He heard machine gun fire right outside his hut, grabbed his weapons, fled the hut and found that everyone was lying on the ground with their weapons ready to fire.

Sanya, Pasha and Otto had been packing their important equipment in bags and throwing them on the wagons with the horses already harnessed to them and ready to go. It was daylight and Kuba saw the commander and the commissar kneeling near the path that led to their main guard post and went towards them. The shooting was getting closer. "What's happening?" Kuba asked.

"The Germans are attacking our camp," Commissar Grisha answered.

Toliya was on guard when he spotted the enemy and began shooting. "Follow me!" the commander shouted and left in the direction of the guard post. They found the guards several hundred yards from the camp, at the rim of the forest, lying behind a log, firing their machine guns. Sasha and Shalik were with Toliya, reloading the machine gun belts. Opposite the forest from the direction of Lopatichi, German machine guns were firing toward them, so the partisans had to lie low in order not to be hit.

"Form a defense line!" the commander ordered. They took up positions in a long chain along the edge of the forest. Kuba was between Nikolay and Grisha. "Remember, don't waste any ammunition!" the commander shouted.

Kuba released the safety on his submachine gun. "Fire!" came the order. They started shooting, taking aim between the trees near the village, where the Germans were located. The German fire weakened. The partisans were beginning to think that the Germans were retreating and they slowed their fire. Orlovsky got to his feet and went over to the commissar, when suddenly a hellish machine gun fire opened on them from both sides, right and left. They turned immediately and returned the fire, lasting several minutes. Kuba was changing the second clip in his gun, when an explosion threw him several feet away. Sand and dust covered him immediately. He wiped his eyes and then another explosion sounded a little further behind him. He heard a shout.

"There are too many of them for us and they have mortars with them!"

"We will have a hot day today!" Grisha shouted back. Again mortar shells exploded around them.

The commander shouted to Grisha, "We will retreat immediately! There is no one left in our camp!"

"Where will we retreat to?" asked Grisha.

"In the direction of the village of Mashuki." Kuba could hardly hear them. The shooting and mortar explosions didn't cease for a minute.

"Follow me. Retreat!" shouted Grisha. Their left wing retreated first. Kuba was in the center and one after the other they retreated in order, with the ones that were still in position continuing to shoot at the Germans. Kuba got to his knees and wanted to run after Grisha and turned his head toward Nikolay, who was behind him, when at once, a terrific flash blinded him and something hit him on the left side of his face and everything went dark. When he regained consciousness, he had the feeling of riding on a wild horse in a rodeo, but it was no horse. It was Nikolay carrying him over his shoulder while running. From behind, they could hear heavy gunfire and in his mouth, Kuba had the sweet, bitter taste of blood.

"Let me down," said Kuba. His face hurt him when he talked. Nikolay put him down very carefully and then Grisha came over.

"You are still alive?" Grisha asked, smiling. Kuba held onto Nikolay's arm then touched his nose and lips. They hurt and his hands were bloody. A piece of small shrapnel from a hand grenade had hit him.

"Are you thirsty?" Nikolay asked. Grisha gave him a drink of whiskey from his canteen and Kuba's strength began to come back. He took his submachine gun from Nikolay's shoulder and started forward, followed by Toliya and Shalik, as the rear guards of their group. Far behind them the Germans were still shooting. The partisans crossed a swamp and entered a forest not far from the village of Mashuki, where they met their commander and the others of the group. No one else was hurt so Major Nikolsky,

Sanya and Loris left them to do some scouting in the area. Anna took care of Kuba's wound and put a dressing on it. His nose swelled up quickly.

The commander was studying his field map and then said, "There are several Nazis after us." Several months earlier, they had built a road of logs to an "island" and had left their equipment and wagons there. Now, they were destroying the roads so that the Germans could not have the "island." Anna gave everyone bread and salt pork but Kuba could hardly chew the food because of his pain. They drank water from the swamp and after awhile Kuba fell asleep.

A few hours later, Major Nikolsky returned with the others and reported that it was quiet in Mashuki but all other surrounding villages were occupied by Germans. It was quite obvious that they were surrounded. One of their collaborators from Mashuki, Ivan Bobko, returned with Nikolsky's group and told them that the Germans had arrived there at sunrise, led by two peasants from the village of Galina. One of the peasants was Koslowski, who before the war, had served as a forest ranger in the same forest and knew every tree in a radius of about fifty miles. Now, he served in the German Gestapo.

The commander asked, "Did many Nazis come by train?"

"Not too many," Bobko answered.

The commander sat down and started to think. Ivan went over to Kuba. "What happened? Did somebody give you a kiss?" he asked, smiling.

"A very hot one," Nikolay answered for Kuba.

The commander came over, took Ivan's arm and said, "Listen, Ivan, we left our horses and equipment on Devil's Island."

"I know where that is," Ivan answered.

"Take care of it."

"I'll try my best," Ivan answered.

The partisans finished their meal and the commander gave the order to get ready to move out. "We'll try to cross the railroad tracks and join the Jewish partisan group near the Wygon Lake," said the commander. Ivan led them to the railroad tracks. At a distance, they could still hear heavy machine gun fire and then a mortar shell exploded. Darkness had set in by the time they reached the tracks. Sanya and Pasha went ahead to investigate the situation. Dogs barked continuously in the surrounding villages and the skies were cloudy. It looked as though it was going to rain.

Sanya and Pasha returned and with no one on the railroad tracks. They began walking in a single line, crossing the tracks quickly and entered the forest on the other side of the railroad. The partisans tried their best to move quietly, but suddenly something unexpected happened. Nikolay always carried his accordion on a belt over his shoulder and when he jumped over a small hole in the ground, the belt came loose and the accordion opened up with a tremendous noise. For a second, everyone froze and almost instantly, at their left, machine guns opened fire. The partisans began to run. Sanya, who was first, took the wrong direction and before they knew it, they were in swamps up to their hips. Ivan Bobko did not cross the railroad tracks. He returned home. The machine guns didn't cease firing for a minute but the partisans, finally, crossed the swamp. They were wet and Kuba had fallen several times, but now they were marching through a dry forest toward the east.

It was nearly sunrise when they came to the Babin Chutors. On the other side of the chutors, they entered the "grobla," a dike built from logs across the swamps, to Novosielski. They were tired but didn't stop because it was still a long way to the village of Svecice, their destination. The partisans continued marching all day until late afternoon, stopping near the village of Novosielski for a short rest. Kuba sat down and fell asleep almost instantly. He didn't know how long he had slept, but someone pushed him and he got to his feet. Everyone was up. Toliya was telling the commander something, so Kuba went over and listened. Toliya was reporting that the village they were about to enter was occupied by Germans. There was only one way left for them, and that was to circle around the village through the swamps, and the swamps around Novosielski were treacherous. It took a lot of nerve and desperation, but finally they did it.

Late in the evening, when the "Eagles" entered the forest near the Wygon Lake, they rested for awhile without fear of a German surprise attack. They were safe once again. It was nearly midnight when they marched through the paths that were very familiar to them. Far behind them, in the village of Novosielski, a machine gun was barking.

Chapter Eighteen

In 1941 there were two kinds of partisans in the Belarusian and Ukrainian forests. The first were active fighters who attacked Germans systematically and crippled their means of transportation. The second were groups of non-combatant partisans, composed mainly of women, children and aged people who had escaped from the Jewish ghettos. They built their camps in very isolated parts of marshes and forests. Neighboring combat groups supported them with food and clothing. The noncombatants, in return, took care of the wounded and manufactured supplies for the men. For example, they manufactured boots and clothing from material delivered to them. They also set up a soap factory. One noncombatant group, consisting of several Jewish refugees from the ghettos of Baranovichi, Kleck, Pinsk and other nearby cities, was located in the vicinity of the Wygon Lake. The commander of that group was a Russian by the name of Misha Sain. A lieutenant of the Red Army in 1942, he had escaped from German capture.

Misha was a born coward. He actually tried to avoid any confrontation with the enemy and he was capable of great cruelty particularly against women and children if they interfered with his plans. There was a young Jewish couple with two small children in his group. One day German troops attacked the camp. The entire group succeeded in escaping into the surrounding marshes and wheat fields. Misha was the first one to run. He hid behind a haystack and watched as his group made its way across the marshes and fields. There were forty some people in his group. They separated into several smaller groups and headed off in different directions. Misha decided to play it very safe by joining a small group which headed his way. There were eight people in that group including the young couple and their children. "This is great," Misha thought. "If the Germans catch up with us, I will just turn the Jews over to them and they will not harm me."

Night came and the group stopped for rest near a tree in a field covered with haystacks. There was no sound of Germans approaching. Yet Misha walked around with his pistol in hand and warned everyone that he would kill anyone that made any noise. In the middle of the night the children began to cry. Without any warning Misha grabbed the two children, dragged them behind a haystack and shot them to death. The Germans were not even chasing them.

Many of the members of Misha's group had been in combat groups previously in different parts of the country. They had been expelled from those groups for various reasons. But the main reason was a deep anti-Semitic trend amongst the partisans. In 1942, there was a Jewish group near the Wygon Lake who had distinguished itself with great bravery. The commander of that group was an eighteen year-old boy from Baranovichi by the name of Misha Zalmanovich. The group did not have enough weapons. Despite having nearly one hundred members, they had only thirty rifles. In spite of this, their bravery brought them fame in the surrounding area. Several of the group's members received medals for their actions.

One of their neighboring partisan groups was called Zhorkincy. Their commander was a Soviet officer named Cigankov. Although relations between the two groups were very good in the beginning, they changed under anti-semitic influence. Eventually, the Zhorkincys began to attack the Jewish partisans, robbing them of their weapons and belongings, and committing many murders. Commander Cigankov and his deputy, "the Politruk," political leader, named Dzvankov, who had graduated from a Communist Party school, actually approved of the anti-semitic actions committed by their men— even accusing the Jewish partisans of attacking the non-Jews. It got worse. There were several open fights between the groups. Many were killed on both sides. But the Zhorkincys were larger in number and better armed, so they forced the Jewish groups out of the forest.

After that, the Zhorkincys stopped fighting the Nazis. They found an easier "enemy" to fight, Jewish refugees from the ghettos. They did the same thing to the Jews as the Nazis—undressed them and shot them. Among those killed by the Zhorkincy was the well-known surgeon from the Baranovichi General Hospital, Dr. Abramovich. They also murdered many women and children. Altogether they killed about 120 Jews, mostly women and children.

A new partisan unit, called the "51st Group," arrived in the vicinity from the marshes near the city of Slonim. They were commanded by a heavyset Russian named Pugachov. The group was strong and had many Jews amongst them. The "51st Group" began to defend the Jewish group of Misha Zalmanovich. Later, they combined into one group. They took back their old camp from the Zhorkincy. Everything was quiet in the area for awhile. But Pugachov was a terrible drunkard and became very friendly with Cigankov. Pugachov's deputy, Misha Sain, was very much against the friendship between the two. A quiet struggle began between Pugachov and his deputy. Nothing was being done to fight the common enemy, the Nazis. When the Germans attacked, they burned down the village of Svecice, forcing the peasants to seek refuge in the forest and build their own earth huts. This happened in the winter of 1942.

After the German raid, Pugachov divided his partisan group in two. He selected all the gentiles and only a few Jews. Well armed, they went east toward the city of Kopul where a mighty partisan division was active under the command of General Komarov. The group that Pugachov had left behind was divided again into two. No one was armed. They were Jews from the nearby ghettos. The only gentile was Lieutenant Misha Sain, who became the commander of one of the groups. The other group was led by a young refugee from Warsaw, Leon Melnik. Later on, those two groups and several others merged and became very active.

Orlovsky's group parachuted down in the vicinity of the Wygon Lake after the merger. The Jewish partisan group was still in bad shape because they did not have many weapons or much food. There was little food to be had in the surrounding area. The villages had been burned. The peasants who survived were partisans themselves, living in the forest and, due to the large number of German troops concentrated in the area, could hardly go out and search for food.

Kuba's commander, Colonel Orlovsky, decided to help the Jewish group. About fifteen miles from their camp was a village called Wygonowschina. Several months before, the Nazis had burned the entire population to death inside their houses. There were now only burned skeletons of houses with burned human limbs and bones sticking out from among the ashes. These were the remains of about two hundred peasants, men, women and children.

There were cellars beneath the ruins where the peasants had kept their food. Orlovsky ordered two men from his group, Yasha and Kuba, to lead a group of twenty-eight Jews on an expedition to that village. Their assignment was first, to bury as many bodies as possible and second, to bring back as much food as they could. The Jewish group had three wagons with horses. It was a hard journey. They couldn't go by road because there were too many German vehicles, so they cut through the swamps. The journey was especially hard on the horses. At times the partisans had to pull the mired animals out of the swamp. It took two days to travel the fifteen miles. But at last they came to a dry road near the village.

They entered the village near midnight of the second day and got to work. The group was divided into two, Yasha took one half and Kuba the other half. Kuba and his group went to the north side of the village, while Yasha and his group stayed on the south side. This way both ends of the road were protected against sudden attack. There were bodies everywhere and several big bomb craters. The partisans moved the bodies to the craters and covered them with dirt. One of the partisans made a cross out of tree branches and set it up at the center of the grave site. Then they started to hunt for food.

The first three cellars they opened were almost full with potatoes which they loaded onto the wagons. Potatoes were also fed to the hungry horses. It was already daylight when they finished loading the wagons and left the village to reenter the swamp. Because of the loaded wagons, it was even harder than before. So they took a little different route and reached an island near noon on their way toward camp. They emptied the wagons and left one wagon and five men to guard the potatoes and to transfer them to the camp. The other partisans then went back to Wygonowschina.

They returned the next evening with two additional wagon-loads. After several days, of repeating the procedure, they had secured a large amount of food. On the third morning, while the campers were sitting around a fire eating, Kuba noticed that Yasha was whispering something to two of the Jewish partisans. The three approached Kuba and Yasha said, "Why shouldn't we get some meat?"

"Where from?" Kuba asked.

"From a village just five miles from here. But the village is only two miles from the city of Telechan, and in that city there is stationed a German garrison," Yasha replied.

"Who knows how to get there?" asked Kuba.

A Jewish blacksmith by the name of Mukasy from Baranovichi came forward and said, "I do."

"Will you go with them?" Kuba asked Yasha.

"I'll take five men and go with them," Yasha answered.

They discussed the matter for a while and Yasha assured him that he would be very careful. Kuba agreed, and in the evening Yasha left with his group. He was the only one who was armed; the others had only hand grenades. That entire night, the partisans talked about Yasha's group. Kuba didn't know why, but he was very worried about the entire affair.

In the morning, the partisans were back on their "island." They had built several huts with tree branches covered with leaves and dirt. Now they built a fire and sat around it, baked potatoes and dried their clothes, wet from the previous night's rain. And they worried about their six comrades. It was late in the morning when they heard the characteristic sound of a Russian peasant wagon. Yasha and his men returned and had brought two hogs, a calf and a sack full of salt, a luxury at that time. "Telechan is full of Germans," Yasha said.

"Are you sure no one saw in which direction you left?" Kuba asked.

"Yes, I'm sure of that," he answered.

"Any news about the German raid on our forest?" Kuba asked again.

"The peasants told us that the Germans were returning to Pinsk and other cities in the west," answered Yasha.

The partisans kept one hog for themselves. The other hog, the calf, and some potatoes were put in the wagon and sent to the main camp. In the evening, they went again to Wygonowschina and on the way met a peasant. Yasha stopped and asked, "Who are you?"

"I'm from a burned out village and am living now in the forest."

"What are you doing on the road now?" Yasha asked.

"I'm on my way to meet some partisans for whom I am doing some scouting."

The peasant was unarmed and they let him go, but Kuba did not feel right about it, he was suspicious and worried. "Who knows," Kuba said, "maybe he's a spy."

"Do you think so?" asked Yasha.

"Yes. Who knows?"

"I think we can still overtake him," Yasha said. With several others, he started running in the direction where the peasant had gone. They returned after about fifteen minutes.

"The devil knows him! He disappeared," Yasha said. They didn't talk about the incident any further.

That night they finished their work a little earlier than usual and decided that the next morning they would return to the main camp on the Wygon Lake. When they got to their island, the sun was beginning to rise on the horizon. It was very cold. They built a fire to warm themselves and roast some pieces of pork which

Mukasy had cut up. Several of them fell asleep. A seventeen year-old boy from Baranovichi, the son of a rabbi, was on guard duty.

It was already daylight and very quiet as Kuba began to sleep. Suddenly, the stillness was broken by heavy machine gun fire and bullets buzzing all around. The partisans immediately rose to their feet. A young Jew from Warsaw, named Abelman, who was sitting next to Kuba earlier, fell immediately, hit by several bullets. The partisans ran toward the swamp and into the forest to hide. The German bullets followed them all the way, hitting the water in the swamp around them with tremendous force. Five machine guns were firing at them. Over the noise, Kuba could hear the Germans yell, "Halt! Surrender!"

Running next to Kuba were three others from the Jewish group. They didn't stop. When they entered the forest Kuba stopped, turned his head and saw his comrades running along the entire width of the swamp. Kuba could not keep from looking behind. There were several bodies on the island and in the swamp. From his right, he heard an outcry, "Halt!" He fired his submachine gun in the direction of the voice. Followed by the three other partisans, he continued to run through the forest. He heard the Germans yelling far behind them. When there where no more bullets buzzing around them, they slowed and then sat down. The shooting ceased but for quite some time they could hear the Germans yelling and laughing. Later, they heard their wagons departing. When it became quiet once again, they got up.

"What do we do now?" asked one of the Jewish partisans.

"We'll go back and see what happened. Maybe there is someone left behind who is wounded and needs our help," Kuba said. They returned to the island, very carefully. A gruesome sight awaited them. Sixteen nude bodies of their comrades were lying in the swamp near the island, among them Yasha and Mukasy. Now they would have to piece together the facts and find out what had happened.

It seems that the peasants of the village where Yasha had taken the hogs and the calf the night before reported the event to the Gestapo. One peasant had followed Yasha. And the peasant they had met the night before had led the Germans to their island. The young boy who was on guard that morning had fallen asleep. The guards took him alive. A week later, after he had been terribly tortured by lying nude on broken glass, and after he had refused to provide the information the Germans wanted, they decided to hang him. It was to be a public execution in the town square— a forced event before the town's entire population. The young martyr himself put the noose around his neck but the German SS officers decided to change the program. Instead of hanging, they decided to release a few specially trained dogs. He was undressed by the Germans. The dogs were set upon him and allowed to devour him alive in front of the spectators.

Special services were held for the fallen men of the camp, concluding with the singing of the Jewish Partisan Song, which originated in the Jewish ghetto of Vilno:

Don't ever say that you are on your final way,

When angry clouds blot out the clear and sunny day,

Our yearned for hour, it will finally appear,

When we shall proclaim to the world that YES, WE ARE HERE!

This song was written not with ink, but human blood,

It's not a sing-song by a bird that's free and proud.

Among the ruins of their burning, crumbling towns,

A people sang this song with rifles in their hands!

Two weeks later, Colonel Orlovsky's Special Partisan Group No.258 vengefully burned the village to the ground and executed the guilty peasants who had led the German troops to the ill fated "island."

The following week, it was raining off and on. There was very little activity in the area since the Telechan incident because all the roads were heavily guarded by German troops. Only partisan reconnaissance parties were actively keeping an eye on the German and other enemy movements. Most of the Jewish partisan camp spent their time inside the earth huts. The guards, manning their posts on a two-mile circle around the camp, were forced to face the bad weather bundled up in their clothing, walking along paths among the trees and watching the approaches to the camp.

Kuba was sitting on a straw mattress in his hut, writing down some notes about the events of the last few weeks. He kept a diary of sorts about the war behind enemy lines, hoping that one day this information would be the basis for a book.

He shared the hut with about a dozen people from the camp. On the other side of the hut, on a mattress, a middle-aged woman, very slim with brown-gray hair and wearing steel-rimmed glasses, was mending some clothing. She reminded Kuba very much of his mother. He closed his eyes for a moment and could vividly see his mother sitting behind an old Singer machine, sewing dresses for a living. She was a gentle, warm and very worried woman, worrying about their future when she was urging him to do his homework. He was overwhelmed by his love for her and his little sister when he pledged silently, "some day I will take care of you both." Little did he know that the "some day" would never come.

"Kuba, are you all right?" a girl's voice asked as he felt her hand on his arm. He opened his eyes and looked at her. It was Rachel, the girl who occupied the mattress next to his. She was nineteen, very beautiful with thick chestnut-colored hair and a doll-like complexion. He had been watching that girl since she had come to the Jewish camp, and experienced an inner surge of warm feelings whenever he saw her.

"Yes, I am all right. I was watching that woman over there. She reminded me very much of my mother. So I closed my eyes and began to drop into remembrances about my family and what might have happened to them."

"I understand your feelings very well, Kuba. I too can see my family before my eyes every day," Rachel said. Her green-turquoise eyes began to fill up with tears. They sat in silence for a long time while the rain was pounding on the roof of the hut.

"Where are you from?" Kuba asked.

"From a small town in Silesia, the coal mining district of southwest Poland."

"How many children are there in your family?"

"Four. I have a brother about your age, a sister two years older than I and a little baby sister, who was six last time I saw her."

Kuba looked at Rachel's tense face. Her eyes had darkened and he knew that she was full of bad memories and emotions that must come out. Otherwise she might break down. "Can you tell me what happened to them?"

She looked into his face, took his hand in both of hers and began to talk. "When the Germans invaded and took our city, my brother escaped to the east with some of his friends. We received a letter from him and he was somewhere in Russia. My older sister was picked up by the Germans one day when she was with a group of her friends and sent to a concentration camp." Rachel began to cry and Kuba put his arm around her, pulling her towards him. Her body was shaken by deep sobs.

"Let's stop talking now, you can tell me the rest some other time."

"Oh, no, Kuba, now you must hear everything that happened," she said. She was silent for awhile and then she began to speak again. "One day in the spring of 1942, the Germans assembled all Jews of our town on a square near the railroad station. They called that place 'Umschlagplace.' There were two gates in the fence around the square. When every Jew of our town was there, the Germans began the segregation; all the young people were ordered to pass through the gate on the right. They were sent to slave-labor camps. The children, their mothers and middle-aged or old people were ordered to pass through the gate on the left. My parents and little sister went that way."

She was crying freely now, her body shaking. Kuba held her close to his chest as she continued. "They took all the people that passed through the left gate across the railroad tracks into a little forest and then we heard machine gun fire. They were all killed there!" The rain was pounding on the roof of the hut and Kuba and Rachel were sitting there with their arms around each other, crying. The woman at the other end of the hut looked at them, wiped her eyes and continued with her job of mending the clothes in her lap.

"How did you get away?" Kuba asked.

"I was working at that time as a spot welder in a factory and I had a special identification card. All the people with such cards were sent back to their factories."

"How did you get out of it and get here?" Kuba asked.

"There was a young couple in that factory who had made arrangements with the Polish underground to escape to the east. I went with them and here I am. The young couple eventually went to Lithuania."

There was some machine gun fire in the distance. Kuba jumped off his bunk and went outside. A young partisan came up to him and said, "It is only one of our groups getting some provisions!" Kuba smiled at him and went back into the hut. Rachel was still on her bunk and was looking at him. Kuba took her arm and she embraced him.

"You know, Kuba, you look very much like my brother," and she kissed him while putting her arms around his neck.

Kuba pulled her close to him and said, "I have to check the guards right now, but I will be back soon and . . . Rachel, I really think that I love you." Kuba left the camp, heading towards the stables. Rachel looked after him with a warm smile on her face, shining through her tears.

The next day the rain stopped. The sky was clear and blue and the partisans began to move around. There were reconnaissance missions going out as far as the city of Pinsk and toward Baranovichi. Kuba got an order to prepare a special group for a dangerous mission against a German garrison at the city of Nesvizh.

When he returned to the hut from a meeting with his new commander, he found Rachel sitting on his bunk. She did not notice him as he approached. He did not call her name but put his arms around her and started talking without looking at her. "My dear Rachel, I was telling the truth when I told you that I love you. I am about to leave on a mission, and you know how it is. I cannot promise you that I will return, but if I survive this mission I will come back to you and if you love me, you will be my wife!" She put her arms around him and drew him down on top of her.

"Oh, Kuba, I have never been with a man before, but you are the one for me. I want you to take me now before you leave. I want you with all my soul and body, in spite of everything that my parents have told me!" In the semidarkness of the hut, Kuba took Rachel, whispering words into her ears that he had never heard from his parents.

"In the name of our Patriarchs Abraham, Isaac and Jacob I take you as my wife! And may the souls of our parents approve of this union!"

"Oh my dear, I want you so much and forever and I am sure my parents approve. I want to have sons from our union, to continue our heritage!"

A bell rang at the kitchen site of the camp and all the partisans assembled for lunch. Kuba and Rachel joined the group around the kitchen and there was something in their eyes that made everyone take notice. They realized that Kuba and Rachel were a family.

About four in the afternoon, Kuba was preparing to mount his horse. The other partisans were already on their horses. Rachel came running toward Kuba, put her arms around his neck and said, "My dear, will I see you again? I don't want to be without you."

"Rachel darling, if we survive this war, we will be together for the rest of our lives," Kuba said, kissing her. Then he mounted his horse and rode out of camp, followed by the others.

When Kuba and his group returned to the camp early the next morning, they were met by a ghostly sight. The camp had been burned to the ground. Dead bodies of Jewish partisans were on the ground throughout the campsite. The previous evening, SS troops had raided the camp. Judging by the number of spent cartridges fired by the partisan weapons, it was a bitter fight.

There was no sign of Rachel.

Kuba searched among the bodies to no avail. He and his group rode off to a nearby village. There they learned some of the details of the German raid of the previous night. One peasant told

Kuba that about twenty young men and women were taken to the railroad station and were loaded on a freight train headed west, toward Poland.

Sitting on his horse under a tree, Kuba began to think about the events of the last few hours. He had a sharp pain in his heart. He was very angry. He began thinking aloud. "I have lost Franca and my son Victor. Now they have taken away Rachel. My parents and sister are all dead by now. How much can a man endure?" Suddenly he began to cry, and that made him even angrier. He looked around and saw his men not far behind him. He turned his horse and rode over to them. "I swear that we will get every German son-of-a-bitch that had anything to do with this. We will kill anyone wearing a German uniform until they are all dead or out of our land. And if I perish during that process, you, my friends and all the others, will have to continue and fulfill this oath. Let's go!" The group crossed the railroad tracks and moved swiftly westwards.

Chapter Nineteen

In the winter of 1943, Orlovsky's group once again occupied their old camping ground in the forest between the village of Lopatichi and the railroad station at Budi. As their old huts were destroyed by the Nazis, they built new ones and prepared them for the cold Russian winter. In each hut, they installed a heater made of empty oil drums. There was plenty of dry wood around to use as fuel.

They received winter clothing by plane from Moscow which included sheepskin coats and hats, even felt boots. Using the parachutes, they made white camouflage uniforms so that they could safely move through the snow territories and not be detected by the enemy. There wasn't a single raid on partisan infested forests during the winter and the partisans, in turn, began to travel to distant parts of the country on special assignments. Because it was difficult to walk through the snow, the partisans did their traveling on horseback or in sleighs. There was a lot of work to be done. New orders came and all members of the Orlovsky group were always out on missions with only a few left at the camp to guard their equipment. At that time, the Germans were in full retreat from the front lines. Since their defeat near Stalingrad, all highways were full of German troops. Kuba's group had to travel over the frozen swamps, but that wasn't too bad. They were on firm footing.

One morning their peasant friend, Ivan Bobko, arrived with very important information and went straight to the commander's hut and stayed there for some time. There were about ten men in camp at that time, having breakfast in one of the huts, when Colonel Orlovsky and Sanya entered, sat down on bunks and the commander said, "We'll have company today." The partisans stopped eating. The commander lit a cigarette and continued, "The German Military Governor of Belarus, SS General Friedrich Fenc, is coming to our forest to do some hunting. Ivan Bobko just brought the news. The General is already in the village of Mashuki and has eleven other German officers and about forty Belarusian SS police with him. The Germans got about thirty peasants together from the nearby villages to serve as 'beaters' to chase the animals toward the hunters."

Furthermore, he told them that the hunting party was organized by the chief forest ranger from the town of Shinavka. "They'll start out at noon today and we should prepare a reception committee for them," added the commander.

The partisans began making their preparations immediately, checking their weapons and ammunition. Each man took about a half-dozen hand grenades and Sanya prepared several cakes of explosives with fuses. They put on their camouflage uniforms. There was only one machine gun in the camp at this moment and Sanya and Vlodik were assigned to serve as machine gunners. When everything was ready, the partisans left their camp. There was a road leading from the village of Mashuki through the forest and about two miles deep into the forest, the road came to a crossing with another road. At the crossing, there once had been a hill, but when they built the roads, they dug through the hill so that, now, where the crossing was there remained one hill on each corner. The peasants called the spot "roskop," or dugout. This was the spot where the Eagles decided to set up an ambush. The group was divided into five units, two men to a unit and at the base of the farthest hill, Sanya and Vlodik set up their heavy machine guns, while the rest of the partisans took up positions on each side of the crossing. Kuba was with Colonel Orlovsky on the far left side of the road.

Even before the partisans were settled in their positions, the Germans began to move in. A sleigh loaded with Belarusian police was in the front, followed closely by sleighs occupied by German officers. The forward partisan positions let them pass through and then allowed the whole column to pass because Orlovsky did not give the order to attack. Kuba asked him why and Orlovsky answered, "They will return the same way loaded up with wild boar, elk and maybe bison."

"What happens if they do not return by this road?" asked Kuba.

"They will, there is no other way for heavy sleighs," Orlovsky replied. The other road led from the crossing to the railroad station at Budi, a narrow, difficult road over a swamp, and it would be difficult to maneuver the sleighs on that road.

A half hour later, the partisans heard rifle fire. The German general and his party had begun their hunt, about three miles from the ambush. The rifle fire lasted about two hours and then it was quiet. The hunt was over. It was very cold and the partisans were moving around in order to keep warm.

When the hunters' shooting had stopped, Orlovsky ordered, "Take up your positions. Don't fire until Sanya opens up with the machine gun!" The partisans took up their assigned positions, Sanya and Vlodik dug in next to the road in the snow so that only the barrel of their heavy machine gun could be seen from Kuba's position. From a distance, they could hear singing and loud laughter. The Germans were returning. The partisans anticipated that the Belarusians would lead the hunting party back and the idea was to let the Belarusians pass at the end of the ambush line and then attack the Germans with full force. However, the General and the other Nazis were in high spirits after the hunt and let their security slip. The first four sleighs were occupied by German officers, with General Fenc in the first sleigh. When the sleigh was about twenty yards away, Sanya opened up with his machine gun and the rest of the partisans began firing their weapons. Colonel Orlovsky was lighting the fuses on the tolulol cakes and throwing them at the horses which panicked the horses and caused the first four sleighs to tangle and turn over. The Germans fired only a few shots before they were all killed. The General's body was pinned down under a sleigh. The sleighs carrying the Belarusian police also got tangled in the skirmish at the center of the ambush but several policemen jumped off the sleighs and took up positions behind trees. Sanya pulled up the machine gun to the top of the nearest hill and began firing at the police and Orlovsky was still throwing the tolulol cakes. Kuba was about twenty feet to the left and farther ahead of Orlovsky when an explosion behind him knocked him to the ground. He was not hurt and turned around immediately. The sight that he faced caused him to scream at the top of his lungs. Orlovsky was lying on the snow, turning it crimson. The Colonel's right arm was ripped off past his elbow, his left hand was bleeding and some fingers were missing. Otto and Nikolay picked up the commander and carried him deeper into the forest. A tolulol cake had exploded while Orlovsky still had it in his hands.

During the commotion that followed, several policemen escaped along the road to Budi. Sanya took over as the commander and ordered everyone into open attack. Kuba hurled a hand grenade at a group of policemen behind some bushes, about forty feet away. After the grenade exploded, the partisans got up and ran toward the enemy positions with Sanya in the lead. When they saw the enemy retreating, the partisans let out a blood curdling yell, used by the Russians when attacking with bayonets. "Hurra! Hurra!"

It was soon over and there were no enemy soldiers or policemen left alive. The partisans returned to the ambush site. Otto and Nikolay succeeded in uprighting one of the tangled sleighs and placed the unconscious Orlovsky on some blankets in the sleigh and started out for the camp. The other partisans fixed up more sleighs and loaded them with the carcasses of elk, deer, wild boar, rabbits and some birds which the Germans had killed during their hunt. They also pulled off the uniform from the dead Germans and gathered all the weapons and ammunition, then returned to camp, leaving the dead enemies in the forefront. Before leaving, Sanya pinned a piece of paper to the undershirt of General Fenc, on which Kuba had written in German "Welcome to the land of the partisans."

The following day, Pasha picked up the frozen body of the German general and dumped it next to a German bunker near the Budi railroad station. The Germans did not avenge the action of the partisans.

Meanwhile Colonel Orlovsky was in very bad shape. Anna said that she would have to amputate his right arm and some more fingers on his left hand. However, her surgical instruments were lost during the last raid by the SS. "We must find a hacksaw somewhere so that I can cut through the bones." Toliya went to the village of Mashuki and obtained a hacksaw from the local blacksmith and, also brought back information about the impact of the ambush on General Fenc.

The German garrison in Budi was in turmoil. The few Belarusian policemen who had escaped the partisan ambush were arrested by the Germans and later executed in the city of Baranovichi. There were rumors that a special SS division would arrive shortly in the area to take care of Special Group No.258, the Orlovsky partisans. It was clear that the partisans would have to move to another area and they decided to do this after they took care of Orlovsky.

The twelve men who had been on a mission with Major Nikolsky returned that night and Sanya contacted Moscow by radio. It was a long conversation. Sanya did not have any more batteries for the radio, so the partisans had to take turns cranking a portable generator. After the radio session, Sanya decoded the instructions from headquarters: "Nikolsky was promoted to the rank of lieutenant colonel and appointed commander of the Special Partisan Group No.258, known officially as the Eagles. After surgery and a short rest, Colonel Orlovsky is to be transported to a clandestine airport maintained by partisans, somewhere in the eastern part of Belarus, for a return flight to Moscow. He will be accompanied by two partisans. Details for his return will be transmitted at a later date."

On the next day, after breakfast, Anna began preparations for the surgery. Kuba and Otto were ordered to assist. Anna had only a small bottle of ether, so they got the Colonel very drunk and then, using a piece of cloth, Anna applied the ether to Orlovsky's nose and mouth until he fell asleep.

All this took place in the "hospital" hut. A special operating table was built and Orlovsky occupied it now with blankets under his head as a pillow. On a small table nearby Anna placed all her surgical tools including the hacksaw, a small screwdriver with a wooden handle and a primus burner.

Anna said to Kuba, "You stay at the table and hand me the tools as I call for them. We must work as a team very quickly. Otto, you stay at the head of the table and monitor the Colonel's breathing."

Anna washed Orlovsky's right arm with alcohol and said, "Scalpel!" Kuba handed her the little knife and Anna quickly made a circular incision around the arm, half way between the elbow and shoulder and rolled up the skin a few inches. Then she cut the muscles to the bone. There was a lot of blood and Kuba had to fight sudden nausea. "Hacksaw!" Kuba handed the hacksaw to Anna and she began to cut through the bone. It was hard work and Anna was perspiring.

Kuba wiped her forehead and Anna said, "You finish it, Kuba, and I will get ready to seal the blood vessels." Kuba began to cut through the bone using a lot of force. The hacksaw was not too sharp and Kuba could feel the pain that this must have caused. He clenched his teeth to hold back his own sickness, and cut through the bone. Anna pushed him aside, removed the arm and using the screwdriver, which she had heated up to a purple color on the primus, she sealed off the blood vessels until there was no more bleeding. Anna then rolled down the skin like a sleeve.

"Sutures!" Kuba handed her the special threads, clamps and suture tool and Anna quickly closed the exposed stump, cutting away any loose skin. The whole procedure lasted only minutes, but it seemed to Kuba like ages. "Kuba, bandage the arm please."

While Kuba bandaged the arm, Anna was working on the fingers of the left hand. When it was all finished, Anna listened to Orlovsky's heart, checked his blood pressure and pulse and finally said, "Comrades, I believe that we have saved the Colonel's life, provided that no infection sets in." From beginning to end the operation lasted about an hour and a half. Orlovsky moaned a few times, but he slept through the entire surgery. As a matter of fact, he slept all day. Kuba and Otto took turns watching Orlovsky and Anna checked the arm and hand frequently for any sign of infection.

Nikolsky ordered most of the partisans to guard duty around the entire perimeter of the camp. They even planted mines on the trails leading to their camp. Kuba could not eat all day. The gory details of the surgery were too fresh in his mind. Orlovsky awakened in the middle of the night, in great pain and complained that the fingers of his hands were itching terribly. He did not know that there were no fingers left on his hands.

The next morning, the Eagles dismantled the camp, loaded all equipment on sleighs and left immediately, heading for the forest in the vicinity of the village of Novosielski , some fifteen miles away. Kuba, Otto and Anna were riding on a sleigh with Colonel Orlovsky. He complained that he could not hear very clearly. At two o'clock in the afternoon, the group crossed the railroad tracks and entered the Novosielski forest, with no incidents on the way. The partisans found a suitable dry "island" and began immediately building earth huts. The new camp was ready at sundown.

After dinner Sanya summoned Kuba and Loris and took them to the commander's hut. Nikolsky just finished sealing a large canvas bag which he then placed in an old gasoline drum. "This drum contains some important documents which we must bury somewhere in the forest. Only the four of us will know the exact hiding place. I want you to pick up some shovels and let's go," Nikolsky said.

While Nikolsky was speaking, Kuba noticed a funny smile on Sanya's face and he suddenly realized that there was a lot of animosity between the two. He could not figure out what it might be. They got some shovels, picked up the drum and went into the forest. Nikolsky found a suitable spot between two young birch trees.

"Let's dig a hole right here," Nikolsky said. Loris and Kuba started digging a hole about four feet in diameter and five feet deep. They lowered the drum into the hole and covered it with dirt. The excess dirt was then shoveled away between other trees, at some distance. Then they camouflaged the spot with some moss and leaves. Sanya rearranged the branches of the birch trees in such a manner that they formed an arch over the hiding place. He tied the branches of the two trees together with some white string, which could not be detected from the ground. After they finished, they returned to camp. No one asked any questions and they were silent during the entire procedure.

That night in their earth hut Otto began asking questions. "What were you guys up to this evening?"

"Oh, nothing much. We had to do some errands for the commander," Kuba replied.

"What do you think of Nikolsky?" Otto asked again.

"He seems to be a straight shooting officer. I kind of like him."

After a few minutes of silence Otto began to laugh quietly and Kuba asked him, "What are you laughing about?"

"Toliya told me today that Nikolsky is carrying on a romance with a sixteen-year-old Jewish girl from another partisan group. Toliya accompanied him several times to the girl's camp."

"Boy, that could be serious and disastrous for a man of Nikolsky's stature and age," Kuba said smiling. It began to rain outside and the two partisans went to sleep.

Sanya contacted Moscow and reported the outcome of the operation on Orlovsky. The reply from headquarters contained a message from the Supreme Command of the Red Army, congratulating the Eagles on the occasion of their victory in the action against General Fenc. There were also instructions concerning the return of Orlovsky to Moscow. Kuba and Loris were to take Orlovsky to a forest in the vicinity of the city of Minsk, where the partisan division of General Komarov was stationed. The two partisans were to accompany Orlovsky to Moscow. A special plane would pick them up on November 18, at eight o'clock in the evening, ten days away. Furthermore, all members of their group were awarded special gold medals for valor.

During the next ten days, the partisans kept a low pro file. Then on November 11, after dinner, Kuba and Loris got ready for the journey east. Anna took care of placing Orlovsky in the sleigh. Nikolsky issued Kuba and Loris brand new submachine guns with ten clips containing seventy-two rounds of ammunition each. Before they left, Nikolsky took Kuba aside and handed him a heavy envelope. "Give this to the commissar in charge of our operations. I hold you responsible for the safety of Colonel Orlovsky."

"Yes, Colonel!" Kuba replied.

Sanya came over with a bottle of vodka and some cups. They drank a toast to the health of Orlovsky and to the success of this journey. Nikolsky and the rest of the partisans embraced Kuba and Loris and kissed them on the cheeks. The sleigh was loaded with food provisions: venison, wild boar meat, salt and several bottles of vodka. There were also four cartons of cigarettes.

Nikolsky shook hands with them and said, "Farewell, my Eagles." Kuba took the reins of the horses and they moved out. A light snow was falling when they crossed the Berlin-Moscow highway but they traveled all night, taking turns at the reins and in the morning they stopped in a forest not far from Stolbtsy and spent the day resting. They ate half-frozen meat and drank some vodka. Loris made a fire and brewed some tea. Orlovsky was awake. Loris took care of all his needs and then at sundown, they continued their journey.

They stopped briefly at the chutor of a friendly farmer who belonged to the "Starovery" sect. The farmer knew Orlovsky and had heard about the ambush on General Fenc. His son was in Stolbtsy on the previous day and had brought back a Belarusian newspaper published by the Germans. On the front page was an announcement about the "heroic" death of SS General Fenc. The farmer told them about the various safe roads to take toward their destination and shortly afterwards the partisans left.

Kuba, Loris and Orlovsky arrived at the Komarov camp on the morning of November 16. The General greeted them personally and installed them in his own hut. There was a military doctor in General Komarov's camp who examined Colonel Orlovsky, gave him some medicine and said that Anna had done an excellent job. Kuba and Loris stayed close to Orlovsky during the remaining two days. Komarov, who was a Red Army general had a strict military discipline in his camp. Everything was very orderly and they even had a few pieces of artillery.

Loris was a withdrawn man who seldom smiled and there was something very hard in his face, particularly in his eyes. He was very friendly to Kuba, but there was a language barrier between them. Loris spoke even less Russian than Otto. The conversations between the two partisans were in a combination of French, Latin and Russian, making it difficult to express one's feelings. However, the two sang songs together and even told jokes, but their conversations during the journey were limited. Kuba felt that Loris understood much more Russian than he made believe.

THE ODYSSEY OF A PARTISAN

A correspondent of the Soviet news agency was at Komarov's camp and interviewed Orlovsky, Kuba and Loris for the Soviet press and took some photos of them, informing them that he was going to return to Moscow with them when they left.

On November 18, a detail of Komarov partisans took Orlovsky, Kuba, Loris and the TASS (Russian news agency) correspondent to meet the plane at an airstrip only a few miles from the Komarov camp, on the shore's of a frozen lake. Torches were set up along the runway and about fifteen minutes before the plane was to arrive. The partisans lit the torches and then returned to the forest for safety, in case a German plane should fly over the area. The plane arrived at a few minutes past eight. It was a Soviet built twin-engine biplane with a heavy machine gun mounted at the rear of the plane. The door opened and a ladder was lowered. A Soviet airman descended from the plane and greeted the partisans and after awhile the pilot joined them. They talked a bit and then Orlovsky was taken on board. Kuba shook hands with the Komarov partisans and thanked them.

The sergeant in charge of the detail told Kuba, "We shall keep the sleigh and horses for you." Kuba boarded the plane and the door was securely closed. There were no seats in the plane, only benches along the walls. Orlovsky was stretched out on one of the benches and Loris secured him with straps that were fastened to the wall of the fuselage. Kuba went forward to the cockpit section to find out why the plane was not taking off. The pilot was talking to someone on the radio and when he saw Kuba, he said, "I have orders to stay on the ground for a while. There seems to be a lot of German aircraft activity on our route. Moscow will give me the signal for takeoff."

Kuba looked outside and saw the Komarov partisans standing near the plane. The pilot opened his side window and told them to put out the torches. The pilot, a captain, introduced Kuba to his copilot, a young, blonde lieutenant. In addition to those two, the crew had only one more man, the tail gunner, whom they had met before at the airstrip. It was past one o'clock in the morning when the plane took off. Flying over the snow-covered plains and marshes of Belarus and Western Russia, the pilot circled north in order to avoid German anti-aircraft emplacements, as well as the Luftwaffe. The sky was turning light blue when the plane approached Moscow. Kuba went to the cockpit to watch the landing procedures.

Suddenly, the copilot yelled out, "German planes!"

"Where?" asked the pilot.

"At three o'clock!" was the copilot's reply. Kuba returned to the cabin and looked out the window. There they were, about a dozen German planes flying in formation above and to the right of them. Even as he watched them, Kuba saw three planes peel off in sharp loops and come towards them. It took only a few seconds before bullets ripped through the fuselage of the small plane.

The tail gunner was firing his machine gun at the German planes and let out a yell, "I got one!" and then he fell silent.

One of the German planes was flying on the left side, firing at the small Russian plane and Kuba could see the large, black swastika on the plane's tail. Loris pulled Orlovsky down from the bench and covered him with his body. The tail gunner was dead and the TASS reporter replaced him at the machine gun. However, after firing only a few rounds, he was also hit and stumbled down from the gunner's platform. Kuba bent over the man and noticed that he was bleeding from the right shoulder. The correspondent told him that he was all right and pointed to the gun. Kuba looked up and saw the belly of a German plane, very near. He jumped up on the platform, grabbed the two handles of the heavy "Maxim" machine gun and started firing. The bullets ripped through the body of the German plane and it began trailing black smoke and flames as it went down. Kuba searched for the third plane and spotted him far behind, also in flames. The TASS correspondent must have hit him, after all. No other aircraft were in sight, so Kuba came down from the platform and fell to the floor as the plane lurched to the right. He realized that the plane was flying very erratically. He made his way to the cockpit and found the pilot was dead and the copilot, with blood all over his head, was moaning. Kuba unbuckled the copilot's seatbelt and placed him on the floor, turned to the pilot and removed his ear phones and then lifted the pilot's body out of the seat and placed him alongside the copilot. There was blood in the pilot's seat but Kuba sat down and grabbed the controls and succeeded in steadying the plane.

A crackling noise alerted Kuba to the earphones on the floor. He put them on and heard the airport operator in Moscow say, "...and congratulations on shooting down three enemy planes."

"Thank you, but what do I do now?" Kuba asked.

"What did you say? Who are you? "

"This is Lieutenant Kuba of the Special Partisan Group No.258."

"Where is the pilot?"

"He is dead and the copilot is badly wounded." There was silence at the other end. Kuba looked outside. He could see the streets of Moscow illuminated by the rising sun.

The operator at the airport tower spoke again, "Lieutenant, can you fly the plane?"

"No, I am not a pilot."

"You will be by the time we bring you down. Now listen carefully."

"I am listening," Kuba replied.

"Khorosho. All right. Look at the center of the instrument panel. There you will see an indicator with a bar across its center."

"Yes, I see it."

"That is the horizon indicator. There are two markers at both sides of that bar. When the bar is in line with the markers, it means that the plane is flying level to the ground. If the left marker is below the bar, the plane is banking to the left, and if the right marker is below the bar, the plane is banking to the right."

"I understand," Kuba said.

"Now, if the bar is above both markers, the plane is coming down or diving. If it is in the opposite direction, the plane is climbing."

"I got it," Kuba said. He banked the plane a few times in both directions and then climbed and descended, watching the instrument. If it were not for the dead and injured people in the plane, he would have enjoyed this flying lesson.

The operator continued, "Now you can turn either by banking or depressing the pedals on the floor in front of you. Look around and you will see the runway, because you are approaching the airport. We lit the guidance lights so that you can see them. I want you to line up the plane with the center of the runway."

Kuba looked down and he spotted the airport and the designated runway and guided the plane to the center of the runway, then started to push down on the controls. "No. Don't do it so fast or you will crash. Level off. That's right. Now you are about two kilometers out. Press down at the controls very lightly. That's fine, now some more. Now, there are a number of buttons to your right. One has a red dot on it and the other a blue dot."

"I see them," Kuba said.

"Start pushing in on the red one. That will decelerate the engines. Now hold the crossbar at about two degrees over the markers. That's good. You are five feet above the ground. Push in on the button with the red dot about five notches. Fine. Jiggle the controls downwards slightly and when you hit the ground, push the red dotted button in all the way." The plane hit the ground and bounced a few times. Then it just rolled along the runway. "Now, Lieutenant, push in on the blue dotted button all the way. That's right. Look on the floor, there is a large mushroom like button there. Step on it with both feet. Those are your brakes."

Kuba stepped on the brakes. The plane turned slightly to the left and came to a full stop. The propellers stopped turning. Kuba tried to get out of his seat, but as the full impact of the events of the last few minutes hit him, he fainted.

Hands pulled Kuba out of the plane. He was in a daze and continued asking, "What happened?"

"Comrade Lieutenant, you are in Moscow, at the airport, and everyone in the plane, who is alive, is being cared for."

"Where is Colonel Orlovsky?" asked Kuba.

"He is in the terminal right now. We shall take you to him." His legs were wobbly, but Kuba managed to walk across the terminal to an office where he found Orlovsky stretched out on a cot, with Loris beside him. Loris' right arm was bandaged.

When Kuba approached him, Loris said, "My companion, you are a brave man and the Colonel was asking for you."

Orlovsky grabbed Kuba's hand with both stumps of his arms, kissed him and said, "My son, you have returned our lives to us and we are so grateful." Kuba bent down and kissed the man on the forehead. Orlovsky was openly weeping. Loris put his arms around Kuba and he, too, was weeping. A short, heavy set commissar pulled Kuba away from the group and greeted him by patting his cheek. This was Commissar Goldsmith, the man who had saved Kuba's life twice before.

"Hey, Kuba, you are alive! Have good luck," he said in Yiddish. Kuba embraced the little man and asked about his family. The two then got into a car and departed for headquarters. In the car, Kuba handed him the envelope that Nikolsky had asked him to deliver. The Commissar looked at it and then said, "Oh, those things. My staff will take care of it."

The next day, the Commissar took Kuba to headquarters and Kuba was promoted to the rank of first lieutenant, a grade above lieutenant first class, which he was at that time. They also pinned a medal on his chest, for defending the air space above Moscow. The commissar also told him that in two days Kuba and other people would be returned to the Eagles camp. Kuba did not even have a chance to see what life in Moscow was like at that time. He was carted off to the airport on the morning of November 21. When he asked about Loris, he was told that the Spaniard would remain with Orlovsky in Moscow. Two other people who were to go with Kuba behind enemy lines consisted of a doctor, who was a major of Special Services, just out of school and a radio operator. The plane landed at the Komarov airstrip about a half hour past midnight and a detail under the command of the same sergeant greeted them and took them to the Komarov camp. Kuba and the two newcomers then got on a sleigh and left for the Eagles camp immediately. There were no incidents on the way and the three arrived at the camp early in the morning of November 24, 1943.

Chapter Twenty

During the first week of December, Kuba served as officer of the day. His duties included the posting of guards and their rotation, tour of the campgrounds, inspection of all camp facilities and weapons, as well as the compound where the horses were kept. The camp was spread in the forest over an area of about ten acres, and there were twenty-two partisans in the group at that time. In one area the partisans stored quite a large amount of captured German weapons, including a forty-five millimeter cannon with ammunition.

Kuba kept one souvenir from the raid on the Tucha Estate, a 7.65 mm., thirty-two caliber, semi-automatic Beretta pistol, made in Italy. He kept the pistol fully loaded in a special pocket constructed into the collar of his sheepskin jacket at the back of the neck. Many of the other partisans had done the same with their small hand guns. This had been suggested by Sanya as a precaution. When the Germans captured a partisan, they ordered him to put his hands behind his neck. It was very easy to extract the gun from its hiding place and use it on the enemy or himself, if necessary. The Nazis never kept partisans as prisoners. They always killed them in a most terrible manner.

One day, Kuba left the "arsenal" area and headed for the stables. The former Belarusian policeman, Shalik, was cleaning the stalls. "How is everything?" Kuba asked.

"Everything is fine except for that black devil of a stallion."

"What do you mean?" asked Kuba.

"When I tried to brush him, he pinned me to the side of the fence with his hip. He even tried to bite me," Shalik replied.

Kuba walked around to the front rail of the stall and stopped in front of the black stallion. The horse laid his ears down flat and bared his teeth, making a threatening sound. When Kuba went closer, the horse started lifting his front legs, but he was restrained by the confinement of the stall. Kuba stretched out his right arm toward the horse, carefully. The horse backed off slightly and Kuba talked softly to him, "You are a beautiful devil. Diablo, that's what I will call you." The stallion continued to make noises but they did not sound angry any longer. Suddenly, the stallion stretched his neck in Kuba's direction and began sniffing at the left side pocket of his jacket. Kuba remembered that he had there a part of a sugar cone which the partisans had brought back from the raid on the Tucha Estate. He took it out and held it in his open palm and the stallion picked the sugar up very gently with his lips. His ears were up again and his eyes did not have the angry glow in them as before. Kuba reached out and petted the horse's nose and mane. The stallion did not make a move.

Kuba began to visit the stallion several times a day, bringing him pieces of sugar or salt. After three days he went into the stall and began brushing the horse, while talking to him softly. The stallion liked this and he even put his head on Kuba's shoulder and made friendly sounds, as if he were talking to Kuba. Finally, Kuba got on top of the stallion and kept talking to him. At first, the horse jumped up and then he just turned his head, looking for more sugar or salt pieces.

A week passed and Kuba put a saddle on Diablo. The horse did not like it at first and tried to shake it off. However, when Kuba came near him, talking softly, the stallion did not object, even when Kuba jumped into the saddle. Shalik lowered the restraining bar and the stallion took off and responded to Kuba's directions. One week later, Diablo was Kuba's horse. No one else could touch him! He still lowered his ears and tried to bite anyone that approached him, except Kuba. And so, Kuba got himself a new horse.

On December 12, Colonel Nikolsky called Kuba to his hut and gave him an assignment. "Kuba, I want you to ride out to the vicinity of Budi and find out what the situation is there. Also, check out our old camp. We have some documents and supplies buried there. See if they are still untouched. Take Vasili Muravyets with you. He was born in the village of Budi and that might prove helpful."

Kuba found Vasili and told him to saddle up and get ready for a trip. They took extra clips of ammunition and hand grenades. In about a half hour they were ready to travel so Kuba reported to the commander and waited for additional instructions. The commander looked at them and then said, "Kuba, if you see anything extraordinary, like a high concentration of tanks, artillery or anything else of importance, investigate it. Do not try anything foolish. There are only the two of you."

"Yes, Colonel. I understand," Kuba replied, and they took off during the night. The two partisans traveled through the snow covered forest, frozen rivers and swamps and finally reached the familiar area around the railroad station of Budi. It was daylight when they found a place to hide out. They took turns sleeping for a few hours, and then began to scout the area. They came out to the rim of the forest and watched the railroad tracks for a while. A German patrol walked by on the tracks toward the bunker near the station. The two partisans began walking in that direction, following the forest along the tracks. When they got near the station, they noticed many vehicles, mostly tanks, parked near the edge of the forest, covered with tarpaulins.

"We will take a look at that equipment when it is darker," Kuba said. They dismounted and Kuba tied Diablo to a tree branch and hung a feed bag, filled with grain, over the horse's ears with the horse's mouth inside the bag. Vasili did the same with his horse. The two partisans sat down near the horses and began eating some bread and salt pork. They were only about a mile from Budi and could hear noise coming from the station and German bunkers. It was the sound of a German song and the music of a harmonica. It was getting very dark, and began to snow. A German patrol again walked by along the railroad tracks.

Kuba turned to Vasili and said, quietly, "If anything goes wrong tonight and we are separated, we shall meet at the Novosiele estate." Vasili nodded and closed his eyes trying to take a nap. Kuba was also very tired but one of them had to be awake, so Kuba kept a watch of the tracks. Diablo bent his head down and nibbled at Kuba's ear. Kuba petted his nose. The stallion was content and returned to feeding. At nine o'clock Kuba shook Vasili's shoulder and said, "It's time. Let's go." They left the horses in the forest and made their way toward the railroad station. Opposite the station, they watched the tarpaulin covered vehicles for a while, until they saw a guard walk by.

Kuba looked in both directions, and said, "Khorosho, Vasili, let's go. Don't forget about our meeting place at the Novosiele Estate!"

They headed straight for the line of vehicles, hidden in the dark. Kuba reached the first vehicle and stopped. There were no signs of movement anywhere near the area. He lifted the tarpaulin and saw a tank, one of the latest German "Tiger" tanks. Kuba examined the vehicle in detail. It had a rapid fire, heavy machine gun and sixteen millimeter cannon. The front plate was about a foot thick and made of steel. Kuba came out into the open, calling for Vasili, quietly, when suddenly two figures appeared behind him and they heard the order, "Halt!"

Kuba froze. He could feel the hardness of a gun muzzle against his spine. The two partisans were lined up against a German tank, facing two SS troopers. The German in charge was a Feldwebel, sergeant, of the Wehrmacht SS. He ordered the two to lay down all their weapons on the snow in front of them. Kuba unbuckled his belt and put down his submachine gun, extra clips, hand grenades and ammunition. Vasili was doing the same. The other German had a rifle with a fixed bayonet, which he was pointing at Vasili's stomach. The German sergeant began to search Vasili, patted him down, until he came to his crotch. There he found a hand grenade, which Vasili had missed. "Aha, he still has weapons!" he said.

The German sergeant fired two shots into Vasili's stomach. The partisan slumped down soundlessly and the Germans then turned to Kuba. They began to search him in the same manner. Kuba had his hands behind his neck and the Beretta pistol was in his right palm, ready. The sergeant was searching Kuba's pant legs and Kuba was watching the soldier with the rifle who was in front of him. In a split moment the soldier looked down at the sergeant and Kuba brought the pistol butt down on the head of the sergeant with full force, while squeezing off two shots into the soldier's stomach. The soldier fell backwards and Kuba pointed the gun at the sergeant's head and fired once. Kuba looked up and listened. There was no change in the sounds coming from the bunker. He turned Vasili over and found him breathing hard, but still alive. The sound of songs coming from the bunker continued. Kuba picked up Vasili and dragged him toward his horse, where he put him over the saddle and tied his feet and hands together across the back of the horse. Kuba held onto Vasili's horse while he mounted Diablo and they took off across the forest toward the Novosiele estate. Before they left, Kuba succeeded in planting a mine under one of the tanks. The fuse was very short and the mine exploded before Kuba and his wounded companion had left the forest.

They took off at a gallop toward the south. The horse carrying Vasili, fell behind considerably, so Kuba slowed down to allow the other horse to catch up with him. A large, black object loomed before him in the middle of the road, looking like a small hut. As Kuba came near it, he realized that this was a German tank. He pulled at Diablo's reins and turned left. The tank's machine gun fired one burst and Kuba felt a sting in his right leg, but he felt that Diablo was hit also. The horse was spewing red foam from his nostrils, but continued running until he reached the front yard of the Novosiele Estate. Then, the horse stood up on his hind legs and fell sideways, pinning Kuba beneath him.

Kuba was awakened by a sharp pain in his leg. He looked around and realized that he was in the parlor of the Novosiele Estate, stretched out on a couch. Aniela Zablocki, the mistress of the estate was bending over him and speaking softly. "It's all right, Kuba. I cleaned your wound. The bullet went straight through. However, your horse is dead. He saved your life and then he died. Also, your friend is dead but his horse is alright. We will take care of you. Here, drink this and go to sleep."

Kuba could think only of his horse, Diablo. He had become like a human being to him and had saved his life, giving up his own. Kuba, the hardened partisan was actually crying for his horse. He had not cried like that since he had learned about the death of his mother, sister and father. Somehow, all those events became concentrated in the death of one noble animal, and Kuba could not

THE ODYSSEY OF A PARTISAN

help but cry for his family. The next day, the Zablocki's and Kuba buried Vasili and Diablo on the estate.

The Novosiele Estate was located about six miles from the railroad and about eight miles from Mashuki. The main house, a beautiful white mansion, was surrounded by a huge apple orchard. It had been built by a Polish settler after the First World War. The owner, Stanislaw Zablocki, was arrested by the Soviet NKVD in 1939 and sent to Siberia. No one heard from him again.

Aniela, his wife, and their two children, Jan, seventeen, and Kristine, a beautiful sixteen-year-old girl, remained at the mansion. Mrs. Zablocki, an attractive chestnut-haired woman in her early forties, contacted Kuba's partisan group in the fall of 1943. She and her children did a lot of work for the partisans and were often helpful in many ways. The partisan group used the mansion for various purposes. Many times, the group stopped there overnight and other times, stayed for several days. Mrs. Zablocki was not too happy about that arrangement because of her young daughter. The soldiers looked at Kristine with hungry eyes, but there was not much she could do about it. She was just as frightened of the Russians as she was of the Germans. Kuba liked the family. They were honest Polish patriots and made no secret of it. This was the only place where he could speak Polish with someone. Mrs. Zablocki told him many times that she was very happy when he came alone to see them. She always treated the partisan group with the best of food and drinks that she had, but she tried very hard to keep Kristine away from them, usually by locking her into one of the upstairs rooms. Kuba visited the estate by himself several times and Kristine would then join them in the living room. They had come to trust him.

"You are not a wild Russian, and you would not try to rape my girl," Mrs. Zablocki once told him. Whenever he went there, she talked about his home town, Warsaw. She was very fond of that city, as was he. She knew all the nightclubs and cultural centers and talked of the good times she had had there before the war.

One day in late December 1943, Toliya and Kuba were returning from a mission. They had had a few drinks in a village on their way and Toliya was singing. After a while, he began to talk about women. He said he would give anything to sleep with Kristine. "You know," he said, "I never had a virgin in my life. This is a rotten country, no virgins. The only virgin I ever saw was my little sister." Kuba did not answer. It was quite common, whenever he got a little drunk, for Toliya to talk that way. "Let's stop in Novosiele. We can stay there overnight," Toliya said.

"Why not ride straight home?" Kuba asked.

"Who's in charge here? I said stop in Novosiele," Toliya insisted with drunken stubbornness. They argued this way for a long time. Finally, Toliya won and they stopped in Novosiele, arriving about eight o'clock in the evening. Jan was outside picking up wood for the fireplace.

"Good Evening," Jan greeted them and ran toward the house. Toliya stopped him.

"Wait. I will go in first," Toliya said, dismounting. Kuba followed very closely behind Toliya as he knew what he had in mind. When they entered the mansion, Jan disappeared through one of the many doors in the hall. They went into the living room, which was large and contained beautiful oak furniture and bookshelves covered the left side wall. A fire was burning in the fireplace and Kristine was sitting there in a rocking chair with a book in her lap, her long, blonde hair hanging loosely over her shoulders. Her mother was resting on a couch on the opposite side of the room in a pink, silk nightgown which showed from her opened housecoat. When they entered the room, Mrs. Zablocki quickly got up. "Oh, how nice of you to stop by," she said in Polish. Standing up, she pulled her housecoat together, then noticed Toliya and said, "Only the two of you? Where did you come from?"

"We are on our way home after about ten hours of riding," Kuba answered.

"Then you must be very tired and hungry. I will go and see about some food for you," she said, smiling. When she passed Kuba on her way to the kitchen, she whispered in Polish, "Watch Kristine. She has a cold and this is the only heated room in the house. That is why she is here now."

After she left the room, Kuba walked over to the fireplace. Kristine greeted him, smiling. "What are you reading, Kristine?" asked Kuba.

"A Polish classic," she answered. He took the book from her hand. It was the Nobel Prize winner, *The Peasants*, by Wladyslaw Reymont. They talked for a while about the book. Toliya was sitting on a chair near the bookshelves, watching Kristine with gleaming eyes. He got up, walked over to Kristine and stood behind the rocking chair. "

You are the most desirable girl I have ever seen," he said and tried to put his hands on her breasts. Kristine jumped up, Toliya tried to catch her, but Kuba was in his way. Toliya pushed him but Kuba stood firm. Kristine was hiding behind Kuba now and was crying. Toliya succeeded in pushing Kuba aside a little and grabbed Kristine's arm. The girl pressed her body to Kuba's back and put her arms around his waist and held tightly. Kuba grabbed Toliya's arms and tried to bend them backwards.

"Let go of me!" Toliya shouted. At that moment the door opened quickly and Jan rushed in with a rifle in his hands. Toliya stopped struggling with Kuba, and Kuba turned around, led Kristine out of the room, and took her upstairs to her bedroom.

"Lock the door," he told her, starting down the stairs.

"Kuba!" she called, still sobbing. Kuba stopped and she threw her arms around his neck and kissed him, wetting his face with her tears. "Thank you. You are so very different from the Russians," she whispered. Kuba waited until he heard the key turn in the door lock and then he went downstairs. When he entered the living room, everything was quiet. Toliya was sitting in a chair with a glass of vodka in his hand. Aniela was standing near him with a glass and bottle in her hands. Jan was there. His rifle was gone and he was standing near the kitchen door.

"I'm sorry for the little argument you had here," Aniela said. "All Toliya needed was a drink." Kuba sat down in the rocking chair. Aniela poured vodka into a glass, handed it to him and whispered in Polish, "The minute I saw Toliya, I had a feeling something like this was going to happen. Is she safe now?"

"She locked herself in her room," Kuba said.

Jan came over, still a little pale. "Can I have a drink, Mother?" he asked.

"Well, you are a little young for that, but you can have one," she replied, and poured a little in a glass.

Jan drank it and his face turned red as he wasn't used to vodka. Then he asked, "Can I go to the village? You are safe without me when Kuba is here."

"Oh, you are lonesome for Alice," Mrs. Zablocki said.

"Who is Alice?" Kuba asked.

"Jan's girlfriend," she answered, and Jan blushed. "All right, go. But don't be late, and be very careful."

"I will, Mother," he answered, leaving the room. They were all silent. Aniela was standing next to Kuba.

Toliya turned toward them. He was drunk but poured himself some more vodka and then said, "What are you two doing over there? Having a good time?" Kuba and Aniela broke out laughing.

"Well, all right, I'll go to Kristine," he said and started toward the door. Aniela caught his arm.

"Please! Don't, Toliya. She is still a child," she pleaded. Toliya put his arm around her waist. "Will you drink with me, Lady?"

"Yes," she answered. Toliya gave her a glassful of vodka. She looked at him and said, smilingly, "That is too much for a woman, Toliya."

"Drink it or I'll go to Kristine," he said. He was quite drunk, unable to stand straight. He held on to her waist. Aniela drank the vodka and made a funny face. It burned her throat. Toliya poured some more for her and led her to the couch. After they sat down, Aniela drank the second glass and was quickly getting drunk. They no longer noticed Kuba and Toliya opened Aniela's housecoat and put his hands under her nightgown. She began to giggle.

"Oh, you bad boy," she said. "I'm old enough to be your mother." Toliya started to undress her. Kuba turned toward the fireplace. After a while he heard the door open and looked back. Toliya and Aniela were leaving the room, Toliya hardly able to walk. Kuba poured himself another drink and was just about to drink it when the door opened again and Aniela reappeared, staggering toward him, no longer wearing the housecoat and her nightgown torn all the way down the front. Her naked, full breasts almost touching his face, she said in a low voice, "Toliya was asleep the minute he lay down on the bed." Kuba's pulse began to beat faster. She began to play with his hair and her hot breath hit his face. She pressed her breast to his cheek. Kuba wanted to push her away but he did not dare move. Finally, she sat down on his lap. Her face was red and her eyes were half closed.

"How long has it been since you had a woman?" she whispered. Kuba drank his vodka and got up. He was getting drunk now and his shirt collar was wet from perspiration. She pulled him toward the couch. He had not seen when she had removed it, but her torn nightgown was on the floor at his feet. With the last strength of his will, he stopped her, as she pressed her body to his. He looked into her face and suddenly came to his senses. This was the face of a mother, not unlike his own. Gently, but firmly, he pushed her away and started for the door. She took a few steps toward him and stopped. "You fool," she whispered in Polish. Kuba left the room and went outside.

In the early part of January 1944, the Novosiele Estate was raided by the Nazis, but the Eagles got word about it in sufficient time and, as one of their groups attacked the Nazis in the village, the rest of them went to the mansion. There was a brief fight with the Nazis who were already there, and the partisans rescued the Zablocki family, taking them to their camp, where they were given one of the huts. Jan became a partisan and participated in some of the missions while Kristine and her mother spent most of the time in their hut because Kristine did not dare to go outside when the partisans were about. Mrs. Zablocki guarded her most of the time, but that state of affairs did not last long.

Kuba noticed that Sanya began to visit the Zablocki hut quite often and after a few days, he even ate his meals there, staying through the evenings, and Kristine's laughter could be heard. Sanya brought gifts for the girl. He seemed to have changed a lot even after he returned from missions. A few weeks later, Sanya took Kristine for a walk into the forest and Aniela promptly followed them.

About that time, the partisans received a message from Moscow that they were to receive three special partisans who were to arrive that same day. In the afternoon, Toliya and Kuba were sent to the air drop area to make all necessary preparations and during the time they were getting some wood together and preparing five signal fires, Toliya spoke to Kuba about Kristine.

"How do you like that, Kuba? I have been after that girl for almost a year now, and Sanya got her just like that."

Kuba lay down the axe he was holding in his hand and looked at Toliya. "What do you mean he got her just like that?"

"Don't be childish, Kuba. What do you think they are doing all day by themselves in the forest — playing dominoes?"

"I don't believe it," Kuba said. "Kristine is a nice girl."

"You are a funny guy," Toliya said laughing.

"And who do you suppose is coming to us tonight by plane?" Toliya asked a little later.

"I don't know and I don't care," Kuba answered angrily. They didn't talk anymore and returned silently, to their camp.

At midnight the entire group was at the air drop area. The five bonfires were burning and they awaited the plane. Finally it arrived. Twelve parachutes dropped from the plane. Three carried men and the rest had equipment. When the three men landed, Nikolsky greeted them and they replied to Nikolsky's greetings in very poor Russian. Kuba was standing nearby and recognized Polish words in their speech, so he asked permission from Nikolsky and approached the three new men who were dressed in Soviet army uniforms. "Are you Polish?" Kuba asked.

The oldest of them, a captain from Warsaw, grinned and said, "Of course we are Polish, and so are you." They shook hands and told Kuba they had been trained in Moscow in the same school from which he had graduated. They were Polish prisoners of war, held by the Russians. After the German attack on Russia, many

Polish officers and soldiers joined the Soviet armed forces and were sent here on a special mission. They would not talk about it further. The captain stayed with Kuba in his hut, and they spent most of the night talking about their hometown.

After the arrival of the newcomers, things began to happen fast. About a week later, two young Poles joined the Eagles partisan group. They had served in a German labor brigade known as "Organization Todd" and together with thousands of other young Poles, these two were drafted by the Germans and assigned to that forced labor unit of manual work for the German army near the front. These two finally succeeded in escaping and, in one of the villages, they met Sanya and Commissar Grisha.

Apparently, Commander Nikolsky did not trust the Poles very much, even the ones that were sent to him from Moscow. He called Kuba into his hut and said, "Kuba, I want you to keep an eye on all the newcomers. You are the only one in our original group who speaks Polish. If you hear something suspicious, I want you to let me know immediately. That's an order."

"Yes, Colonel," Kuba answered. The two young Poles were kept in camp for about a month. They were issued rifles and participated in several missions. The older one didn't return after one of the missions and no one knew what had happened to him. There had been a lot of shooting and he may have been injured or killed, but no one knew anything about it. The general impression was that he had escaped and had returned to the Germans. The younger one, Ludvik, felt very badly about it and told Kuba many times that he didn't believe the other one had escaped. Ludvik thought that he was most likely dead!

Ludvik was about seventeen years old. He and Jan Zablocki became great friends, just as any other two boys of the same age would have done. They were always together and even on the missions of great danger, they tried to stay close to one another.

Kuba was sitting in the Zablocki hut because the two women were washing their hair and they had asked Kuba to guard them. He watched the graceful movements of Kristine's arms and memories began to flood his mind: Rachel! Where is she? Is she still alive? If so, what had the Germans done to her? Maybe she is in a concentration camp. Where? Auschwitz, Teresienstadt, Gorlitz, the death camps of Maydanek and Treblinka? Every moment he had spent with her was fresh in his mind, the softness of her green-blue eyes, the milk-and-honey skin and that fluffy hair. But, most of all, he remembered her full lips and the way she put her arms around his neck and kissed him, for the last time. He remembered the last conversation with Rachel, when she had mentioned the demise of her family, and then he recalled the name of Rachel's brother, Motek Walaski, who was a refugee somewhere in Russia. In his mind, he talked to Rachel, "My dear Rachel, I will try to find your brother in Russia, even if I have to go as high as the Kremlin. They must have some record of Polish refugees and somewhere I will find your brother's name." And then Kuba thought about a possible future for himself if he survived the war and Rachel was alive. They would build a new life, have sons and propagate the rich and noble heritage of their people. Otherwise, there was no purpose for living.

Meanwhile, there were new developments in the Eagles camp. The German army was in full retreat and the Eagles received new orders from Moscow. There was a report that a Polish partisan brigade, a part of the Home Army (Armja Krajowa in Russian), known by its initials A.K., had moved into the area. The three Polish officers from Moscow became very busy. It became clear that their mission would be to establish contact with the Polish A.K.

One day, right after supper, the three Polish officers had a long conference with Nikolsky in his hut. Then late in the evening, Nikolsky called for Kuba. When Kuba entered the hut, he saw all of them sitting around the table, watching as he entered. Nikolsky observed Kuba for some time and then said, "Kuba, you know our area pretty well by now, so tonight you will lead the three Polish comrades on a mission. I want you to be extremely careful because it is more dangerous than you might think. As you probably know, there is a Polish partisan division in this area and they are not too friendly toward us or the Jews. No matter what happens, I want you back here by noon tomorrow." After that he briefed Kuba on the situation, then he said, "Now, all of you go to your huts and rest. You will leave the camp at ten o'clock sharp. Horses will be ready for you." They left the officer's hut and the three

Polish partisans headed for their huts. Since Kuba didn't ask them any questions, and they didn't talk, they separated silently.

Kuba lay down on his bunk and tried to sleep, but the door opened and Nikolsky came in, sat down on the bunk and began to whisper. "Check your pistol and machine gun carefully, Kuba. You are going to meet some of the Polish A.K. Be very careful and shoot first if necessary, but remember one thing, no matter what happens, don't let them disarm you for they are even more dangerous than the Nazis."

Kuba promised to follow his advice and Nikolsky produced a flask of vodka from his side pocket. They drank some and then spoke about many things. Nikolsky left Kuba's hut about nine-thirty p.m. and there was not any time left for him to sleep, so he started to get ready. The four men quietly mounted their horses and left. The Polish officers told Kuba where they wanted to be taken, the vicinity of a village about thirty-five miles away. He knew the area very well. It was a beautiful June night. The moon was very bright and the four partisans enjoyed their trip, arriving at a farm near Nesvizh, which the Polish officers seemed to know. They walked straight up to the house and knocked three times on the window, two long knocks and one short. After a while, an old man with a long, gray mustache opened the door and greeted them, without fear. Kuba was about to enter the house when Alexander, the Polish captain, told him to stay outside on guard. After the three went in, Kuba started to walk around the house when Alexander returned, saying, "Kuba, if you hear anyone approaching, ask them for the password, and they should say 'The Battle of Grunwald,' a victorious battle in which the Poles fought against the crusaders in 1410, near the Prussian city of Grunwald." Alexander returned to the house and Kuba was on guard duty for about three hours, but no one showed up.

It was already four o'clock in the morning. The darkness began to fade and a new day was about to be born when Alexander and his companions joined Kuba outside. "They didn't show up," Alexander said. "Do you know a safe way to get back to our camp in the daytime?"

"No way is safe at any time, especially in the daytime, but you heard the commander's orders, we must be back by noon, so let's get going." Silently the Poles followed Kuba and headed straight for the Brest-Moscow highway, arriving there at about seven in the morning. No one was around, so they quickly crossed the highway and kept on riding and avoiding villages and main roads until they came to the village of Mashuki at about nine o'clock in the morning, where they stopped at a house of a friendly peasant. Kuba was worn out and lay down on a cot in the peasant's house and fell asleep while Alexander, and the other two, sat at a table and ate the food which the peasant's wife prepared for them. She wanted Kuba to eat, but he was too tired. He slept until past noon and then the four partisans left the village.

When they arrived near their camp, Kuba suddenly felt sick to his stomach. It must have been the amount of vodka he had drunk with Nikolsky the night before. He told Alexander to follow the road to the camp, and he cut through the bushes, to the place where their latrine was. He was only about a mile from their camp when he heard voices. He stopped his horse and dismounted, listened again and heard someone talking, not far away. He went in the direction of the voices, came to a clearing and stopped. He realized now that Toliya was right that day at the air drop area, for here under a tall pine tree, lying on a green army blanket, were Sanya and Kristine. She was almost nude and Sanya was holding his hands on her naked breasts as she tried to push him away.

"Don't. Please don't do that to me," she whispered.

"But I love you, so what's the difference?" Sanya said. Kuba looked at them and was so shaken that he could not move. Kristine tried hard to get away from Sanya, but he had her pinned down and succeeded in pushing his knees between her legs, while she was crying quietly in a funny way. Kuba wanted to interfere, but something held him back from doing so. He turned away and started to leave, then heard the giggle and laugh of Kristine. After that, Sanya also laughed. Kuba ran away and returned to the camp and found Alexander was there and already talking to Nikolsky.

That evening, the partisans had a campfire and for the first time, Kristine was present, sitting next to Sanya and they were appearing to have a good time together.

Jan and Ludvik were on guard duty. Several nights later, the Polish officers and Kuba were on the move again, going to the same house as before with Kuba again standing guard outside the house, but this time not in vain. About one o'clock in the morning, five Polish partisans arrived, gave Kuba the password and shook hands with him. They left one of their men on guard and told Kuba to go into the house.

Alexander wasn't too happy about this arrangement, but the commander of the Polish group said, "He won't betray us. Kuba is a Pole from Warsaw and I like all Poles." Alexander and the Polish commander left the room, returning after about two hours.

"Let's go," Alexander told Kuba. They were on their way back and were very hungry. This time, they returned by way of a different road and stopped at the Babin chutors. Ivan Bobko told Kuba that his brother was brewing moonshine, and Kuba knew where the still was located. They entered the house and the farmer's three daughters greeted them. They sat down at the table.

"Where is your father?" Kuba asked Marusia, the youngest of the three girls.

"He is outside. Come on, I'll show you where," she said. They left the house. Marusia was a nice-looking girl, a little on the heavy side. "He is in the stable, brewing some whiskey," she said, taking Kuba's arm. He put his arm around her and they walked toward the stable.

"Well, how are you, Kuba?" her father, Mikhail Bobko, asked. "Come over here and have a drink." He handed Kuba a cupful of whiskey, but it was warm and Kuba could not drink it. "What's the matter, are you still a sissy?" the old man said. "This is a real man's drink. Look." He filled another cup of warm whiskey and drank it like water. Kuba did the same although it tasted terrible, like castor oil. Marusia thought that Kuba was going to fall, so she put her arm around him tightly, much tighter than was necessary. Suddenly the whiskey took hold of Kuba and he was drunk.

"Put him on the hay, Marusia," her father said, picking up several bottles of whiskey to take into the house. "When he gets well again, bring him to the house and we'll have a party," Mikhail said, leaving. Marusia took Kuba to the back of the stable and laid him down on some hay, then pretended she was going to leave, but he got hold of her skirt and pulled her down. She giggled and lay down beside him.

"Do you like me?" she asked.

"Sure," Kuba said and began to play with the buttons on her blouse. He was quite drunk and awkward.

"Oh, you are clumsy," she said and unbuttoned her blouse. She was not wearing anything beneath her blouse and her large breasts fell heavily on Kuba's chest.

It was obvious that Sanya was in love for he had changed very much. No longer was he the cold-faced Soviet officer, raised and trained by the Communist Party. He was now a young man in love with a girl and he began to shave every day and to keep his clothes in neat order. Kuba noticed that their commander, Nikolsky, didn't like the situation very much and often they argued. Whenever Sanya had any spare time, he spent it with Kristine. Her mother, Aniela, no longer cared, having become involved herself in romantic affairs with several partisans.

Kuba was still accompanying Alexander and the other Poles to the meeting with the Polish A.K. In the middle of February, the commander told Kuba that it would not be necessary for him to work with Alexander any longer. He had assigned Jan and Ludvik that task. "Jan is a native of this region and a Catholic so he will be of more use than you are."

Kuba felt strange when the commander told him this. There was something suspicious about it. He had been present during a conference between the commander and Alexander where the commander read some instructions from Moscow regarding the Polish Home Army. Among other things, Moscow demanded that the leaders of that movement be liquidated and the partisans taken over by Soviet trained people. Alexander had promised to do his best to fulfill the Moscow order. When Kuba left the commander's hut, he was very angry because he understood what it meant, and he knew that it was a preparation of the Soviet government to take over Poland after the war.

Several days later, their Polish group returned from one of their routine trips and Kuba noticed that Alexander was very excited. One of the Polish paratroopers who had come to them with Alexander was missing. A few minutes later, Kuba learned that he had been killed in a clash with the Polish A.K. Alexander spent over two hours in the commander's hut and no one was allowed to enter. Then, Nikolsky ordered Kuba's partisan unit to move out of their huts and head for their old camp. Commissar Grisha, Pasha, Ludvik and Jan disconnected the stove, which Kuba had made from a gasoline drum, put it on a wagon, filled the wagon with some more equipment from the hut and left the camp. Kuba was ordered to remain with the others in the camp. Sanya was with Kristine in her hut, at that time, and Aniela was in one of the partisan's huts. No one paid any attention to what was going on with them any longer.

After an hour, Pasha and the commissar returned alone and entered Nikolsky's hut and closed the door behind them. On a wagon, covered with straw, were the uniforms worn by Ludvik and Jan when they left camp. Kuba suddenly became sick, vomiting, and disregarding the others. He cried for the two Poles and wondered whether the Communists would kill him, also. Nikolsky called Kuba. "Kuba, I want you to take two men and go to our old camp. There is a little job waiting for you. You'll see what it is when you get there."

Otto and Nikolay went with Kuba. He knew exactly what the job would be. In their old camp, they found the bodies of Jan and Ludvik, both lying in their underwear, with bullet holes in the back of their heads. Kuba's job was to bury them. He watched Nikolay throw the two bodies into a single grave. Two young boys. What terrible crime had they committed that they should be shot like this? Kuba was sure that the boys did not do anything contrary to Nikolsky's orders. Their misfortune was that they had been selected by the Communist rulers of Russia to be stepping stones on the road to the conquering of Eastern Europe, victims of Russia's attempt at purging themselves of all intellectuals, professionals, landowners, high military and Polish diplomats, before the anticipated takeover of Poland.

When the partisans returned to camp, they found that Kristine and her mother were under arrest in their hut, a guard posted at their door. Kuba looked for Sanya and found him at the kitchen, sitting on a boulder and watching the fire. He tried to talk to him, but Sanya would not answer.

Kuba went on guard duty at nine o'clock in the evening. When he passed the Zablocki hut, he noticed that the door was open and Nikolsky was there. Aniela saw Kuba and called, "Everything is okay, Kuba. The Communists just told us that Kristine and I are going on a very dangerous mission tonight and that our assignment will be very useful to the Soviet government."

"Good luck, Aniela," Kuba said, but he had a very painful, choking feeling in his chest. He was on guard duty for about a half hour when he heard a wagon approaching from the camp and saw Pasha was driving the horses, and that Aniela, Kristine, the commissar and the chief of staff, Volodiya Botin, were on the wagon. They drove by quickly and Kuba noticed that instead of taking the road out of the woods, they turned left, leading to a swamp. Several minutes later, he heard a pistol shot followed by a series of sub-machine gun shots. The wagon returned but the two women were not on it.

The next morning Otto, Nikolay, Vlodik and Kuba were sent out to bury the "dangerous spies," Kristine and Aniela. They were lying face down in the grass, the ground red with their blood, two more victims, Polish landowners, of Russia's purge.

Sanya took the event very hard, hating Nikolsky and not trying to hide his feelings. He was a captain of NKVD, People's Commissariat for Internal Affairs, known as the Secret Police. He began to build up a case against Nikolsky and several times called Kuba and other partisans into his hut to question them and to learn more about Nikolsky and his misbehavior. He once asked Kuba to sign a document to this effect. Kuba knew that their commander had buried many important documents near Mashuki, which were to be delivered to Moscow when their tour of duty was over. When that day came, the documents were missing and never found, and Nikolsky was degraded and paid a heavy penalty. Kuba knew who was responsible for lifting the missing documents but did not reveal the knowledge. Kuba was completely shaken by these events. In his imagination, he pictured the execution of his mother and sister in a similar way. He realized that this was the way the Russians would deal with the leaders and intellectuals of the countries they conquered, including Poland. He decided that night, that he would rather die than participate in this type of activity, especially against Poland, and that his own situation was not too promising. He gripped the handle of his machine gun and said to himself, that when the time came, he would take a lot of Communists with him. He would not die alone.

Chapter Twenty-One

The struggle of the partisans behind the German lines entered into a new phase. The high command in Moscow issued an order to all partisan groups throughout the German occupied Soviet territories to begin "Operation Destroy German Railroads." The Eagles received an order over the shortwave radio some time in February of 1944. Their commander, Colonel Nikolsky, ordered all of them to assemble at the parade grounds of the camp. He stood in front of them, a tall man dressed in a leather jacket and trousers, taking in the entire group with his deep, penetrating dark blue eyes. He did not wear a hat and his blondish gray hair was weaving with the wind. "The war against the Nazis is in its final phase," he said. "The Germans are in full retreat on all front lines and we must make a special effort to quicken the advance of the Red Army." With his right hand stuck behind his belt, Nikolsky looked around at the group. "The high command of the partisan movement in Moscow has issued an order to all partisan groups to start a war against the German transport facilities. It is important to destroy German soldiers but it is much more important to destroy the railroad tracks, bridges and installations. There is no more steel in Germany to replace destroyed railroad tracks, therefore, we declare war on the German railroads."

That same evening Nikolsky sent out units of the group, with copies of the order from Moscow, to all partisan groups in the area. Kuba was sent with the orders to partisan group No.56, known as the Shchors partisan group. The commander of that group was a young electrician from Warsaw named David Liker. He had many citations for bravery, having destroyed forty trains carrying German troops. He was decorated with the highest medal of the Soviet Union, a gold star with the title, "Hero of the Soviet Union." In spite of all this, he was not a Communist. Rather, before the war he was a very active Zionist in Warsaw.

Otto and Kuba carried the order to that group, arriving at the campsite at midnight. The guards stopped them, "Stop, who is coming?"

"The Eagles," Kuba answered.

"Password?" the guard asked.

"Seventy-two," was Kuba's response.

"Twenty-seven," the guard replied.

When they approached the guard, Kuba said, "We must see your commander, immediately." One of the guards pulled a rope which was hanging from a tree branch and they could hear a bell ring at a distance. A few minutes later the officer of the day (O.D.) appeared.

"Two Eagles to see the commander," the guard reported.

The officer knew Kuba and Otto and shook hands with them. "Follow me," he said. They entered the a large camp with many earth huts constructed in three rows and in the center, a square with several tables, covered with rags and nearby, the kitchen. Kuba, Otto and the O.D. entered the commander's hut. David was sitting on his bunk, rubbing his eyes. It was past midnight.

"Hello, Eagles," he said, smiling. They sat down on the bunk next to him. David Liker looked up at the officer of the day and said, "Go get us something to eat. We are hungry." The officer left the hut. "What's up?" Liker asked them.

Kuba handed him the order from Moscow. After David read it, Kuba said, "Tomorrow, at eight in the evening, you must be with your group near Mashuki. What will the password be?"

"The password for tomorrow is sixty-six and the answer is twenty-two," replied the commander. The O.D. returned to the hut with a basket of food and a bottle of whiskey and the three men began to eat. Liker asked more questions about the order and they talked about various things including the latest news from the front.

It was past three o'clock in the morning when Kuba and Otto mounted their horses for the return to their camp. It was a very bright night and they rode fast through hidden forest paths. Several times along the way, a rabbit darted out under the feet of the horses and from a distance they could hear the frightful howl of wolves. It was daylight when they arrived at their camp. Commander Nikolsky met them in front of his hut and the two dismounted.

"Our mission was carried out," Kuba reported.

"That's fine," Nikolsky said. "Now go get some sleep." Kuba and Otto took the saddles with them into their huts and used them as pillows. It was one o'clock in the afternoon when Kuba awoke and everyone was eating lunch. Otto and Kuba took some clean underwear from Dr. Anna and went to take a bath in a separate hut. There was a big kettle of boiling water and the fire was kept going under the kettle by Vlodik, who served as bath attendant that day, the bath day for everyone. A low bench was at the side of the hut which held wooden bathtubs and in one corner a pile of large rocks was stacked which were heated, and then water was poured over them to create steam.

After lunch the partisans were busy preparing several hundred small mines with fuses, each one weighing one-half pound. They worked at it all afternoon. At six o'clock in the evening the partisans ate dinner and by six-thirty, they were all on horseback, each one carrying four mines in addition to their usual weapons and ammunition. Also, a wagon was loaded with several sacks full of mines for the partisans from other groups, who were to participate in this particular action.

Nikolsky was carrying on a conversation with Volodiya. The commissar and Kuba were standing next to Pasha and Toliya. Everybody was laughing and kidding Vlodik who was sitting on a very small horse and he was so very tall and skinny. It was a funny sight.

"Don Quixote," Otto said, and everyone laughed. At this moment the chief of staff, Volodiya, came toward them.

"You ride out first and be our scouts," he said, naming Pasha, Toliya and Kuba. The three started immediately. It was already dark and the forest seemed to be mysterious and quiet. The moon was shining brightly above them as the three partisans rode in single file, Pasha first, Kuba in the center and Toliya brining up the rear. They came to the end of the forest and ahead of them was the village of Mashuki.

Suddenly, from the bushes came a command, "Stop, who is coming?"

"Sixty-six," said Pasha.

"Twenty-two," someone answered.

The three Eagles approached the bushes from where the voices came. This was the No.56 partisan group, already in the village, along with several other partisan groups. One was a partisan brigade by the name of Molotov, stationed near the Bobrow village which consisted of three large partisan groups. Half an hour later, all partisans were assembled, about 450 altogether. The commanders of the groups had a conference in the house of Ivan Bobko and when the conference was over, the partisans left the village. Each group went to take up its position on the railroad tracks of the Wilno-Lwow line, and while riding, the commander gave the Eagles final instructions. "Remember, after planting your mines you will watch for a red signal from my flashlight. You will then immediately light the fuses and run."

When they reached the tracks, Pasha, Toliya and Kuba went to investigate the area, leaving the horses in the forest. Kuba lay down several yards from the tracks. It was very quiet and they waited for the German patrol to pass. "When the Germans pass us, we can start out," Pasha said. They waited for some time and because they were lying motionless, they were getting very cold. Finally, the patrol passed them. Ten Germans, all wearing helmets and rifles, passed along the embankment resembling a silhouette on a movie screen. The Germans were pretty far away when Pasha told Kuba, "Go call the rest."

Kuba returned to the forest and found the entire group sitting on logs smoking, keeping the cigarettes in the palms of their hands so that no one could see the glow. "Let's go," Kuba said. The partisans got up and quietly followed Kuba. Shalik, with his machine gun, went to the right and Sasha, with the other machine gun, to the left. They were to protect the others. They spread out along the tracks, each one having four rails to destroy, they moved swiftly. Kuba planted his first mine and put a white piece of paper next to it so he could find it and then went to the next rail and planted another one. When he finished the last rail, he jumped down into a ditch and lit a cigarette, as did everybody, using the cigarettes to light the fuses. They waited several minutes. Kuba was afraid that his cigarette would not last long enough. They saw a red light from a distance, going on and off three times. This was the signal.

"Light them up," Pasha said. They went to the tracks again. Kuba found his first mine and lit the fuses with the cigarette, ran to the next one and did the same, and so on. No matter how careful they were, they made a lot of noise and soon machine guns started shooting far to their right, the bullets zooming high over their heads. The cigarette was very short and Kuba burned his fingers on the last mine but when he was assured that all fuses were lit, he turned and ran toward the forest.

"Faster! Faster!" Kuba could hear the commander yelling somewhere in the distance. He ran as fast as he could, but it was hard to run through the forest because of the swampy terrain and the snow. He fell several times and when he was about a dozen yards into the forest, he fell over Nikolay, who was on his knees, swearing like a drunken sailor.

"What happened?" Kuba asked him.

"I lost my cap," Nikolay said. Kuba began laughing. Nikolay's cap was hanging on a tree branch just above his head. They ran together and suddenly there were several flashes and almost immediately the mines began to explode. The partisans lay flat on the snow as pieces of torn steel flew overhead, counting the explosions, fourteen, fifteen, and sixteen. Soon they lost count. From a distance, they heard the explosions of mines planted by the other partisans. At the same time, there was a continuous hail of bullets from the machine guns which the Germans were firing from the bunkers along the tracks. All the partisan mines had exploded. Kuba and Nikolay went to the place in the forest where they had left their horses and found the entire group already there.

"Anybody hurt?" Nikolsky asked. Everyone was all right and they rode fast, Toliya and Kuba several yards ahead of the group. In Mashuki they met the other partisan groups again and assembled at the rim of the forest, near the house of Ivan Bobko.

All commanders were in the center and Nikolsky made a little speech. "Comrades, we accomplished a very important job. We have destroyed about four kilometers of railroad tracks and the enemy won't be able to repair the damage for a long time. This is only the beginning of that operation. From now on, day or night, we won't let the enemy rest until we chase them out of here." They returned home in a good mood. Everyone was happy and the horses galloped fast as they felt the nearness of camp.

Chapter Twenty-Two

In the early days of 1944, many German soldiers and officers were trying to establish contact with the partisans. There already were Germans, who had deserted their army in many of the partisan groups. Sometimes Sanya, Otto and at times, their commander, made trips at sunrise to a farm near the town of Hantsevich. The fact that they undertook such dangerous journeys during daylight hours indicated that they were working on a very important project. Kuba also was present on several occasions when they met a very mysterious man in Mashuki, a pleasant looking man who always arrived in a limousine, accompanied by two civilians. The commander and Sanya would lock themselves into a room with the mysterious man. All kinds of gossip was circulating among the members of the partisan groups about this man, some guessing that the mystery man was a plain-clothes German officer. Shalik assured them that on several occasions he had seen the man in Siniavka in the company of high German officers. One evening the partisans received an order to get ready for a journey to the Brest-Moscow highway the next morning. They readied all of their equipment and went to sleep early that night. Kuba did not have guard duty that night so he fell asleep without any worry. Sometime during the night, he was awakened by Sanya. Kuba looked up at him, in surprise, and said, "I'm not on guard duty tonight, you made a mistake," and he tried to go back to sleep, but Sanya laughed.

"The commander wants you," he said.

Kuba strapped on his belt and pistol around his waist and followed Sanya to the commander's hut where he met a partisan by the name of Petrushka, who had just returned from an assignment. Also present were Commissar Grisha and the chief of staff,

Volodiya. The commander handed Kuba a sheet of paper filled with typewritten words.

"Translate it," he said. Kuba took the letter. It was written in German and was addressed to Herr Colonel Nikolsky: an invitation for Nikolsky to come to a meeting on a farm the next day at nine o'clock to meet a man by the name of "Vladimir." The letter emphasized extreme caution and secrecy regarding the meeting and was signed, Stephan Orban, Major of the German Army. After translating the letter, Kuba wrote it in Russian and handed it to the commander, who read it. The commander then turned to Kuba and Petrushka and said, "Thank you. Now go get some sleep."

Kuba returned to his hut, and completely forgetting about the letter, went to sleep. At five thirty in the morning, the partisans were awakened. They hastily washed, ate their breakfasts, saddled their horses and waited for further orders. Grisha and Volodiya came out of their hut, took the reins of their horses and ordered the others to mount up, then left the camp silently, Grisha and Kuba bringing up the rear. Suddenly, the commander came out of his hut and called Grisha. The partisans stopped. After a while Grisha motioned to Kuba and said, "Kuba, you stay here. The commander needs you."

Kuba turned his horse back, put him in the stall and started to take off the saddle when the commander called to him. "Leave the saddle on, we're riding in a short while."

"Shall I wait here?" Kuba asked.

"No, follow me." Kuba followed Nikolsky into the hut. The commander checked Kuba's clothes, boots, everything as Kuba watched in surprise. The Colonel went over to a heavy chest that was standing in the middle of the room and took an expensive leather coat from a drawer and handed it to Kuba. "Here, put this on," he said. He also gave Kuba a new fur hat, while Kuba looked at the commander in astonishment, but didn't dare ask any questions. The commander noticed Kuba's gaze and said, smiling, "You see, Kuba, we'll be diplomats today, so we will have to be dressed nice and neat." Kuba silently changed his clothes, and then Nikolsky asked, "Do you have enough ammunition for your pistol and submachine gun?"

"Yes," Kuba answered.

"Go saddle my horse, will you?"

"Yes, comrade."

A half hour later they were riding quickly through the forest in the direction of Hantsevich. It was quiet. The forest was still asleep. Only the sound of the horses' hooves disturbed the stillness. They came to a river and crossed it slowly. When they reached the other side, the commander stopped. "We will rest here for a while," he said and dismounted. Kuba followed him. They tied their horses to a tree and sat down on a log. Nikolsky offered him a cigarette. The commander did not smoke but always carried cigarettes or tobacco with him. After Kuba lit the cigarette, Nikolsky said, "Kuba, it is possible that we may meet that German officer whose letter you translated last night. We will act as if we don't know him, because there may be other Germans around. We will only be several yards from the city limits, therefore, always be alert and on guard to take action, if necessary."

"I understand perfectly," Kuba said.

After a short while they mounted their horses. "Remember, this is a very important, secret mission and no one should find out about this meeting."

"Yes, Colonel."

They were riding through the forest again and when they came to the rim of the forest the sun was very bright. They went into a small birch grove. They could hear dogs barking and somewhere, a child was singing a song. They were traveling slowly as the path was almost invisible. Finally, they came to a chutor farm. "We'll leave our horses here," the commander said. Kuba tied their horses to trees and then they walked toward the house, stopping first behind some bushes not far from the house. The commander whistled several times and a peasant came out and approached them.

"Good day, comrades," he greeted them.

After they shook hands with the peasant, the commander said, "We left our horses a little farther back. Send your boy over and tell him to feed and take care of them until we return."

The peasant turned toward the house and started calling, "Stiopa! Ey, Stiopa!"

"I am here," a boyish voice answered from a distance.

"Come over here," the peasant called. A boy, about twelve years old, came running toward them. His face was covered with freckles and he was wearing his father's sheepskin and big boots. The sleeves of the sheepskin touched the ground. Stiopa got a little scared when he saw the partisans.

"Good day," he said shyly. His father told him what to do and the boy ran toward their horses, whistling happily.

"Now take us to 'Vladimir," said the commander. They followed the peasant and went straight to the forest and after about half an hour, they came to a clearing. In the center was a big white, brick building with a terrace and behind that were several other buildings that looked like barns. The house looked like a mansion — two stories and a red-tile roof. There was no one around.

"Here lives Vladimir," the peasant said. They looked around behind the house and the other buildings. Kuba knew by now that Vladimir was a country doctor, appointed by the Germans, and had made a lot of important acquaintances among the German high officers. "I'll wait here for you," the peasant said, and sat down under a tree.

Nikolsky and Kuba entered the yard. The gate made a squeaking sound as they opened it, and inside, they stopped and waited with the expectation that someone would come out of the house, but nothing happened. "Let's go inside," said Nikolsky. Kuba opened the door and went in. There was a small hall and to the left was a door, which he opened and jumped back quickly. By instinct, they both had their guns in their hands, ready to fire. The room was the kitchen. An old woman was standing near the stove, dressed much better than any of the other peasants they had ever met. On the left side, near the window, was a table and two German soldiers were sitting at the table with rifles in their hands. Next to the table, there was a door leading to another room. The Germans were more surprised than the partisans and turned pale, not knowing what to do.

"Order them to raise their hands," Nikolsky whispered.

"Hande hoch," Kuba said. The Germans raised their hands slowly, their guns falling with a crash to the floor. At this moment the other door opened and Vladimir came in from the other room.

"Don't shoot! They are with us," he said, very calmly. Kuba and Nikolsky put down their gun. The Germans bent down to pick up their rifles and were still pale.

"You must forgive us. We didn't know," Nikolsky said. Vladimir came over to them and shook hands.

"Let's go into the other room. We have been waiting for you long enough," said Vladimir. They entered the other room and again their hands went automatically to the guns. In the middle of the room near the table there was a German officer. He looked at them and smiled.

"Gentlemen," he said.

Vladimir introduced them, "This is Colonel Nikolsky."

"My name is Stephan Orban, Major of the German Wehrmacht," the German officer said.

They sat down at the table and the officer called his two soldiers and said to one of them, "Bring in the package."

The soldier left and returned immediately with a package wrapped in newspaper. He put it on the table near the officer and the Major then ordered the soldiers to go outside and keep guard. After they left, he opened the parcel, took out a German "Walter" automatic pistol, two hand grenades and several cakes of chocolate and handed all of this over to Nikolsky and said, "This is our token of friendship and willingness to fight alongside you against the Nazis."

Nikolsky thanked him and they began to talk about the main objects of the meeting. Kuba had the job of translator of German to Russian and Russian to German and from their conversation, he learned that the regiment commanded by Stephan Orban was made up of non-Germans. Most of them were Czechs and Hungarians. The Major himself was a Czech.

The Major looked at Nikolsky and said, "The regiment had returned from the front lines several weeks ago. The German armies are retreating and it is our desire to fight against the Nazis. We hope in this way to regain our human dignity."

The Major told them also that another of their plans was to join the partisans and bring with them their entire equipment of artillery, tanks and ammunition. Additionally, he said that they could not wait too long, because there were many Nazi officers in their regiment and if the Nazis found out what was going on, the entire regiment would be liquidated.

They discussed the problem for quite some time, then Major Orban contacted the partisans about three times a week and they supplied him with propaganda leaflets in the German language which he distributed among the German troops and, in turn, he sent them information through Vladimir.

Nikolsky said, "I cannot make a decision about this problem, alone. I'll have to contact my superiors in Moscow, but until I receive an answer from them, we can start working together immediately. I'll give you several assignments to perform and by the time you are through with them, we'll have an answer from Moscow. Yes, Major Orban, I can assure you, personally, that after you complete the assignments, it may be possible for you to fly to Moscow."

Major Orban was silent for a few moments. Then he said, "What are the assignments you have for us?"

"First, I will send you a package of literature for the German Army, pamphlets and booklets and you are to distribute as many as you possibly can among the soldiers of the German garrisons in the area. Secondly, you will have to meet with one of us, once a week, or write a report covering all important information about the plans and movements of the German troops."

The Major was quiet for a long time. He lit a cigar and offering one to Nikolsky and Kuba, said, very sternly, "I agree," and shook hands with them. Nikolsky then informed him as to when and where they were to meet. The German soldiers saluted them, making Kuba feel uncomfortable. An hour later, they were approaching their camp and Kuba thought about the strange meeting and the possibility of the war ending soon, but he still was not completely certain that he would actually live to see it happen.

Several weeks had passed with this arrangement, when the Major decided it would be more convenient for him to keep his contact through Vladimir only, as it was not safe for him to come directly to the partisans so often. About a month later, in reply to their report on the case of the Major and his regiment from Moscow, they also received a message for the German Major. Kuba translated the Moscow message into German which stated that the Major was to destroy the German garrison in the city of Hantsevich and then join the partisan group. The soldiers were to be divided among various partisan groups and then the Major was to fly to Moscow the next month.

Petrushka, accompanied by a new partisan by the name of Moshe Top whom they had recruited from a Jewish group, were to deliver the message to Vladimir and wait there for an answer. At this time, the Eagles were living in a new camp on the other side of the Brest-Moscow railroad tracks. Kuba's guard duty was in the early morning hours, so he went to sleep. After a few hours, he was awakened by noise and excitement in the camp. He went outside and found all of the partisans gathered near the commander's hut. Nikolsky was talking with Ivan Labanovich, who had just arrived. When Kuba joined them, Ivan was finishing his tale. "...they stepped on a mine. The little one is dead and the Jew's legs are seriously wounded. He succeeded in crawling to my farm and when I put him on the bed, he whispered a few words to me, 'Petrushka has a letter' and 'the Germans are all over the place.' Then he lost consciousness."

Nikolsky interrupted Ivan's story and said, "Sanya, take twelve men with you and get going. Ivan will lead you." They got ready fast. Kuba was amongst the twelve as well as Shalik with his machine gun. They rode fast through the woods and then left their horses at the edge of the forest while they continued on foot, crossing a frozen swamp with ice so thin that it was breaking under their feet. It was making a lot of noise as well as getting them wet. From a distance the partisans could see the railroad tracks. They were moving very slowly.

"He should be around here someplace," Ivan said. They strained their eyes looking and eventually detected a dark object in the snow not far from the tracks. It was the torn body of their comrade, Petrushka. They hoped that the important reply from Major

Orban would be on his body. The partisans ran toward the body, and then suddenly stopped, frozen in their tracks. Several men in camouflage uniforms were near the body, but were unaware of the partisans nearby. One of the uniformed men lit a cigarette, giving himself away. They were Nazis. The partisans lay down on the snow immediately. Shalik lay down next to Kuba, but he slipped and his machine gun made a lot of noise and the Nazis opened fire almost immediately shooting very low. The bullets were whistling closely over the heads of the partisans giving Kuba a sense of his skin shrinking at the places where the bullets passed. Shalik, the first one to snap out of it, opened fire with his machine gun and they then all joined him.

The Nazis slowed down their fire and Sanya gave the order, "Everybody retreat." The partisans nearest to the forest began to retreat.

Nikolay, Shalik and Kuba remained in their places and continued firing at the Nazis. The others had time to reach the forest and then to open fire on the Germans, so that the three could retreat. Several long minutes passed; the longest in Kuba's life. Shalik changed the third magazine on his machine gun and started to shoot again but stopped suddenly. Kuba did not notice it right away because he was deafened by the barking of his own submachine gun. By instinct, he looked up at Shalik and a cold shiver went through his spine; Shalik was lying, face down, on his machine gun, his head covered with blood. Kuba crawled toward him and at that moment, the others opened fire from the forest, bullets flying high over their heads toward the Germans.

Nikolay threw Shalik over his shoulder and began to retreat and Kuba carried Shalik's machine gun and turned around every so often to fire at the Nazis. Nikolay placed Shalik on his horse and the group left the forest for Ivan Lobanovich's farm where they found Moshe Top lying on a bed, his feet wrapped in a piece of bloodied linen. He was unconscious and Ivan's wife was sitting near him and crying. Shalik had a bullet in his cheek and one in his shoulder so Nikolay washed and bandaged him. "Get your wagon ready," Sanya ordered Ivan.

In a bitter mood, they returned to camp and when the commander greeted them, he had a very serious expression on his face. "Do you have the letter?" he asked.

"No," Sanya answered. Nikolsky's face darkened and he asked Sanya to follow him into the commander's hut. Several partisans carried the two wounded soldiers into the first-aid hut so that Dr. Anna Aksakova could attend to their wounds. Shaliks' condition was not too serious because the bullet had gone through his body, but Moshe Top was in bad shape. The bones in both of his legs were shattered. Anna performed major surgery on him, amputating both legs just above the knees. Moshe suffered very much and was unable to sleep when he regained consciousness. Sanya then came into the hut, went over to Kuba and took his arm.

"Let's go for a ride," he said. Kuba didn't ask any questions. He got some fresh ammunition for his submachine gun and they rode off. Kuba did not feel very tired, in spite of the terrible night before. They rode quietly for about twenty minutes when Kuba realized that they were heading toward Hantsevich.

He asked Sanya, "How far are we going?"

"To the farm near Vladimir's house," he answered.

Kuba did not ask any further questions, but in a few minutes Sanya continued, "You understand that we must get in touch with Major Orban and bring him to our camp immediately. All because of that damned letter that the Nazis took from Petrushka."

It was about ten in the morning when they came to the railroad tracks which they had to cross. They were dangerous to cross at night, but it was almost an impossibility to cross them on horseback in broad daylight. They stopped at the rim of the forest and observed the area. To their left was a crossing. A little further on some farms and to their right was a German bunker. There was no one on the tracks, so they waited several minutes. Then Sanya said, "To hell with it, let's go."

He was a little ahead of Kuba and they both rode like the devil to cross the tracks, the horses running wild, and they continued in this manner for about ten minutes, then finally slowed down on the other side of the tracks, deep in the forest. It was hard to stop the horses because they were running so wild that they did not obey. An hour later they came to the chutor. Sanya whistled and the peasant came out of the house, looking quite pale. "What's new?" asked Sanya.

"Nothing good," answered the peasant. "Vladimir was arrested this morning."

"How do you know?"

"His mother is in the house now," the peasant answered.

"Call her out here." In a few minutes the old woman was with them.

"Oh, my Eagles, they beat him so much," she cried out, wringing her hands.

"Tell us what happened," Sanya demanded. She told them that in the morning, the Nazis had surrounded her house, searched it thoroughly, then demanded that Vladimir tell them where all the partisans were. When he did not reply, they beat him terribly. Also, she remembered that several times they repeated the name of a German officer who they claimed was in contact with partisans.

They took Vladimir away, she said, then asked, "What should I do now? I'm so worried."

Sanya was silent. The peasant kept his head down and was very nervous, then said, "I'm afraid they will come to get me today."

Sanya lit a cigarette and looked at the peasant. "Take your family and Vladimir's mother and leave immediately for Mashuki."

"What should I do with my belongings?" asked the peasant.

"Take whatever you can on your wagon, but you'd better hurry. It's getting pretty bad around here." The partisans left the chutor about two in the afternoon and arriving at Mashuki, they stopped at Bobko's house. Sanya ordered Ivan to go to Hantsevich to find out what had happened there. After he left, Kuba and Sanya went to sleep. Ivan returned about midnight and brought some very bad news. The Nazis had succeeded in reading the Major's coded letter and also found several of the partisan leaflets on him and his soldiers. The major and his soldiers were placed under arrest and Vladimir and several others in town were also arrested after they had been questioned. They later learned that the Major was sent to Berlin, tried for treason and executed.

After telling Ivan to take care of his family and Vladimir's mother, Sanya and Kuba left for their camp. They were in a bad mood and tired when they arrived at camp just before sunrise. They reported to Nikolsky then went to their huts. Kuba entered his hut and found his comrades sitting on their bunks quietly. No one was asleep and no one asked any questions. Pasha rolled up his sheepskin and put it under Kuba's head and covered him with another sheepskin, but it took Kuba a long time to fall asleep. Moshe Top regained consciousness that evening. He was very hungry and after eating told them the story.

Petrushka and Top were returning home on foot. He said, "We left our horses in a village because we couldn't cross the railroad tracks with so many Nazis around. When we came to the tracks, I went ahead and Petrushka followed behind. He had the letter from the Major. On the other side of the tracks, we began to run toward the forest when suddenly there was a terrific explosion behind me. It knocked me down into the snow and I was deafened for a while. I wasn't in pain but I looked back and saw Petrushka's torn body, his head separated from the body. I wanted to get up to get the letter from Petrushka, but I couldn't, my legs were numb. I began to crawl on my hands, losing blood all the time and eating snow to remain conscious. I got to the forest and it took me a long time to get to a house. I knocked on the door of a house and a peasant came out. I told him about the letter and Petrushka and then recognized the peasant as Ivan Lobanovich. Then I lost consciousness."

This was the hardest day in their lives as partisans. There weren't any songs that evening, not even by Nikolay, the Cossack. They all went to bed early.

Chapter Twenty-Three

It was spring of 1944. All roads and paths in the Polesiye part of Belarus became torrents of water flowing like rivers and streams towards the main rivers of the area. The roads became a giant swamp under a layer of water and the Polesiye marshes became a watery mass, covered with hundreds of islands of green trees and blooming meadows. The rocks and trails in the birch and pine forest were crisscrossed by numerous footprints of rabbits, deer, elk, wild boar and occasionally bear.

The Germans were in full retreat. There were persistent rumors about the imminent opening of a second front by the Americans and British in France and Radio Moscow reported daily on the rapid advance of the Soviet Army as town after town was being liberated from Nazi occupation. Soviet troops reclaimed over half the territory of Belarus. In the Ukraine, the Russians captured the capital city of Kiev, crossed the Dnieper River and were rapidly approaching the border of Rumania, as well as the pre-war border with Poland.

The instructions from the Moscow military headquarters to the various partisan squadrons were now directed towards the preparation of local conditions for the advancing Soviet Army. The immediate order for the partisan units dealt with the problem of accumulating information on the strength, movement and equipment of the retreating German troops and of particular importance were areas of high troop concentrations. This information was immediately transmitted to Moscow via shortwave radio. Every night, aircraft of the Soviet Air Force were bombing and strafing the areas and positions pointed out by the partisan units. Floating magnesium flares, dropped by the aircraft and suspended from small parachutes, illuminated the dark landscape into daylight. There was no rest for the retreating armies of the Third Reich. The once mighty Luftwaffe all but disappeared from the sky.

The large concentration of retreating German troops in the area forced the Eagles partisan group to return to its old camp near the Wygon Lake. In order to carry out their new assignments effectively, it was necessary for them to go out on missions as far as the village of Hantsevich, only nine miles from the major city of Baranovichi. The village was their meeting point with collaborators and contacts from the city who were Polish and Belarusian members of the under- ground and relayed vital information to the partisans. One evening, the commander entered the earth hut which Kuba shared with several other partisans. He looked at Kuba and said, "Get ready for a mission at once!"

"Who is coming with me?" Kuba asked.

"Otto," he replied. Kuba and Otto saddled their horses, checked their submachine guns and sidearms and mounted up. Colonel Nikolsky grabbed the reins of Kuba's horse and spoke quietly, "You will ride to the chutor just east of Hantsevich. Your old friend, Shary, will meet you there. He will give you a detailed map showing all vital German positions in and around Baranovichi. Guard it with your life. We must have this information before sunrise. Be very careful."

"I understand, Colonel," Kuba answered. The horses started at a brisk pace, riding along a winding path through the thick forest.

Shary, a Polish machinist, was at the power plant of the Baranovichi railroad depot. He and Kuba had worked together on underground assignments on many occasions. Shary and his wife, Maria, had hidden Kuba at their apartment many times. Those two lovely people helped Kuba and saved his life during a particularly nasty and painful act against the man responsible for the death of Kuba's wife and infant son. That had been four months ago, during the second week of December 1943. Dressed in German officers' uniforms—even their weapons were German; Kuba and Otto were on a special assignment in the city of Baranovichi. Each of them carried in his coat pocket a small three inch by five inch Bakelite box of British manufacture which had four magnets on the back side and a small steel rod with evenly spaced notches on it, magnetic mines. When the steel rod was pulled out slightly, it activated the firing pin which, by means of a spring mechanism, caused it to explode after a predetermined period of time. Each notch determined the moment of explosion at half-hour intervals. Shary had provided them with forged German documents which entitled them to perform a routine inspection of the power plant, semaphore and radiotelegraph communication systems of the railroad depot.

The two partisans in their German uniforms were admitted to the power plant without any difficulties and the civilian manager of the plant, a German electrical engineer, took them on a tour of the facilities. He was proud of his clean, efficiently operated power plant. They came to the generator room. The generator was powered by a three piston steam engine, and next to the engine, separated by a short brick wall, stood a huge boiler which provided the steam which, in turn, activated the engine.

Before leaving the room, Otto and Kuba managed to stand with their backs next to the equipment and quickly attached the magnetic bombs to the engine and boiler, the timers set for one hour. It was hard to detect the mines because they looked like component parts of the equipment. Kuba and Otto left the plant and walked unhurriedly towards Shary's apartment on the other side of the railroad tracks, about a mile and a half away and once there, they quickly changed into their civilian clothes and Maria got rid of the German uniforms. Shary had just returned from an errand and was closing the door when the mines exploded. The house shook violently. They went to the windows and looked at the power plant just as the tall, brick smokestack toppled over in a cloud of dust, smoke and flames.

Within minutes, Gestapo and SS troops blocked off the entire area and began a search for two German officers. Shary hid the two partisans in a coal cellar behind the apartment where they spent the rest of the day and most of the night. Early in the morning, Shary called them back into the apartment. They washed up and Maria prepared some breakfast. As they were eating, they heard a commotion on the street. Many footsteps could be heard.

Kuba went to the window and the others joined him. A column of raggedly dressed men and women were marching slowly in the middle of the street towards the power plant. On the front and back of their coats, large, yellow Star of David signs were attached. Their faces were very skinny and gray looking, like living skeletons.

Kuba grabbed Shary's arm and asked, "The Jewish ghetto still exists?"

"Yes," Shary answered.

"How many Jews are still alive in the ghetto?"

"About one hundred and fifty," Shary answered.

"And who is their Head of the Jewish Council?" Kuba asked.

"Chaim Steinbeck!" Shary answered.

The traitor? Kuba's brain was inflamed with memories; the grave of his eighteen-month-old son, Victor, in the back of Steinbeck's house and the scaffold with his wife Franca's body hanging from it. The muscles in his face tightened as he turned to Otto and said, "Otto, go back to the camp and report on the success of our mission. I will return tomorrow as I have a personal mission to carry out and I will see you tomorrow at the camp."

Otto embraced Kuba, kissed him on the cheek and said with tears in his eyes, "I understand, my brother. I will not be too far away." Shary and Otto went down to the back of the apartment, across some backyards and headed towards the forest where the horses had been left.

It had been snowing all day and the city was covered with a white blanket. Kuba was restless, pacing the room back and forth in nervous anticipation. Shary returned at noon and reported that Otto had made it safely to the place where they had hidden the horses. He also told them that the Gestapo arrested several Wehrmacht officers in connection with the explosion at the powerhouse.

Shortly after six o'clock in the evening, many footsteps could be heard again in the slushy wet snow. Kuba put on an old, black coat which Shary found for him and to which Maria had attached two roughly made yellow Stars of David. Kuba kissed Maria goodbye and Shary accompanied him downstairs into the hallway. They embraced each other and Kuba opened the front door. A column of Jews were passing by and, in the semidarkness, Kuba slipped into the column unnoticed by the German and Belarusian police guards.

Half an hour later, the column passed through the heavily guarded ghetto gates and the Jews slowly dispersed into the surrounding houses. Kuba turned right, towards a vacant lot. The ghetto was much smaller than Kuba remembered it to be in 1941, only one square block. Several houses stood at the far side of the vacant lot with no lights shining through the windows, appearing to be unoccupied. Kuba walked along the empty lot toward the right side of the street and suddenly stopped. A light was showing through a drawn shade in the window of the second house on the right side: Chaim Steinbeck's house! Kuba stood next to the window and listened and the only sound that he could hear was that of a man crossing the room and of papers being shuffled.

Kuba remembered that by order of the Gestapo, all doors in the ghetto must remain unlocked at all times. He approached the door and again listened and heard the clank of a cup being placed on a saucer. It was very quiet in the ghetto. Kuba noticed that the doors and some windows in the surrounding houses stood open. No one lived in them. Their occupants had been exterminated by the Nazis long ago. The entire area gave one the feeling of being in a cemetery.

Kuba pulled out his German nine millimeter Luger gun, opened the door, stepped quickly inside and closed the door behind him. Now he was in the kitchen. The room was illuminated by a kerosene lamp on a table and in a chair behind the table sat Steinbeck, drinking hot tea from a cup. He looked up at Kuba and sudden recognition and fear were reflected in his eyes. He turned very pale and his right hand, which held the cup, froze half way between the table and his mouth. Kuba looked at the man. He was well fed and dressed in good clothes, unlike the other Jews of the ghetto. Some jewelry and paper money were lying on the table. His left hand was resting on a ledger and he was holding a pencil between the fingers. Kuba glanced at the open door leading to the other rooms of the house. There was no light coming from there. Kuba asked, "What happened to your family?"

Steinbeck's mouth fell open, but no sound came out. He shifted his eyes to the gun in Kuba's hand. "So, you sold them out too, in order to save your own rotten life," Kuba said. Steinbeck did not reply. His hands shook. The time had come. Kuba looked deep into Steinbeck's eyes and said, "Remember, Steinbeck, I promised you that I would be back." Kuba leveled the gun at Steinbeck's head and fired twice, Steinbeck fell backwards, upsetting the chair and table, breaking the kerosene lamp. Bank notes flared up into the flames.

Kuba left the house and closed the door, and made his way along the path of empty houses towards the ghetto fence on the eastern side, picking up a long plank on the way, to help him get over the eight-foot, barbed-wire fence. He passed the last house and stopped in the shadow; the fence was about twenty feet in front of him. He could hear some laughter and two men conversing in German. They were the ghetto guards on the other side of the block. Kuba approached the fence, stopped and listened. To his left, he could hear someone whistling the first bars of a Russian Army song quietly, a signal among the partisans of his unit. He looked beyond the fence toward a clump of trees about fifty yards away and saw someone standing there. He walked in that direction and immediately noticed an opening in the fence. He crawled through the opening and ran toward the clump of trees. When he reached the trees, a man stepped out and called, quietly, "Kuba, here!"

It was Otto! He had cut the hole in the fence and waited for Kuba and now led Kuba to the back of the tree clump where their horses were waiting. They mounted and took off at a gallop toward the village of Hantsevich. "Well, how did it go? I did not hear any pistol shots, but that was some fire you set to the house," Otto said.

"Oh, I shot Steinbeck twice in the head, and then flipped over his kerosene lamp on the table, which was loaded with money and papers. That started the fire."

"How did he react? Did he say anything?" Kuba was silent for a few minutes, recollecting the events in Steinbeck's house. He did not feel any remorse for his action, but he felt a deep contempt toward Steinbeck for his behavior and for what he did to his own family.

"Can you imagine that son-of-a-bitch delivered his family to the Nazis for execution in order to save his own life?" Kuba said.

"Those are the facts of life," Otto said. "Each nationality has its own rats!"

Now, in the spring of 1944, Kuba and Shary would meet once again, this time for the purpose of getting the information that the commander had requested from Shary. At a gallop, they passed the Babin chutors, the village of Tsiganie and several other villages on the road to Baranovichi where they would find Shary at the home of a farmer. They crossed the River Shchara and galloped across the Brest-Moscow highway without even looking for German patrols or ambushes and reached their destination after two hours of hard riding. From a distance, they could see the crisscrossing beams of the German anti-aircraft searchlights. "It will be nice to meet Shary again. He is a real nice person," Otto said.

"Yes. He is also the truest friend we have."

"Looks like our air force is really a living hell to the Germans in Baranovichi."

"Looks that way. There is not much resistance on the part of the Luftwaffe," Kuba said.

Kuba, with Otto behind him, entered the farm house, a typical East European farm house, consisting of one large room with a huge, brick, flat-top oven taking up almost half of the room. The oven was attached to the center of the right wall, dividing the house into two parts and behind it, the room was occupied by a large oak table with crude benches.

The remaining walls of the room were lined with attached, wide, wooden benches which folded out into beds at night. The benches and the flat top of the oven served as the bedrooms for the entire family. "Ah, how good to see you again, Kuba and Otto. Your friend is waiting for you," the farmer greeted them.

"It is good to see you too, my friend. How is your family?" Kuba replied, shaking hands with the man.

"Everybody is fine, thank you." The farmer went outside to stand watch. His seven children were sleeping on straw mattresses on the benches along the walls and the farmer's wife, a pleasant blonde woman in her middle thirties, looked down at them from her bed on top of the oven. Shary was waiting for them at the table with a glass of hot tea before him. The "tea" was made from burnt bread crumbs and boiled water and was sweetened by a chunk of yellowish sugar and called "Kipyatok" by the Russians.

Shary greeted Kuba and Otto with an embrace and produced a bottle of vodka. They looked at each other, remembering the events of their last meeting four months ago and drank in silence. After a while, Kuba inquired about Shary's family and the situation in Baranovichi.

Shary began to speak, "The German troops in the city are very demoralized. They kill people on the streets for little or no reason. Looting and rape are common everywhere and they are now talking openly about the fact that they are losing the war and will be leaving the area soon. However, the SS officers have warned the citizens that their orders are to see to it that the approaching Russian hordes will not find a single living being or any whole buildings and farms here."

"And it will get worse," Kuba replied. "The Germans know that their end is near and they will try to destroy as many of our people and property as they can. We must double our efforts to get rid of them as quickly as possible."

The Germans did not waste any time in carrying out that threat. Hundreds of villages in Belarus and the Ukraine were being burned to the ground. In most cases, the local population was herded into churches or other large structures and burned alive. The Jewish population in these towns and villages had been exterminated long ago by special units of the German Security Service, known as "Sonderkommandos." The houses in the larger towns and cities were systematically dynamited by special German squads. There was no one strong enough, not even the partisans, who lacked the manpower or equipment, to defend the cities and stop the murder and vandalism performed by the ever increasing numbers of retreating German troops. The roads and streets were full of retreating armored columns, tanks and artillery.

Shary also told them about the hasty attempts of the Sonderkommandos to erase any evidence of their crimes by rounding up hundreds of local men and boys and forcing them to dig up the mass graves of executed Jews. The corpses of the slaughtered men, women and children were then thoroughly searched for hidden valuables, including all anatomical cavities, and then were piled up into mounds, soaked with petrol and burned. The local men, forced into the operation, were then executed.

The hour was getting late, and Kuba and Otto had to prepare for the return trip to their camp. Shary handed Kuba a small envelope containing the information requested by Colonel Nikolsky. "Don't forget us after the victory!" Shary said as the partisans departed. The horses were well fed and rested and they took off at a gallop into the forest. When they approached the railroad station at Lyesnaya, the horses became nervous, causing the men to slow down and to stop. A loud roar of many aircraft was shattering the stillness of the night. Looking up, they saw that the sky was covered with hundreds of planes.

After listening for a while to the sound and pitch of the engines, Otto said, "Our planes!"

The planes were headed for Baranovichi and soon the horizon in that direction was lit up as in daytime by the floating magnesium flares dropped from the planes. The two partisans were about fifteen miles away from the city, but they could hear distinctly the noise of many bomb explosions. They smiled with satisfaction and continued looking at the spectacle as strings of tracer bullets and puffs of anti-aircraft shells made it appear like a display of fireworks. They continued their journey and Kuba, without thinking, began to finger the little padlock in the left pocket of his shirt. The comforting coolness of the padlock gave him some kind of assurance that he would be all right. He did not think about it because he was afraid that somehow the padlock would disappear, like the rest of his dreams.

After about an hour and a half, they came to the Sovietski chutors and stopped at a secluded farmhouse. The farmer was a friend of the Eagle partisans. Kuba knocked on the door, three slow raps, a pause, and again three slow raps. This was their signal. The door opened shortly and the farmer, Pyotr Vashkevich, greeted them and invited them into the house. He had expected them and was aware of their mission. Pyotr served them cold baked potatoes and homemade vodka while Kuba told him about the air raid on Baranovichi! Pyotr said that he had heard the planes fly by. Then he reported on events in his area. They had not seen many Germans, because the chutors were far from any highway. However, there were many strangers passing by. "As a matter of fact," Pyotr said, "two Soviet POW's, a boy and a girl, came last evening asking for a contact with partisans. They claimed that they had escaped from a camp in Volkovysk."

"Where are they?" asked Kuba.

"At my neighbor's house," Pyotr replied.

"Go get them now," Kuba said. Pyotr grabbed a sheepskin coat and left the house, returning several minutes later followed by the two fugitives. The girl was about nineteen years old and had a beautiful face, deep, dark eyes, black hair and a short, slightly upturned nose. She was dressed in an old Russian army coat and a gray woolen scarf on her head, tightly knotted under her chin and clutched a small canvas sack in her hand. Otto, standing near the door, waved his hand at Kuba and pointed to the boy. Kuba nodded his head and Otto took the boy out into another room of the house.

"What is your name?" Kuba asked the girl.

"Darya Korolenko," she answered, smiling at Kuba.

"Ukrainian," Kuba said. "Where were you born?"

"In Kamenetz Podolski."

"How old are you?" Kuba asked.

"Twenty-one." Kuba looked into her eyes and she gave him a big, somewhat coquettish smile which Kuba could not help but return. He looked at his watch, almost midnight.

"Unpack your things and empty your pockets. Put every thing on the table. I want to see all your documents and papers," Kuba ordered. Still smiling, she reached into her dress between her breasts and produced a "Komsomol" (Communist Youth Organization) membership booklet, then emptied her pockets and her sack. Kuba opened the membership booklet. The name and other information agreed with her statement, however, the photograph was missing."

"Where did you come from now?" Kuba asked suddenly in a much harsher voice.

She looked up at him somewhat frightened and said, "I worked in a kitchen for German officers in Volkovysk. Anton worked there as a mechanic and we both decided that now was the time to escape."

"Who is Anton?" Kuba asked.

"The boy that came with me," she replied.

"How did you get to Volkovysk?" Kuba asked.

"I worked there in the railroad cafeteria before the war," she answered.

"How did you manage to conceal your Komsomol booklet during all that time?" Kuba asked, watching her facial expressions very carefully.

Darya blushed slightly and answered with some embarrassment, "A woman can always hid things on her person so that no one can find them."

Kuba burst out laughing and looked through the rest of her belongings, consisting only of a few items of clothing and personal hygiene. He got up from the bureau and walked over to the door. Darya followed him. He opened the door and told her to go into the other room. Then he called in the boy. The young man was distinctly Russian looking, high cheekbones, blue eyes and blonde hair. He was dressed in an old and dirty army coat, worn out boots and no head covering. His face was pale and there was a scar on his left cheek. Kuba looked through his possessions. All he carried was a small pocket knife, some matches and a pack of German cigarettes.

"What is your name?" Kuba asked.

"Anton Fedorov," the man replied.

"Where were you born?"

"In Petrozavodsk," he answered.

"Where did you get that?" Kuba asked, pointing to the scar.

"During the battle of Veliki Luki in 1941, where I was captured by the Germans," said Anton. He was an auto mechanic by trade. According to his Red Army I.D. card, he was twenty years old. The rest of his story was in accord with Darya's statement.

Kuba called Otto and said, "We will take them with us." As a precaution, Otto found some rope and tied Anton's and Darya's hands. Anton got on the horse with Otto and Darya rode with Kuba. They rode in silence until they reached the partisan camp. The sky was turning lighter. It would soon be sunrise. They left the two strangers with a guard, unsaddled their horses, put them in their stalls and went to the commander's hut.

Nikolsky was waiting for them. He was standing with his chief of staff and the commissar, Grisha, of the Eagles partisan group. Kuba handed the envelope, which he had received from Shary, to the commander and reported the conversation he had had with Shary and the air raid on Baranovichi. They discussed the events for some time. Finally, Kuba told them about Anton and Darya.

"They may be spies!" Nikolsky said.

"That is why we brought them here."

"Bring them to my hut," Nikolsky ordered. Several minutes later, Kuba returned to Nikolsky's hut with Darya and Anton. In addition to the commander, there were now Sanya, Volodiya and Grisha in the hut.

"Kuba, go get some sleep," Nikolsky said. Kuba returned to his hut and found Otto already sound asleep. Kuba stretched out on his mattress and fell asleep almost instantly, his right arm wrapped around his weapon.

Darya and Anton were accepted into the partisan group. Darya was assigned to help Anna with the cooking and other chores and Anton was assigned to various tasks, including the care of the horses. After a week had passed, the partisans took Anton with them on a minor mission. He behaved to their satisfaction and helped them repel an attack by a German patrol by firing his rifle at the Germans along with the rest of the partisans. He even took extra chances by exposing himself to the Germans and drew away their fire.

Two weeks passed and Kuba became very friendly with Darya. She often approached him and asked if she could clean and mend his clothes, and Kuba agreed. One day Kuba was sitting on his mattress cleaning his submachine gun, when Darya came in with a bundle of his clothes. She moved so quietly that Kuba did not hear her enter, but as she stood behind him, he turned around and saw her. She was wearing a skirt and blouse, open at the top, so that Kuba could see her firm, unrestrained breasts swelling out.

She put down the bundle of clothes, came nearer to Kuba and said, "How long has it been since you were with a girl, Kuba?"

Kuba looked at her and his heart began to pound. Her black hair cascaded down to her shoulders and her eyelids were narrowed so only the black pupils were showing. Her lips were slightly turned in a sensuous smile as she looked into Kuba's eyes." There was a fragrance about her that disturbed him to such a degree he could only think of her nearness and femininity. She came closer to him and he stood up, her firm breasts pressing against his bare chest. "How long, Kuba?" she repeated.

"A long time! Too long," he replied and took her into his arms. Her lips met his, her tongue pressing against his teeth. With trembling hands, Kuba unbuttoned her blouse and touched her gently, but with purpose, and they tumbled back on the mattress. That day Darya moved in with Kuba, so Otto was forced to find other quarters. After that, Kuba's clothes were clean, his face shaven, his hair trimmed and he kept a well groomed, neat, clipped mustache.

Nikolsky looked at him, smilingly and said, "That woman is really taking care of you. How did you get so clean looking here in the forest?"

"Well, Colonel, I can't help it if I am so lovable. That girl is really something, the soul of Ukraine!" Several days later, Colonel Nikolsky called Kuba to his hut. Otto and Nikolay were already present. The commander informed them that he had just received an order from Moscow to blow up the main bridge on the River Shchara and that it had to be accomplished that night. The bridge was located only three miles from the major city of Stolbtsy, on the prewar border between Poland and the Soviet Union and was part of the Berlin-Moscow highway, the main road used by the retreating German troops. Kuba was ordered to lead an advance reconnaissance mission accompanied by Otto and Nikolay. The rest of the partisan group was to follow them three hours later. A special unit was busy assembling a forty-five kilogram bomb consisting of explosive toluene compounds, related to TNT. Kuba went to his hut and began to clean his equipment for the occasion.

Darya came up behind him and put her arms around his neck and, purposely, began to excite him erotically, while asking a very specific question. "Where are you going, Kuba?" Kuba did not respond. Instead, he began to undress her playfully and succeeded in getting her aroused to the point where she submitted to him with a cry escaping her lips. With a peculiar smile on her face, she left the hut shortly.

It was a warm day. The partisans had a special dinner consisting of broiled pork and potatoes. Kuba was looking for Darya, but she was not present. Nikolsky sitting next to Kuba pulled out a flask of vodka and passed it around. After dinner, Nikolsky asked Kuba to follow him into the forest for a last minute conference. They were accompanied by Otto, Nikolay and Commissar Grisha. Nikolsky and the commissar were briefing them on the delicate details of the mission.

They were all dressed in brand new khaki uniforms, received during the last parachute drop from Moscow and armed only with their pistols. "Your main objective is to find a suitable jump off point for our mission as close to the bridge as possible. We must obtain information on the strength of the German guards and the location of their command post," Nikolsky said.

"Where will we meet you?" asked Nikolay.

Nikolsky pulled out a map from his pocket and while pointing to a specific spot on the map, said to them, "We shall meet at this point near the village of Pousevich, about two hundred yards from the river. There is a nice oak grove there." They synchronized their watches with Nikolsky's watch. Suddenly they froze. They were several hundred yards away from their camp and yet they could distinctly hear the sound of a Morse code message being transmitted from nearby. They looked at each other. The only radio transmitter was in Nikolsky's hut, back at the camp. They pulled out their guns and carefully followed the clicking sound of the radio operator's key. Nikolay was in front with Kuba close behind and the others spread out in a semicircle. Kuba stopped and pointed to a branch of a tall pine tree and they all looked at what Kuba had spotted. There was a wire hanging down from the branch. They proceeded in silence. They could hardly believe their eyes. Darya was sitting on the ground with earphones on her head and a very compact transceiver in her lap, operating the key with her left hand. A small caliber gun was on the ground next to her right hand, her back towards them. Nikolay picked up her gun and the others surrounded her. She looked up at them and reached toward the place where her gun had been, then frantically, she started tapping out a message. Too late! Grisha grabbed the transceiver out of her lap and Kuba ripped off the earphones.

"Get up." ordered the commander. Darya got up slowly. She was very pale and as she stood up, she reached for her throat. Kuba noticed that she had slipped something into her dress. He grabbed her roughly by the arm, reached into her dress and pulled out a small notebook from between her breasts. He looked at her with hurt in his eyes and said to her in German, "The game is over, my dear."

Suddenly, Nikolsky asked, "Where is Anton?"

"He is on guard duty now!" said Grisha.

"Nikolay, go get him!" Nikolsky ordered. Nikolay ran off toward the camp. Kuba looked through the notebook and found a lengthy message about the plan to blow up a bridge, written in German, time and location were not given. Kuba gave the information to Nikolsky. The commander slapped Darya across the face and asked, "Did you manage to transmit all that information?"

"No. I was just establishing contact." Otto used Darya's belt to tie her hands behind her back and they returned to camp. Nikolay was waiting for them, holding Anton. His hands also were tied behind his back. The entire group gathered around the interrogators, watching in puzzlement. Anton's nose was bleeding. It seems that Nikolay had had a little conversation with him.

"Lock them up in the bath house!" the commander ordered. Nikolay and several other partisans marched off the two prisoners. The bath house was an earth hut with one exit only, a hole cut in the roof and a wooden barrel full of water mounted over it for showering. On the other end of the roof there was a chimney. Inside there was a fire pit surrounded by boulders and rocks, used as a steam bath by pouring water on the hot rocks.

Nikolsky called a meeting of his staff and when everybody was present in the commander's hut, he looked very intensely into Kuba's eyes and said, almost spitting out the words, "Go bring in Darya!" Kuba went in the bath house and ordered Nikolay to bring out Darya. She came out and Kuba led her toward the commander's hut. The expression on her face was very hard. Her lips were pinched together and she looked at the ground in front of her. She entered Nikolsky's hut, followed by Kuba. All officers were sitting on the bunks. Nikolsky, Grisha and the chief of staff were seated on a bench behind the table. Kuba found a place to sit down and Darya remained standing in front of Nikolsky with her hands tied behind her. The interrogation began.

"Who ordered you to come here?" Nikolsky asked. Darya remained silent, keeping her eyes on the table and avoiding the eyes of the others. She would not answer any questions even after Sanya slapped her across the face a few times. Kuba felt as though he were being slapped. This went on for fifteen minutes, and the commander said "with your silence you have admitted your crime. Take her back, Kuba, and bring Anton here!" Kuba took her back to her prison and in a few minutes returned with Anton. Nikolsky began to interrogate him.

Anton's face was puffed up and his right eye had begun to discolor. He started talking almost immediately: twenty-two Soviet POW's were trained for espionage among the various partisan groups in the area. The training took place at the city of Volkovysk and these two were assigned by the Germans to the Eagles.

Nikolsky said something to Grisha and the latter left the hut returning shortly with Darya. Nikolsky told her, in a quiet voice, that Anton had confessed to everything. He related to her all the facts. Darya gave Anton a bitter look and continued her silence. Finally Nikolsky asked her sharply, "Are all these facts correct?"

Darya raised her head for the first time and looked at him with her dark, defiant eyes. "Yes!" she answered. The partisans looked at the two condemned people in silence, knowing what was in store for them.

Meanwhile Nikolsky continued the interrogation. "How did you get here from Volkovysk?"

"The Germans drove us to the vicinity of the Niskie village. Then we were on our own," replied Anton.

"Did you go through the village?" Nikolsky asked.

"No, we circled the village and followed the forest toward the Babin chutors. Those were our instructions," Anton said, glancing somewhat frightened, at Darya. It was obvious that Darya was in charge of their mission. She stared at Anton, and his answers became more reluctant.

The commander said to Anton, "You don't have to be afraid of her anymore. Now, what did you do next?"

After a pause, Anton continued with a shaky voice, "We continued walking through the forest for the rest of the day. We circled the village of Novosiele and continued until we came into this forest where your camp is located. "

"Did you know in advance where our camp was located?" Nikolsky asked.

"The Germans told us which forest to go to, but we did not know the exact location of the camp," Anton replied.

"Why did you return to Sovietsky chutors?" Nikolsky asked.

"After we discovered the location of your camp by following hoof prints, we hid the radio equipment and guns nearby and returned to the chutors. Our orders were not to contact you directly, but rather depend on the farmers to introduce us to you," Anton replied.

The commander, commissar and chief of staff exchanged a few quiet words, and then Nikolsky turned to Darya with a question. "How many times did you make contact with the Germans since you were with us?"

Her lips were drawn tightly as she answered, "Today was the second time."

"How did you find out about our orders to blow up a bridge?"

"I overheard part of your Morse code conversation and some verbal comments exchanged between yourselves and the commissar," she replied.

"How did you manage to decode our messages?"

"While cleaning your hut yesterday, I found some notes which had gotten stuck beneath your mattress. The rest was simple," said Darya with a sarcastic smile.

Again Nikolsky conferred quietly with his two aides and then said, "Remove the prisoners!"

Kuba and Otto led the prisoners back to the bath house and as they were returning to Nikolsky's hut, they passed Pasha and Toliya who were heading deeper into the forest with shovels in their hands.

Half an hour later the entire Eagles partisan unit was assembled in the forest before two freshly dug graves, Darya and Anton standing in front of the graves. The commander pronounced the verdict of the court martial: "For treason against our motherland, you, Darya Korolenko, and you, Anton Fedorov, are sentenced to death. The sentence is to be carried out immediately!"

Volodiya, carrying two rifles with attached silencers, walked up to Nikolsky, the commander turned to the partisans looked each one of them in the eye and gave the order.

"Pasha and Kuba, step forward!" The two partisans approached Nikolsky and accepted the rifles from Volodiya as Toliya approached the prisoners and offered blindfolds. Anton agreed. Darya declined. They were both very pale and trembling. Pasha and Kuba took up their positions twenty feet from the condemned, Kuba facing Darya, who looked at him through tears. She was still very beautiful. Kuba remembered her nearness and warmth during time they had spent together and began shaking with emotion.

Suddenly, Nikolsky spoke, "Carry out the order!" Pasha and Kuba raised their rifles and took aim. Kuba looked at Darya's face through the sites of his rifle and was unable to contain feelings any longer. He pulled back on the sharp kick of the rifle butt against his shoulder, but he did not hear the shot. Darya and Anton disappeared, their bodies having fallen into the freshly dug graves. Kuba remained standing, leaning on his rifle, overcome with emotion. Someone came up behind him and put a hand on his shoulder. Kuba turned and faced the commander who was looking at him with a stern expression on his face.

He spoke quietly to Kuba, "Get a hold of yourself. Everything is all right. Remember, if necessary, you must be able to shoot your own brother... This is war."

A detail of partisans got busy covering the graves and the remainder of the unit returned to camp Still ahead of them was a more pressing task; the bridge on the River Shchara.

Chapter Twenty-Four

It was a calm, sunny, late afternoon. The earth was wet from the melting snow and the sky to the north was darkening due to a cloud layer that was moving from that direction. Kuba, Nikolay and Otto were riding in a westerly direction through the forest, their horses following an old trail which ran parallel to the Brest-Moscow highway. The events of the day loomed heavily on their minds and Kuba could not forget the forlorn look in Darya's eyes before he pulled the trigger. She was so beautiful and so lost. Who would have thought that such a girl could be a dangerous spy?

They continued their journey swiftly and in silence. It was still daylight when they arrived in the vicinity of the village of Pousevich. Ahead of them was the River Shchara and at a distance, they could see the bridge. The horses' legs submerged into ankle deep water because of the swamps, but finally they reached the edge of the forest nearest to the bridge. Kuba dismounted with the others. They tied their horses to available tree branches and, after a thorough reconnaissance of the area, proceeded on foot. The area was unknown to Kuba. After a few minutes, they reached the edge of the forest and had to lie down because the bridge was only several hundred meters in front of them and between them and the rivers there was only a swampy meadow. They surveyed the area around the bridge and found that there was a highway which continued across the bridge along a swampy embankment to their right. The wide bridge across the river accommodated railroad tracks, plus heavy traffic on the highway lanes. On the opposite side of the river, there was a German bunker, near the bridge, and somewhat further, there could be seen several farmhouses. The partisans explored the area directly in front of them by means of a canal which extended from the forest, cut through the meadow and reached the river under the bridge. "That is the only way to reach the bridge unnoticed," said Otto.

"We have to make sure that it is possible to walk in the canal," suggested Kuba. At that moment seven German soldiers appeared on the bridge and walking in a group, crossed the bridge and stopped at the other end.

As the partisans watched, three more Germans joined the first group and they all stood near the bunker talking and laughing. Then two more soldiers appeared on the near side of the bridge and lit up cigarettes while leaning on the rail and observing the river. One soldier began to sing a German Army song and several of the others joined in.

The partisans noticed that one soldier carried a light machine gun while the rest were armed with rifles and submachine guns. "There must be about fifteen of them," said Nikolay.

"There may be more in those houses on the other side," said Kuba. They watched the Germans, in silence, then after a while Kuba said, "Let's go check the canal."

The partisans pulled back into the forest and reached the canal and Nikolay got into the canal and took a few steps. The water reached below his knees. He took a few more steps and said, "The bottom is solid. It is easy to walk here."

The three partisans returned to their horses. It was getting dark. The sky became heavily clouded and it looked like rain. They started walking, leading their horses toward the meeting place.

"It will be quite a job!" Nikolay said, wet from his walk in the canal. They reached the meeting point and looked around and as it was still early, they tied their horses to trees and lit up cigarettes. Suddenly Nikolay said, "Hey, Kuba, we would have been in a pickle tonight if we had not caught your girlfriend."

"Yes. There would have been a whole bunch of Germans here by now!" said Otto.

Kuba was silent and still in shock. What happened? How could he have been so stupid and not detect the treachery in Darya. He thought to himself: *I must have been pretty desperate for a woman to let my guard down the way I did. That Darya was some actress, and was she ever beautiful. And there I am, a man that killed the woman of his desires.* He went on like this struggling with his conscience. *But wait a minute, you old fool. That woman seduced you and tried to kill you and all your friends and comrades.* It took a long time for Kuba to finally relax, and accept the fact that this is war and he did not commit any crime, and he was not in love with that girl.

At nine-thirty that evening, they heard a noise deep in the forest. The three partisans moved away from their horses quickly and took up positions behind trees, their weapons at the ready. They could clearly hear many horses coming in their direction and soon a rider on horseback emerged from among the trees, moving slowly in their direction.

When he was about twenty-five feet away Kuba ordered, "Password."

"Twenty-three!" the rider said, "Counter password!"

"Thirty-two!" Kuba answered the signal, recognizing Pasha's voice. There were altogether about twenty partisans. Nikolsky asked Kuba what the situation was near the bridge and he reported on all observations which he and his two companions had made.

Nikolay joined in and said to the Colonel, "We even discovered a very comfortable road to the bridge." Vlodik, Kolia and Sasha carried three huge bundles of explosives, which altogether must have been about one hundred and twenty pounds. A timing device was installed in one of the bundles. The whole group tied their horses to trees and one of the new partisan recruits was assigned the mission of guarding the horses. Pasha, Vlodik and Toliya picked up the heavy toluene mines and the entire group moved toward the bridge.

"Remember, we must proceed in silence from now on. No talking, coughing or sneezing!" Nikolsky ordered. When they reached the canal, the group stopped. Two partisans went to the edge of the forest and looked around. It was very quiet and dark and heavy clouds covered the sky. They could distinguish the dark contours of the bridge and the bunker. No sounds came from that direction. Toliya, Pasha and Vlodik entered the canal carrying the heavy mines on their shoulders, and proceeded along the canal towards the bridge.

The rest of the partisans went to a point opposite the entrance to the bridge and spread out in an assault position. The order was that in case anything went wrong, they were to storm the bridge and bunker. Three heavy machine guns were set up at strategic points and the others of the group were armed with rifles, light and submachine guns and each partisan had at least three hand grenades hanging from his belt. The three partisans in the canal were moving forward very quietly; there was hardly a sound coming from their direction. Slowly, they approached the bridge. The minutes ticked away and the tension among the partisans grew as they strained their eyes trying to get a glimpse of the three men in the canal. The Eagles manned their positions in silence. Kuba developed a strong headache. There had been too many events for one day. He could still see Darya's last, desperate look. About twenty-five minutes had passed but to Kuba, it seemed like an eternity, when they heard a quiet noise from the canal. Pasha, Toliya and Vlodik returned, soaking wet.

The entire group got to their feet and retreated deeper into the forest. The Colonel asked, "Did everything go all right?"

"Yes, everything is set!" Pasha replied.

"Where did you place the mines?" asked Nikolsky.

"At the steel crossbars next to the cement columns which support the bridge," Pasha answered.

"What did you set the timing device at?" asked Nikolsky.

"One hour!" was the reply.

The Eagles returned to their horses and from a distance, in the stillness of the night, they could hear the whistle of a locomotive and the noise of the approaching train from the west, several miles away. "Mount your horses!" Nikolsky ordered. The entire group mounted up and at a slow trot followed the forest circling the village of Pousevich and stopped on the other side of the village. Nikolsky looked at his watch. "Five minutes to go!" he said.

Kuba's horse became restless in the excitement. He steadied the animal with whispered words, and looked up at the sky. It was clearing somewhat. Here and there, stars could be seen. The minutes were dragging on like hours. Then it happened! The sudden explosion! For a second, the sky lit up like daytime. The horses jumped and it was difficult to hold them still.

"Let's go!" yelled Nikolsky. They started their long ride back to camp, in silence until they reached the Novosiele "trakt," an ancient road across the swamps, built by the Romans during the third century. The "trakt" continued past the village of Novosiele and finally disappeared in the swamp. They then followed a forest trail toward the village of Niskie where they stopped and gathered around Nikolsky, who was sitting on his horse with a broad smile on his face. Everyone was happy with the success of the mission.

Nikolay started laughing and said, "The Germans will never figure out how we managed to plant those bombs under such a heavily guarded bridge!"

"Yes, there is no limit to their surprise right now," Nikolsky said and then added, "You, Pasha and Nikolay remain in Niskie. Find out all you can about the results of our job!" The two named partisans dismounted and led their horses toward a farmhouse as the remainder of the Eagles rode in the direction of their camp in the nearby forest. It was past two o'clock in the morning, and it was beginning to rain when they reached their camp.

Sanya greeted them, "We had quite a day today. We got rid of two spies and destroyed a major bridge!" The group took care of their horses and then went to the kitchen to get some food. Dinner consisted of cold pork and bread. Kuba was sitting on a log and eating, reflecting on the events of the day with mixed emotions. He thought about his father and mother; his memory of them so strong at that moment, that he could see their faces. What would they say to his part in the events of this day? It stopped raining. The sky was clearing and Kuba arose and walked toward his hut. Before entering the hut he looked up to the sky and saw the seven twinkling stars of the Big Dipper high above the forest.

Kuba awakened at about ten in the morning and heard many voices in the camp. There was quite a commotion, so he went outside. Nikolay and Pasha had returned and were reporting on the results of the previous night's mission. The bridge was completely destroyed and the train that they had heard approaching had already been on the bridge at the moment of impact. It was a troop and supply train, carrying tanks and other heavy war equipment. For the moment, the Brest- Moscow highway could not be used by the German troops in their flight from the advancing Soviet armies.

This situation, however, endangered the existence of the partisans because more and more German troops would be concentrated in the area while waiting for the construction of two pontoon bridges to be built across the River Shchara, which German army engineers had started to construct a few days after the explosion.

The Eagles were now over sixty men strong, due to the large number of local partisans who had joined the group. It became necessary, at times, to split up the group into smaller units in order to avoid detection. The Germans were venturing deeper and deeper into the countryside in search of food, coming to chutors and villages in and around the forest where the partisans had their camp.

The Eagles continued their operations against the Nazis, nevertheless and during the following weeks and months, the partisans attacked many German garrisons, railroads and highways throughout Belarus and the Ukraine. Many units had penetrated into Poland and Lithuania. The Nazi rule over Eastern Europe was coming to an end.

Chapter Twenty-Five

Several weeks passed, summer came and it was warm, so life in the forest became easier. The partisans could move about with less danger of being detected as they kept constant watch over the German movements. The number of enemy troops in the area had increased to such a degree that it became necessary to divide the Eagles into two separate groups. Commissar Grisha took half of the squadron and moved to one of their old campsites near the village of Lopatichi on the other side of the railroad tracks. Kuba was assigned to that group, as was Sanya. The two groups communicated by way of radio or courier.

During that period, the main task of the partisans was to pinpoint strategic positions of the Germans and indirectly control the bombardment of such positions by Soviet and other Allied air forces. The partisans were always in much greater danger than the regular army forces on the front line. The Russians, and others, considered one year of service behind enemy lines to be equal to three years on the front lines.

However, this dangerous situation worsened enormously. The many German divisions in the area were joined by thousands of Nazi satellite forces: Hungarians, Rumanians and Italians. Death lurked behind every bush, tree, farm building and ravine. The sound of gunfire could be heard throughout the day and night and the partisans came across many dead bodies of men, women and children. Most of the bodies were stripped nude and some were badly decomposed. Flies and maggots crawled in and out of gaping mouths, ears and eye sockets. The stench of decomposed bodies was unbearable and a horrible sight. The partisans buried as many of these Nazi victims as possible. Of course, the names or identities of the victims remained unknown.

Among the Soviet-dominated partisan groups, religious feelings or beliefs were almost nonexistent. Kuba had inherited a deep feeling that a destiny, or supreme power, controlled the course of his life. His parents were not religious. They did not observe the ancient laws and rites of their forefathers nor did they attend a church or synagogue. Nevertheless, Kuba had the feeling that someone was watching over him. In his subconscious, he associated that "someone" with his dead parents and his entire immediate family, all victims of the Nazi genocide against the Jewish people. As far as the other partisans were concerned, Kuba noticed that a few of them crossed themselves and their lips moved in silent prayer. On several occasions, he noticed that Pasha took out from his pocket an earring, rubbed it lightly, while his lips were moving as in prayer. Sanya, on the other hand, carried a German bullet which he placed in his blanket behind his saddle during an encounter with a Nazi ambush. Before each combat action, Sanya held the bullet in his left palm and looked at it intensely for several seconds.

In a strange way the little padlock that his mother gave him before the war became to Kuba such a "deity." He could never explain how the little padlock got into the pocket of his pants; possibly it had been there all the time without his noticing it but since its discovery, that little padlock became a talisman to Kuba. Whenever he touched it or looked at it, he could see his mother's face before him and, at times, he found himself talking to the padlock. He knew that he was not cracking up, but something was there that influenced him in that manner.

Before each dangerous action, Kuba reached into his pants pocket to feel the cooling effect of the small padlock and it gave him the feeling of complete security. Even during the fiercest battles in which he had participated, he had the feeling that nothing would happen to him. Somehow, it was like watching the entire event on a huge movie screen.

It was June of 1944. The day was hot and the Eagle partisans were resting in their camp after the previous night's activities when suddenly the stillness of the day was shattered by the earsplitting sound of low flying aircraft. Several German planes passed over the camp at tree top level, flying in the direction of the village of Mashuki. Minutes later, the partisans heard a heavy bombardment coming from the direction of that village. The commissar summoned two partisans and told them to ride towards the village and see what was going on. About forty minutes later, the two scouts returned and reported that the Germans had, indeed, bombed Mashuki in reprisal for the villagers' cooperation with the partisans of the area.

The entire Eagle group was gathered near the commissar's hut to discuss the events when a German spotter plane flew over the camp, a twin-engine, double-fuselage plane. It was so low that the partisans could actually see the pilot. After the plane had passed the camp, it turned around and began to circle the camp again. "He spotted the camp!" yelled the commissar.

"He must have noticed the smoke from our kitchen!" added Sanya. On the second circle around the camp, the pilot began to strafe the area with machine gun fire while the partisans ran for the nearest trees and bushes.

The order from Grisha then came, "Go get our weapons!" The partisans darted towards their huts and came out, armed with two heavy machine guns, one twenty-millimeter anti-tank gun and submachine guns and rifles. They spread out under trees and bushes and got ready. The German plane was continuing to circle the camp at treetop level. The commissar instructed the partisans, "Look at those two fir trees to the south. You will notice that the plane passes behind those trees during each circling pass. Set your sights at the altitude of the plane. The plane is flying from right to left. Pick a point near the left tree and as soon as the plane passes the right tree, open fire!"

The partisans took aim and waited. Kuba had his gun ready next to him, and Toliya took up position with his anti-tank gun. The German plane was approaching the first "target" tree, spraying the area with machine gun fire. "Fire!" yelled the commissar. All hell broke loose! Everybody was shooting his weapon at the designated point in front of the approaching plane.

The plane began to trail smoke and Toliya fired his automatic anti-tank gun. He must have hit a fuel supply tank, because flames erupted around the cockpit. A black serpentine of smoke followed the plane as it went down in an easterly direction, crashing somewhere on the other side of the railroad tracks.

"We got him! We got him!" somebody yelled.

"I don't think that too many of our bullets missed the target!" said the commissar, smiling broadly. The partisans were standing around under the trees and talking about their first victorious encounter with an enemy aircraft when Pasha, the "cook for the day," called them to dinner. They picked up their utensils and lined up in front of the kitchen. It was late afternoon and the air was cooling off. After dinner, Sanya contacted Moscow for his daily report and any further instructions. The partisans who were assigned to guard duty that day left for their posts. Kuba did not have any duty that day, so he stretched out under a tree and lit a cigarette and soon fell asleep.

After about an hour of sleep, Kuba was awakened by some new commotion in the camp. Ivan Bobko, from the village of Mashuki, who was an underground contact of the Eagles, arrived in camp. He was talking to the commissar, to report on the bombing of the village. He related that the villagers were in their houses getting ready for dinner when the German bombers swooped down on them and that when the first bombs exploded, the entire population ran for cover into the nearby forest. The planes, flying very low, chased them and sprayed machine gun fire on the escaping people causing many casualties, dead and wounded. Many houses were blown up and on fire. Grisha assigned two first aid men to get some medical supplies and return to Mashuki with Ivan. After they had left the camp, Sanya emerged from his hut. He had a radiogram in his hand. He called the commissar aside and the two got involved in a lengthy discussion.

It was getting dark and quite chilly when Sanya called Kuba and said to follow him into the commissar's hut. The commissar was sitting on his bunk with a sealed letter in his hand. He looked at Kuba, for what seemed to be several moments, before he spoke, "Kuba, you will carry this letter to Colonel Nikolsky. It is an extremely important document and I hold you responsible for its safe delivery. It must not fall into German hands even if you have to swallow it in case of deadly danger. Do you understand?"

"Yes, Commissar," Kuba replied. Then he asked, "Is someone coming with me?"

"Take Sergey Bazanovich with you. He is a local boy and knows the vicinity well. Be particularly cautious when crossing the railroad tracks," the commissar said and then added, "Get some warm clothes. It will be cold on the swamps."

Kuba put the letter on his chest, under his shirt. The commissar got to his feet and shook hands with Kuba. "Good luck, Comrade." Sanya also shook hands with him and clapped him on the back.

Kuba left the hut, found Sergey near the campfire, tapped him on the shoulder and said, "Come on, we are going on a mission!"

"Just the two of us?" Sergey asked.

"Yes!" Sergey was about nineteen years old, short in stature with light blue eyes and very blonde hair. A typical Belarusian peasant boy who never owned a pair of shoes and walked around wearing native "laptchi" moccasins made of the bark of birch trees. He wore an oversized coat and he had to put an extra short strap on his long rifle, so that it would not drag on the ground when he walked.

The two of them went to their huts to get ready. Kuba changed his clothing, checked his submachine gun and strapped two extra magazines onto his belt, each containing seventy-two rounds of ammunition. Then, after a thought, he also strapped on his pistol and three hand grenades.

He met Sergey outside. Because of the great numbers of Germans in the vicinity, they had to travel on foot. Horses were too noisy for such an assignment. Sergey was armed with a regular Soviet Army rifle and several containers with ammo on his belt. The commissar walked with them as far as the guard post and on the way, gave them final instructions, "You better cross the railroad near the village of Haynin. You, Sergey, keep a sharp eye on Kuba. Don't let anything happen to him. You are his bodyguard on this journey!"

The two partisans saluted and soon disappeared into the forest, circling the villages of Lopatichi[4] and Haynin, which meant they

---

[4] **Lapitchi** (possible reference to Sergey's Moccasins) is a different place than **Lopatichi**, but both are in Belarus. Lapitchi may be the origin of Sergey's

had to walk through the swampy forest. They finally reached the edge of the forest and the railroad was about two hundred yards away. As a precaution against partisan attacks, the Germans had cleared two-hundred-meter-wide strips of land along both sides of the railroad tracks.

It was a clear night. The moon was hanging over the forest on the other side of the tracks. Kuba and Sergey stopped and studied the area, carefully. It was very quiet. The water on the bare strip of swamp separating them from the track embankment shimmered in the moonlight. They were exactly opposite the spot where sometime ago their comrade Petrushka had been killed by a land mine. There were no signs of any German patrols on the tracks. They stood there for several minutes in silence. Not a sound could be heard.

Finally, Kuba told Sergey to follow several paces behind him and to try to place his feet in Kuba's tracks, in case of land mines. Kuba was wearing his army boots which soon filled up with water, but, Sergey with his "laptchi," moccasins, which did not retain the water, had little trouble. A last look around, and they started toward the embankment, moving slowly and with great caution. Sergey was about ten feet behind Kuba. They released the safety locks on their weapons and continued to move slowly. Kuba did not feel right about this mission. He had a vague premonition, but was not frightened. They reached the embankment, which was about two and a half or three meters high, its sides covered with grass.

Kuba stopped and listened. Sergey stopped ten feet behind him, then slowly Kuba started to climb the embankment and half-way up he stopped and lay down, listening for any sounds of approaching trains. It was quiet. Instinctively, Kuba reached into his pants pocket and froze. His mother's padlock was not there. He must have left it in the other clothes. His uneasiness grew and he rested for a few more minutes and continued his climb. He grabbed the nearest steel track with his left hand and pulled himself up onto the embankment. He froze and turned pale as he

---

Moccasins spelled 'laptchi' in this text. Another possibility is the term, 'lapchi' which refers to a particular type of weaving in Nepal. –ED.

came face to face with a German SS trooper, wearing a typical steel helmet. Their faces were not more than five feet apart.

Kuba slid down the embankment in a hurry and started to run toward the forest. Sergey took off like a rabbit, in his "laptchi" and was nearing the forest when the Germans opened up with heavy machine gun fire. Kuba dropped to the ground and turned around quickly. He saw about ten Germans lined up on the embankment and a machine gun on a tripod, set up at the far side of the embankment. As he dropped to the ground, he felt a sharp jerk in his left-hand palm, near the thumb. Also, a bullet whistled past his left ear, ripping out a piece of cotton from his jacket. When he finally faced the enemy, he pushed himself forward because the bullets were hitting the water just behind his legs. A thought came to him that the vertical range of the gun pivot did not allow the gun to be lowered any further.

Kuba lined up his submachine gun on the silhouettes of the ten Germans, resembling ducks in a shooting gallery with the moon behind them. Kuba took aim at the first German to the left, rested the gun magazine on the palm of his wounded hand and opened fire, moving the gun slowly from left to right across the line of Germans. He did not release the trigger until after he had reached the silhouette of the last German, continuing to fire and reversing the motion of his gun to the left. He continued to fire his gun in that manner until the magazine was empty. There was no more movement on the embankment. Nobody was shooting at Kuba anymore.

Kuba lowered his gun and there was a hissing noise when the gun barrel touched the swamp water. He looked at his left, hand, which had begun to throb painfully and saw that the thumb was at an awkward angle, a dark gap between the thumb and the index finger. Kuba placed his gun between his knees and pulled out the empty magazine, replacing it with a fresh one, then got to his feet and started searching for Sergey.

He found him in the forest. The boy was sitting under a tree and sobbing. Kuba kicked him lightly and Sergey looked up at him with fear his eyes. "That'll teach me to go out on a mission with a nineteen year old. Some bodyguard you are!" said Kuba. "Get out your first-aid package!" Sergey ripped open the first aid kit and bandaged Kuba's hand. Then Kuba asked him, "How many shots did you fire at the Germans?"

"None. I was scared. I thought that you were dead," Sergey said quietly. "All right. Let's go!" Kuba smiled grimly.

"What are you going to do?" asked Sergey with a trembling voice.

"We are going across the railroad. Remember our mission!" said Kuba, starting out once again toward the embankment. Sergey followed him, reluctantly. They crossed the railroad, several feet from the dead German ambush without any incidents. The rest of the journey was without event and they reached the main camp by midnight.

Kuba reported to Nikolsky's hut and handed him the sealed letter. Nikolsky asked about their trip and Kuba reported in detail on the incident with the German ambush. He did not mention Sergey's behavior.

"So, you got them all! Good boy!" said Nikolsky and slapped him on the back, then started reading the document. Afterwards he ordered Kuba to go see the doctor and to get some rest. "You will have to carry back a letter to the commissar tomorrow night," said the colonel.

The doctor cleaned Kuba's wound and stitched it up.

"You are a lucky man. No bones were hit," the doctor told Kuba. He found an empty bunk in the doctor's hut and fell asleep immediately and Sergey found quarters with another partisan. Kuba, at that time, did not know that his recent mission marked the beginning of a much larger and more dangerous task which would involve all the partisan units in the area.

Chapter Twenty-Six

It was a hot, humid summer in the swamps of Polesye and a thick layer of swamp fog hung like steam over the ground, covering the shrubs and trees. However, the most severe problem was caused by the swarms of mosquitoes and other insects which breed in swamp conditions. Life in the forest became unbearable. The partisans sported swollen faces and arms as a result of mosquito stings. The insects even found their way beneath the men's clothing during the day and did not let up their attack at night.

It was July of 1944. The air on the swamps of Belarus was filled with the sounds of the approaching front lines. The distant thunder of artillery fire could be heard day and night and, according to radio communiques, the Soviet Army was only some sixty miles from the Wygon Lake. The member of the Eagles partisan group were again united at the Wygon Lake camp and there was a lot of excitement among the partisans due to the approaching Soviet Army, as well as to the frequent, secret meetings of the top command of the squadron in Colonel Nikolsky's hut.

The meetings always ended with a radio conversation, lasting sometimes more than an hour, between Nikolsky and the Supreme Partisan Command in Moscow. The dry cell batteries for the generator were used up and, because of the proximity of the Germans there were no more parachute drops of supplies. So the partisans took turns in cranking the generator making it possible to operate the shortwave radio. The spent batteries, each one weighing about six pounds, were gathered by the partisans and used to play tricks on the Germans. On several occasions, the partisans planted those spent batteries across the railroad or the highway, causing a disruption to the flow of German troops for some period of time because they had to investigate the foreign objects before they could proceed. While this procedure was going on, the Eagles would attack the Germans with machine gun fire. This type of operation went on for several weeks.

Then a more dangerous game began. The different partisan groups in the area received orders that they were now under the unified command of Colonel Nikolsky and their joint mission was to set up ambushes along both sides of the highways and railroad tracks. When Allied planes attacked the retreating German troops, the partisans' job was to open fire at the enemy troops and chase them back into the open. There was no escape for the Nazis and it became very difficult for them to find shelter from the advancing Soviet troops. Whatever aircraft were left of the once mighty Luftwaffe now were engaged in the defense of Germany proper and the immediately surrounding territories. Thousands of German troops ended their retreat to the Fatherland along the Brest-Moscow highway or railroad and, with this type of action continuing through the night, the various partisan groups carried out their assignment in shifts.

Kuba found it difficult to sleep during his time off because of the mosquitoes, and this was true for all of the partisans. As a matter of fact, during one of the secret meetings between Colonel Nikolsky and Commissar Grisha, there occurred an amusing incident. Smoke was pouring out of the commander's hut, accompanied by yells, "Get out, you sons of bitches!" Kuba and some other partisans grabbed their weapons and ran to the defense of their chief. As it turned out, the commander and commissar had set fire to some straw and rags in an attempt to get rid of the mosquitoes, almost burning the hut.

At noon, Sanya emerged from the commander's hut with a radiogram. Nikolsky studied it for a while and then called a general assembly of the partisans. Nikolsky was very serious when he read the order from Moscow: "Due to the fact that the partisan group No.258, known as Orlovsky Eagles, has completed its mission on the territory of Belarus, it is therefore ordered to begin moving west toward the Bug River and the Polish border. If there are any wounded or sick partisans in the group, they are to be transported to the field hospital operated by the Sukhanov partisan group."

Kuba listened to the order and a flood of thoughts went through his mind. They were going west! Maybe, they would reach Warsaw and by some miracle Kuba's mother and sister would be alive. Perhaps, if everything turned out right, he would have a chance to get away from both the Germans and the Soviets.

Nikolsky continued his order. "Start packing your most necessary belongings right away! A large part of our equipment and documents will be hidden underground, right here. Take care of your horses and their needs. We are leaving at six o'clock in the morning. We will be accompanied by most of the partisan groups in the area!"

"Do we take our most ferocious enemy with us, the mosquitoes?" Nikolay asked smiling broadly. Everybody broke out in laughter and Nikolsky shook his finger at Nikolay, smiling. The partisans went to work immediately. Pasha and two other men started digging a hole in the forest where all the excess equipment and documents were to be stored and another group got busy loading the three wagons in the camp with the weapons, ammunition, food and medical supplies. Still other partisans were sent out with official orders to the additional partisan groups in the immediate area.

Kuba went to his earth hut, and started packing his few belongings and cleaning his weapons and the others were engaged in similar activities. Commanders of other partisan groups arrived and congregated in Nikolsky's hut and after about a half-hour, the Colonel emerged from his hut, accompanied by the guests. Several glass containers of homemade vodka were lined up on the grass before him and he called on all his troops to join him in a toast for victory. Everyone got a cup or any type of vessel and filled it with the vodka. Nikolay, the Cossack, got his accordion and started playing, some partisans went inside the circle which had been formed by the rest of the group and began to dance to the music, Cossack style, squatting on their haunches and kicking out their heels in a real "Kozatchka" dance. This went on until well past midnight when finally, the commanders of the other partisan groups left and the Eagles went to sleep, after posting the proper security guards.

Kuba could not fall asleep for a long time. This was a turning point in his life. Was it true? Was the war coming to an end? What would he find in Warsaw? What about the Treblinka concentration camp which served only one purpose— to liquidate the Jewish population of Warsaw? Sanya wakened him roughly. Everyone was dressed and waiting for the commander's order to march. Kuba got up, splashed his face with cold water and went to find his horse, "Blatnoy," who was already saddled.

"Thank you, Otto!" Kuba said silently. Pasha came over and handed him a piece of salt pork and bread. Kuba mounted his horse while chewing on the food.

Sanya rode over to him and said, "Kuba, take your scout squad and ride out ahead of us. We shall follow in twenty minutes." They started on their way west, more than ninety partisans stretched out along the narrow forest trail, following Kuba's advance group. On the way, the Eagles were joined by other partisan groups who had received similar orders and were now under the command of Colonel Nikolsky. They had a variety of weapons amongst them, including several four-inch cannons.

The entire partisan army traveled from village to village and chutor to chutor with no sign of German troops. However, behind them, they could hear the rumble and thunder of the approaching Soviet troops, which were only about ten miles behind them on the main highway.

After two days of travel, the partisans reached the Bobrovich Lake. It was a warm afternoon and Colonel Nikolsky decided to spend the evening and night at the shore of this beautiful lake. Guards were posted, the kitchen detail started a fire, and the preparation of dinner for the group began. Most of the partisans undressed and jumped into the lake. Even the few women joined them in the water. The partisans swam, splashed and chased each other, especially the almost nude girls. The war that was raging around them was temporarily forgotten. This continued for about an hour.

Suddenly Pasha yelled out, "Look! There is someone coming down the road!" Everybody ran for their clothing and weapons. A stranger was approaching them in the company of two partisan guards. Kuba was standing next to Sanya and Nikolsky, listening to the latest radio communique: the Soviet Army had just captured the towns of Sinyavka and Budi, with its railroad depot, the towns in the immediate area of the Eagles camp near the Wygon Lake.

Meanwhile, Pasha and Nikolay brought the stranger into the camp and before Colonel Nikolsky and Sanya. He was a tall man, blue eyes, blonde hair and wearing a dirty German uniform with strange insignias on the collar, looking like the Russian letters "ROA." When the man spotted the partisan camp, he had started running into the forest and Sanya fired a shot to help bring him into the camp. Now, he stood before Nikolsky frightened. His hands were behind his head and on his neck, German style of surrender.

Nikolsky asked, "Who are you?"

"I am Russian," replied the man.

"Why did you run?" asked the commander.

"I thought that you might be German troops," said the prisoner.

"Do you carry a weapon?" asked Nikolsky. The man did not reply immediately. Nikolay searched him and produced a German made pistol.

"So, you are a 'Vlasovyets,'" yelled Nikolsky. Nikolsky looked at the man and his uniform. He did not look German. He had high cheekbones, narrow blue eyes and blonde hair, and looked like a Ukrainian from the Kuban area.

The commander finally said, "So, you joined the traitor General Vlasov to fight against your Motherland?"

The prisoner tried to deny the charge but soon broke down and admitted that he had served as a guard at the Maydanek concentration camp, where thousands of Jews and other nationalities were put to death daily by the German "Sonderdiest" (SD). Nikolsky walked up to the man and slapped him across the face. Then he asked in a halting voice, "Did you participate in the killing of our people, Jews, women and children?"

The man turned very pale and started to cry. "The Germans forced us to do it. They killed many of us who did not obey," he sobbed, looking desperately at the partisans.

"And how did it feel to kill children?" Nikolsky yelled at him. "Did you get a kick out of it?" he asked in disgust. The prisoner did not reply. He looked down at his boots, trembling all over.

In a sudden decision Nikolsky said, "Sanya and Nikolay, take him and get rid of him!" The two partisans grabbed the stranger and went into the forest. Soon there was the report of two pistol shots. Sanya and Nikolay returned without him.

Kuba was hardly disturbed by that incident. However, he could not help thinking, "How many more people do we have to kill without a real trial before that thing is over?"

At four o'clock the next morning, Nikolsky ordered the Eagles to break camp and continue the journey west. By noon they had reached the territory which was under the control of a powerful, mixed Polish-Russian partisan division under the command of General Sikorski—not related to the famous London-based general and statesman. More and more partisan groups joined the Eagles. The majority were Jewish groups. Although poorly armed, the Jewish partisans were among the fiercest fighters against the Nazis. The Jewish fighters, Kuba amongst them, behaved like suicide squads. They had nothing to lose and they did not have the alternative of becoming POW's, as did the Christian partisans. In addition to their fight for survival, these Jewish partisans were on a mission of revenge for the slaughter of some six million Jews. But the Jewish partisans were always in double jeopardy. The Germans were not their only enemies. They were forced to defend themselves against the anti-Semitic partisans of Ukrainian, Polish and Russian origin, who took advantage of the turmoil of war to kill Jews on sight. This is how the most tragic chapter in the history of the East European people's fight against the German invasion occurred. Amongst these groups, Kuba met some old friends from the underground days in Baranovichi: Chaim Stolovitski, Itzhak Medresh, Moniek Dubkovski, Lazar Segal and others, little realizing that one day they would become high-ranking officers in the Israeli Army. Very few of his fellow partisans knew that Kuba was Jewish because of his rank of captain and his flawless Russian accent. Encounters with anti-Semitic partisans were always resolved by gunfire. These episodes left Kuba with a sick feeling, shattering his spirit. He could not help but worry about the kind of life there would be for him after the war.

After four days of hard riding, the Eagles reached the forest near the city of Kosovo Poleski, where they had to cross the Brest-Moscow railroad. Here, they hit a snag. The entire area along the railroad tracks was occupied by thousands of retreating Germans and Hungarian troops and there was no chance of approaching and crossing the railroad tracks. Having no alternative, they set up camp in the forest near the headquarters of General Sikorski. The general invited the Colonel, Sanya, Grisha, chief of staff and Kuba to share quarters with him. Kuba was happy with that arrangement because some more of his old friends from the early days in Baranovichi and Lida were there.

The radio communique that evening reported the capture of the cities of Baranovichi and Slonim by troops and the offensive was continuing towards the fortress city of Brest-Litovsk and Bialystock across the River Bug. The partisans were elated with the news. However, Colonel Nikolsky was worried about the news. He put on a gloomy face and said, "I am afraid that we will never make it across the Bug River before the Red Army gets there!" Everyone broke out in laughter, but the Colonel was quite serious.

Early the next morning, there was a general alarm. The Eagles lined up with their weapons ready. The Colonel had just received a courier from General Sikorski's quarters. It turned out that the German troops had begun an attack on the partisan positions. Sikorski, who ran his operation in a military fashion, set up mine fields and built concrete bunkers around the perimeter of his camp and several of these bunkers had been attacked by German artillery and machine gun squads during the night. The situation was getting serious since there was only a total of some four thousand partisans in the area, facing a combined army of German and Hungarian troops of more than forty thousand who were equipped with tanks and artillery. The partisans had four four-inch cannons that they stole from the Germans in addition to a few antitank guns. Colonel Nikolsky, Commissar Grisha and Chief of Staff Volodiya were summoned to a meeting with the general.

After dinner, the partisans received an order to prepare for an all out fight with the Germans. It was no longer guerrilla warfare. The partisans now had to dig trenches and get ready for direct, front-line combat. The scouting parties reported that the Germans were massing troops around the perimeter of the partisan holdings. The situation was serious, but the day passed quietly. In the evening they received reports that the entire camp was surrounded by German troops. All partisans were very uneasy; the thought of dying a few days before liberation was very distressing. The night passed without event. However, no one slept. Black clouds were gathering over the partisans' heads.

Chapter Twenty-Seven

At dawn, the Germans began bombarding the partisan area with heavy artillery and mortar fire. The entire partisan army immediately took up their defense positions in the prepared trenches and bunkers. The enemy, thus far, was not visible and the partisans did not use their weapons as the German shells exploded at some distance from the partisan positions. It became apparent, however, that the Germans had begun a systematic bombardment of the area, their fire moving slowly from left to right with artillery and mortar shells exploding near the entrenched partisans. Two of the bunkers were hit.

In his trench, Kuba pressed his forehead against the dirt wall. The earth was shaking and heaving from the impact of the exploding shells. Pasha was sitting next to him, trying hard to roll out a cigarette, finally succeeding and handed the tobacco pouch to Kuba. They lit up their cigarettes for there was nothing to do but wait out the bombardment.

Pasha moved closer to Kuba and yelled into his ear, "If this keeps up, we will never make it! If only the Red Army would hurry up and get here!" Suddenly there was a tremendous explosion behind their trench, catching both Kuba and Pasha in a cloud of dirt and dust and throwing them against the bottom of the trench. The frequency of exploding shells increased in their immediate area killing several partisans by shrapnel. There was very little the partisans could do to help their wounded comrades. This lasted until two o'clock in the afternoon and when the bombardment quieted down, Nikolay jumped into Kuba's trench, holding a chunk of semi-cooked meat wrapped in a rag.

"Here, have some food," he said, cutting off pieces with his knife. Then it was very quiet. Pasha crawled out of the trench and ran off somewhere. The partisans peeked out of their trenches wondering what was going on.

Pasha returned after a while, carrying two German helmets. He gave one to Kuba. "Here, put it on. They will attack soon!" he said excitedly. Kuba looked around him. The result of the bombardment was everywhere: uprooted and broken trees, smashed wagons, dead horses and men. They were near the edge of a small meadow and on the other side, about two-hundred yards away, was another stretch of forest. That was where the Germans were. Suddenly, Sanya yelled very loud, "Attention!" Kuba looked through his binoculars across the meadow and saw many enemy troops running from the opposite forest towards them. They were running for several yards, dropping to the ground and then running again. Nikolsky was standing in the open, near a tree, observing the enemy through his binoculars. The Germans were approaching along the entire width of the small meadow.

"Get ready! " Nikolsky yelled an order. Several minutes passed. The Germans were firing occasional shots at the partisan positions while approaching slowly. When the enemy soldiers were about two-hundred feet away, Nikolsky gave the order, "Fire!" The partisans began to fire. Some were armed with grenade launchers. The grenades exploded amongst the approaching Germans. Others sprayed the meadow with machine and hand gun fire. This deafening burst of fire power lasted only a few minutes, but, to Kuba, it seemed like an eternity.

The Germans stopped their advance and began to retreat, having no cover from the partisan fire. Many dead and wounded Germans remained on the meadow as the other Germans retreated into their side of the forest.

It was quiet again. Pasha rolled out two cigarettes and gave one to Kuba. Both of them were very thirsty and hungry, but there was no water around.

After about twenty-five minutes, the Germans again attacked, in two waves from the right and left sides of the meadow, forcing the partisans to split up into two groups and shift their defense positions. This attack lasted much longer and there were many more enemy soldiers, many in Hungarian uniforms. When the enemy was finally forced to retreat, Kuba was out of ammunition.

He made his way back to the nearest supply wagon, which was located deeper in the forest and where a field hospital was to attend to the wounded partisans. In addition to a supply of ammunition for his submachine gun, Kuba also picked up several canteens of water, made his way back to his battle position and distributed the canteens amongst the nearest partisans, including Pasha.

That evening and night, the Germans made two more attempts to overrun the partisan lines and this situation continued for the next two days. The condition of the partisans was rapidly deteriorating. Ammunition was running low and they were practically without food. They had plenty of water which they had obtained from the huge swamp behind their stretch of forest.

On the third day, in the morning, the Germans attacked again, this time sending out three tanks against the partisans. The tanks crossed the center of the meadow and broke through the partisan lines, spraying the forest with machine gun and cannon fire. The front line of the partisans, which included the Eagles group, retreated in two opposing directions, leaving an open path for the advancing tanks. The tanks moved side by side in a straight line across the forest, advancing at a rapid pace, leaving a wide path of destruction behind them.

Then something funny happened. The tanks did not stop at the other end of the forest but continued into the swamp. After traveling several yards over the swamp, the tanks quite rapidly began to sink. The tank crews opened their hatches and crawled out on top of the tanks in a desperate attempt on their part to save themselves. The Sikorski partisans opened fire on them, and the whole incident was over in a matter of minutes.

Meanwhile, at the front positions occupied by the Eagles, something new happened. A not too distant rumble of artillery fire started and all of a sudden shells began to explode in the forest occupied by the German Army. No shots were being fired at the partisans any longer. Kuba stood up and observed the German positions through his binoculars. The artillery fire against the enemy was very dense and cannon shots fired by the Germans were being directed toward the east, away from the partisans. The cannonade lasted for over an hour. All of the sudden, hundreds of enemy troops spilled out into the meadow, running in a westerly direction. The partisans opened fire at them, but the Germans were retreating very fast. By now, the explosions of artillery shells could be heard all around the partisan encampment. Finally, it became very quiet and there was no movement in the German camp. The partisans left their trenches and gathered in groups discussing the new development. They were dirty, unshaven and very hungry.

Nikolsky joined Kuba's group, wearing a German helmet, and said, "Kuba, Pasha and Nikolay, get your equipment and go find out what happened on the other side. Pick up a few more partisans from the other groups."

"Yes, Comrade Commander!" Kuba replied.

Despite his external calm, Kuba was really excited. Now he would have the first chance to see the real destruction of the hated Nazis. That was part of the revenge that he promised his martyred parents, sister and his own family.

After a few minutes, Kuba's group consisted of twelve partisans. They circled the meadow and entered the forest on the other side, and there saw the evidence of the aftermath of a real battlefield. Hundreds of dead bodies of German and Hungarian troops were scattered everywhere. Weapons boxes with ammunition were lying around, and even several artillery pieces with stacks of cartridges were left behind.

They crossed the forest and came out on an open field. A wide, well-used road crossed the field from east to the west. On the other side of the road, the partisans could see a small lake and another forest and to the right, railroad tracks shimmered in the sunlight. Kuba looked to the east and spotted a cloud of dust rising from the road and heard the rumbling noise of many vehicles moving westward. The partisans dropped to the ground in order to prevent detection. Kuba remained standing behind a tree and observed the approaching vehicles.

"It is a column of tanks, trucks, personnel carriers and more!" Kuba said, feeling a slight tremor in his voice. "Now we are in real trouble!"

The convoy left the road and headed straight for the spot where the partisans were. Kuba dropped to one knee and continued looking at the leading tank. As the dust cloud settled after the column left the dirt road, Kuba, using his binoculars, spotted a large, red star painted on the side of the first tank.

He jumped up and started yelling at the top of his voice, "Those are ours. He jumped out of the tree cover and waved his arm in the air while holding his gun and his squad followed the procedure. The leading tank stopped abruptly and the rest of the column came to a clanking stop. Hatches opened up and Russian soldiers came out of the vehicles, smiling broadly.

"You are partisans?" one of them asked.

"Yes, we are," said Kuba. "We are the reconnaissance group of the Eagles squadron."

"Oh, the Eagles!" said the lieutenant, jumping off the tank. "We heard about you way back in Kursk. I wished all my military life to serve in a group like yours. What is your name and rank?" he asked.

"I am Captain Kuba, in charge of this reconnaissance group."

The lieutenant embraced Kuba and kissed him on both cheeks, took off his Red Guard Medal and pinned it to Kuba's shirt, and said, "You deserve this more than I do, Captain!"

"Let's go back to our division camp," said Kuba. The whole column turned into the forest, crossed the little meadow and entered the Eagles encampment and the Red Army set up camp in the partisan held forest. That was a night to remember. The Russian soldiers brought up their field kitchen and everybody helped themselves to food and drinks. Several Red Army soldiers produced accordions, balalaikas and harmonicas. A number of nurses from the Red Army field hospital joined the merriment and there was dancing and singing all night long. The front line was then some twenty miles to the west of the Eagles camp.

That night the Eagles received orders to proceed west along with the Soviet Army and make an attempt to cross the front line and get behind the enemy lines. At four o'clock the next morning, Nikolsky ordered the Eagles to begin their journey west toward the Bug River, traveling along open roads and highways. Kuba found it very awkward to travel openly on roads which only a few days ago were occupied by enemy troops. They traveled at a brisk pace, hoping to cross the Bug River ahead of the Soviet Army, but, to no avail. Fast moving Soviet armored columns passed them, waved at them and occasionally threw food rations to them, including beer and vodka containers. The Eagles were constantly in the company of Soviet troops.

The next two days were uneventful. On a few occasions lonely German planes appeared, dropped a few bombs, made some strafing passes over the moving Soviet Army and partisans, but caused little damage. The Eagles reached the vicinity of the city of Volkovysk, left the road and entered the forest. Colonel Nikolsky decided to head southwest, using forest trails and to try to reach the Bug River north of the city of Brest, the only chance they had to get behind the enemy lines again. They were now well equipped with weapons, ammunition and food. The Soviet Army even provided them a horse drawn field kitchen.

On the second day, the Eagles found evidence of the retreating Germans. They came upon scattered German equipment and ammunition containers in a meadow and that evening, Kuba and Nikolay who were riding ahead of the group, spotted German soldiers. They returned to their group and reported their observation to Nikolsky, who then ordered the group to spread out and advance on the Germans. The partisans caught up with the Germans when the latter were crossing a clearing in the forest along a dirt road. They were Waffen-SS troops, about two dozen, traveling on foot, probably following a larger German regular army unit, in order to prevent the Wehrmacht soldiers from attempts of surrender to the Russians.

At a signal from Nikolsky, the partisans began firing at the Germans. The Nazis dropped to the ground and returned fire. A fierce fight ensued as the SS men threw hand grenades at the partisans. Kuba was in a forward position, crouched behind a tree. Suddenly, a hand grenade landed several feet in front of him. He dropped to the ground as the grenade exploded and a small piece of shrapnel hit him in the upper lip next to the left side of his nose. It felt like a blow from a fist and Kuba was startled for a minute, but resumed firing at the enemy. It was all over in a matter of minutes. All the Nazis were dead. The partisans suffered two dead and five lightly wounded. Kuba had only a small cut near the nose and after Nikolay applied some medication, the bleeding stopped.

The Eagles traveled through the forest during the following two days without meeting anyone.

Colonel Nikolsky said, smiling, "It might be that we are behind enemy lines again!" At sunrise of the third day, the forest came to an abrupt end. The partisans came out into a very large field with a large river crossing it. The Bug River, flowing from south to north and then east where it deposited its waters into the mighty Vistula, is the largest river of Poland. The Vistula continued on to the Baltic Sea.

The partisans stretched out along the edge of the forest, taking in the beauty of the lush, green fields and the blue waters of the river before them. To their right, the forest stretched closer to the river, partially hidden from the partisans' view, and from that direction came a muffled sound of voices and hammering. Kuba, Nikolay and Pasha rode off in that direction to investigate. They rounded the bend and stopped short as they saw a great number of vehicles and soldiers. Kuba observed the activities through his binoculars. After a while, he started laughing and said, "That's the Red Army. They built a pontoon bridge and are now crossing the Bug!"

Kuba adjusted the binoculars and began looking at the opposite shore of the river. A whole army was over there with tanks, artillery and equipment. The three partisans returned to their group and Kuba reported their observations to the Colonel, who then went into conference with the commissar and the chief of staff. Sanya set up his radio equipment and made contact with the Moscow headquarters. One hour later, the Eagles entered the camp of the Soviet Army and Nikolsky reported to the commanding officer, Major General Popov, informing him that the instructions received from Moscow were for the Eagles to remain with the Soviet troops until further notice. Kuba learned that these troops were part of Marshal Rokossovsky's army, who, according to the latest news, had advance units of that army liberating the city of Bialystok deep in Poland at this moment. The only German pocket left near the Bug was in the fortress of Brest. While the partisans were traveling through the forest trails, the Soviet troops had advanced some eighty miles into Poland.

The shrapnel wound on Kuba's face became infected and slightly swollen. Nikolsky told him to go to the field hospital which was set up near the river in a huge, green army tent. Inside the tent there were four rows of cots and at the far end was a partitioned area that was the operating room. The hospital had several doctors and about two dozen nurses, but only a few patients, because most of the wounded had been shipped back to hospitals in the liberated cities. A doctor looked at Kuba's wound and ordered a nurse to prepare a cot for him. He noticed that the sheets and blankets had American inscriptions on them. The doctor injected some Novacaine into Kuba's lip and then proceeded to clean out the infected wound and after applying a dressing with adhesive tape, the doctor gave Kuba an injection of penicillin explaining, "This is the latest and fastest infection fighter we have and which we received from America. You will spend the night here and tomorrow you will be like new."

The nurse, Tatyana, who was assigned to Kuba, was Eurasian. She was of medium height, black hair and eyes and very attractive. She wore a white nurse's uniform which fit her like a glove, emphasizing her perfect body and rather large breasts straining against the cloth of the uniform.

Kuba could not take his eyes off her. He had not been that close to a woman in a long time. She sat on the right side of the cot, checking Kuba's pulse, her hands cool and gentle.

She looked at Kuba, smiled and said, "So how is it to be a partisan? You are the most admired soldiers in our land, you know?"

Kuba smiled back at her, his upper lip still numb from the Novacaine. He held her hand and said, "It is different than on the front line. It's much more dangerous, always surrounded by the enemy."

"Did you have many casualties during your actions?" she asked.

"We had casualties but nothing like those on the front. You see, the enemy never knew how many of us there were or where we were. One partisan equaled ten enemy soldiers because he could see them, whereas the enemy could not see him and we always attacked the enemy from the cover of the forest, mostly at night. The Nazis panicked when we opened fire on them, because they could not see us. This was our greatest weapon—a surprise attack."

"You are the real heroes of this war," she said and suddenly leaned over and kissed Kuba on the lips. Kuba could feel her breasts pressing against his chest and, surprised by her action, he embraced her and held her in this way for several minutes.

After a while she pulled away from him and said, "Now I have to bring you some food and fresh underwear; yours need cleaning. I'll be right back!"

It was getting dark outside and the tent even darker on the inside. An officer and a nurse entered the tent. The officer's left forearm was in a cast, but he held a bottle of vodka under it and his right arm was around the nurse's waist. They went to the far side of the tent and sat down on a cot. They sipped vodka, talked and giggled. The officer then unbuttoned the nurse's blouse and began playing with her breasts. The giggling soon stopped.

Tatyana returned carrying a tray loaded with food. She set the tray down on the ground next to Kuba's cot and then sat next to him. She listened to the noise coming from the cot occupied by the officer and the nurse, then quietly giggled.

She reached into a pocket of her uniform and produced a bottle of vodka, poured some into two cups from the tray, handed one to Kuba and said, "To victory!"

They drank and looked at each other in the semi-darkness. Tatyana touched Kuba's face and said, "In the morning I will shave your face. You look like a Tartar and your mustache tickles." She gave a short laugh and then asked, "What is your rank?"

"Oh, I was promoted to captain recently, but we do not wear uniforms so nobody knows for sure," Kuba replied, laughing.

They ate some sausages and baked potatoes, the best food Kuba had eaten in a long time. Afterwards, Tatyana poured some more vodka and Kuba put his arms around her, when all of the sudden, she jumped off the cot and said, "I forgot something!" She ran out of the tent and returned within several minutes. By that time, it was completely dark.

She sat on his cot and said softly, "Here, let's change your clothes!" She began to pull off Kuba's shirt and pants. "You know, we don't have too much action here now. All seriously wounded are being transported from the front directly to hospitals in the rear. I am off duty tonight. I better sponge you down," she said, as she began to clean Kuba with a soft, wet cloth.

As Tatyana cleansed Kuba with her gentle hands, he reached up and began to unbutton her blouse. She leaned toward him. Still giggling quietly she worked her way down his body, until she touched his erect penis. Kuba pulled her down on top of him, reached under her dress and started to pull down her panties. Tatyana spread her legs and took him inside her with an animal cry escaping her lips. All that time, they had been exploring their bodies with their hands. They twisted and turned until Tatyana was beneath him, resting on her back. Finally, Kuba could not hold back any longer and he ejaculated with a force and passion that made his spine tingle with pain. Tatyana was moaning into his ear, repeating over and over again in Russian, "Give! Give!"

Finally they fell asleep, completely spent. Kuba's face was buried in Tatyana's hair, which smelled of jasmine, his hands holding her firm breasts. Two people from opposite sides of the world joined together in the most natural embrace known to mankind since the beginning of time.

Part IV:
After the War

Chapter Twenty-Eight

The partisans waited in the army camp for four days to receive orders from Moscow. During that time, they helped the regular army with various tasks. An ammunition dump was built and an airstrip was laid out on the field along the river. Sanya was in daily radio contact with Moscow headquarters and, on the fourth day, Nikolsky called together the Eagle partisans and read a short radiogram to them: "A special plan has been dispatched to your camp. The plane will deliver to you supplies and special orders. It should land at your camp at six o'clock this evening."

There was a lot of excitement in the camp after that announcement. Red flags were set up at both ends of the landing strip and everybody was out on the field waiting for the sound of the approaching plane. Army officers, using binoculars, scanned the sky. Kuba was standing a few feet behind Colonel Nikolsky and was looking to the east through his binoculars, when someone put an arm on his shoulder. Kuba turned and faced Tatyana. She smiled at him and asked, "What does this mean?"

"We will know soon, but, I have a hunch that we will be leaving your camp," Kuba answered.

"Don't forget, Kuba, after dinner I have to change the dressing on your wound," she said, smiling at him. Kuba started to say something, but at that moment, the sound of an approaching aircraft could be heard. The plane appeared, flying low over the forest and headed straight for the landing strip. It was a twin engine plane, painted a khaki color with red stars on the fuselage and tail. It circled the field and came in for a landing from the far end of the strip, taxied down the strip and stopped almost in front of the people. The engines were stopped and a door opened downwards, forming a staircase, and several officers descended from the plane. The first one was a major-general. Nikolsky and General Popov greeted the guests and after a short conversation with the new general, all three departed for General Popov's quarters.

Meanwhile, the aircraft crew, helped by some partisans and soldiers, unloaded several crates from the plane, loaded them on a truck and took them into the camp. Half an hour later, all partisans were assembled in front of the crates, facing Nikolsky and the two generals. Nikolsky introduced the newcomer as Major-General Mironov. The crates were opened and inside were brand-new Soviet Army uniforms. General Mironov smiled at the partisans and said, "By now, you must be tired of your old partisan clothing, so I brought you a present— a new uniform for each one of you, according to your respective rank. Pick them up, put them on and return here in twenty minutes."

The uniforms, including new boots, were packed in sets. Each package had a paper band around it and the name of a partisan on it. Kuba picked up his package and went into a nearby tent, put on the new uniform and boots and looked at his shoulder bars with the three little stars forming a triangle, the insignia of a captain. The cap had the same insignia. He left the tent and returned to the assembly area.

The partisans stood shoulder to shoulder, in four lines about five feet between the lines, facing the two generals and Colonel Nikolsky in his new uniform. General Mironov held a sheet of paper in his hand and stood up on one of the crates, which was turned upside-down. Several hundred Soviet troops were lined up along both sides of the partisans. It was very quiet. Mironov looked at the uniformed partisans with obvious satisfaction and began to read: "As of today, 30 August 1944, the Special Group No. 258, also known as Orlovksy Eagles, completed its mission behind German lines. The group is therefore ordered to return to Moscow for reassignment. Tomorrow morning, you will begin your journey east on horseback. In Baranovichi, you will board a train for Moscow. You will take with you all your weapons. The horses will be distributed among the peasants and farmers who cooperated with you during your activities in the area. In the name of the Supreme Command of our armed forces and the Supreme Soviet of our country, I salute you!"

The soldiers and officers began applauding spontaneously, the partisans remained at attention. Three officers, carrying rectangular metal boxes, took their places next to General Mironov. When it had quieted down, Mironov continued, "Several of you have been awarded medals and orders. As I call your names, you will please step forward and line up in front of me." Mironov called out twelve names, Kuba amongst them. The partisans stepped forward and lined up in front of the general, standing according to their rank. Nikolsky was the first one on the left and Kuba was sixth in line standing next to Sanya who was also a captain. Mironov walked over to Nikolsky and the three officers carrying the boxes with open lids were following close behind him.

Nikolsky was decorated with the Order of the Fatherland War, or Patriotic War, the Order of the Red Star and a silver Partisan Medal. Mironov proceeded from one man to the next, pinning the various decorations on them. Kuba was decorated with the Order of the Fatherland War, Second Class, the Order of the Red Star and silver Partisan Medal. It was eight o'clock in the evening by the time the ceremony ended. Everybody went to the kitchen area and lined up for dinner. They had a special treat that night, thick pork chops, potatoes, bread and a glass of vodka. Everyone congratulated the decorated partisans and there were many speeches and toasts.

After dinner, several soldiers produced musical instruments, some soldiers and partisans formed a large circle and the traditional Russian singing and dancing began. The festivities continued until after midnight.

Kuba went to the field hospital where Tatyana was waiting for him. She kissed him lightly and then changed the dressing on his wound. Afterwards, she took his hand and led him to her tent.

The tent was empty and everyone was in the camp celebrating. They quickly undressed and made love for a long time. After they had dressed again, Tatyana took Kuba's face in her hands, kissed him hard on the lips and said, "I wonder if we will ever meet again?"

The next morning, the partisans had breakfast with their army hosts. The wagons were already loaded with their equipment and food. The horses were fed and ready for the journey. The plane and General Mironov were gone, having left early in the morning. At about eight o'clock in the morning, the partisans sat on their horses, lined up two abreast, and again there were speeches by General Popov and Colonel Nikolsky. Many soldiers and officers came over to the partisans for last farewells. Tatyana came over to Kuba and handed him a small package, looked at him with her olive-shaped eyes, and said, quietly, "I shall remember you for a long time!"

And then they were off, riding east along the highway in the direction of Baranovichi. Kuba opened Tatyana's package and found three packs of the finest brand of Russian cigarettes known as "Kazbek," and a bottle of vodka. There was a note scribbled on a piece of brown paper, containing two Russian words: "I love you!" Kuba put these in his saddlebag and Nikolay, who was riding next to him in the uniform of a first lieutenant, gave him a knowing look and said, "You found yourself a nice girl!" Kuba only smiled at him. They rode at a brisk pace for several hours and the column passed through the city of Volkovysk and continued towards Hantsevich, where they set up camp for the night outside the village.

Nikolsky ordered Kuba and Otto to ride out to a certain chutor to find their old friend Ivan Bobko from the village of Mashuki. There were many peasants and farmers gathered at the chutor so one of their boys went to fetch Ivan Bobko, returning in about a half an hour drunk and happy.

Kuba took Bobko aside and gave him the message. "First thing tomorrow morning, you will get together about two dozen of our friends and collaborators from the Wygon Lake area and meet us at the railroad station in Baranovichi!" Kuba and Otto spent a couple of hours at the chutor and then returned to their unit near Hantsevich.

On the way back, Otto said to Kuba, "Well, my dear friend and comrade in arms, this is probably our last mission together. Soon our trails will part. The war is almost over."

"What do you think will happen?" asked Kuba, looking at Otto in his new captain's uniform.

"After we return to Moscow and go through a lot of official ceremonies and parades, I will most likely be sent to Germany on some assignment. You might be assigned to some desk job, or to a mop-up unit. It is certain that hundreds and maybe thousands of Nazis are still hiding out in the forests and swamps, especially SS and SD troops," said Otto. They rode in silence for a while, Kuba with mixed emotions about riding along an open road, looking around for signs of ambush or Nazi troops. They crossed the railroad tracks at the station Budi, the place where they had so often attacked German forces. Kuba remembered how one night, some months ago, he had planted a mine on the tracks near Budi and while waiting for the explosion, he had heard the train whistle and wondered if he would ever have a chance in life to buy a ticket and board a train, the way it was before the war.

They neared Hantsevich when suddenly Kuba said, "Otto, it is obvious that within a few months the American and Soviet troops will be in Berlin. What do you think will happen to Hitler and his henchmen?"

"Oh, they will not surrender. They will most likely blow themselves up in the chancellery bunker," Otto answered. They entered the Eagles encampment near the village and reported to the Colonel. He accepted their report and told them to get some sleep, but Kuba could not fall asleep for a long time, thinking about the past events, his encounter with Tatyana and the unknown future.

The next day, the partisans arrived in the city of Baranovichi. About sixty percent of the city was demolished and construction of the railroad depot had already begun. The burned-out hulks of German and Soviet tanks, artillery, vehicles and, occasionally, aircraft were scattered all over the city. The local citizens were back in their homes or in makeshift shelters. The entire city looked like a military camp, due to the large number of Soviet troops and equipment. They set up camp near the railroad tracks and secured a perimeter of about four hundred feet and, after the tents were set up Sanya contacted Moscow. There were new instructions: the local partisans, who had joined the Eagles during the war, were to be discharged. Each one was to receive a horse, clothing, two thousand rubles and a certificate saying that they had been members of this special partisan unit. The original Orlovksy group was ordered to return to Moscow.

In the evening, a special train with huge red flags on both sides of the locomotive and banners extolling the deeds of the partisans, pulled into the depot for the partisans. The train was to leave for Moscow the next morning. Meanwhile, the partisans loaded the train with all their weapons and equipment. Ivan Bobko and his group showed up, as arranged, and brought with them many bottles of homemade vodka, pork, fish and other food. The whole thing developed into a huge celebration, which involved the entire Soviet garrison and the local population. There was a lot of food and vodka and fights among the various individuals. The horses and wagons were distributed among them, as ordered by Moscow. Kuba, Otto and Sanya found some upper berths in Nikolsky's railroad car and put their equipment there. They cleaned themselves, shaved and went out to join the activities. At six o'clock in the morning, when the train pulled out, heading east from the Baranovichi station, Kuba and the other partisans, including the colonel, were snoring in their berths, unaware of the fact that the train was moving.

They passed many towns and cities on what was former Polish territory and then they were in Russia. The train traveled at top speed and in the morning they stopped in the capital of Belarus, Minsk. A military band was at the station, playing Soviet patriotic songs and there were more speeches. The train continued east toward Moscow.

On the third morning, the train pulled into the Belarusian Voksal station in Moscow. There, General Orlovsky and his daughter were waiting for them in addition to other dignitaries. General Orlovsky, their first commander and for whom the Orlovsky named their group was wearing an artificial left arm but embraced everyone of the partisans and kissed them, tears running down his cheeks as he repeated over and over: "We have won! Victory!

Many more partisans were arriving from different parts of the country and there was a line of trucks decorated with flowers and red flags waiting for them. The partisans got on their assigned trucks, according to the different partisan groups and the trucks began moving along Gorki Street toward the Red Square, when at a side street near the Kremlin, the trucks stopped. The partisans got off the trucks and lined up in columns, their weapons in their hands. From somewhere, a brass band appeared at the head of the column, struck up a Russian marching tune and the parade of the partisans began.

There was a huge red banner stretched high near the Lenin Mausoleum, proclaiming:

"Greetings to the partisans of the war for the Fatherland!"

Kuba was marching next to Sanya and when they approached the Mausoleum, there came a sharp command and the partisans saluted smartly, turning their heads to the right. There on the review stand, above the Mausoleum, were lined up the leaders of the Soviet Union, with Stalin in the center, flanked by Marshal Voroshilov and other members of the Politburo and military. The President of the Supreme Soviet, Mikhail Kalinin, was standing at Stalin's right with the rest of the Politburo members lined up beside him in accordance to their importance. Marshal Voroshilov was on the left side, followed by a number of marshals and generals. They were all saluting the partisans. General Orlovsky and Colonel Nikolsky led the column of partisans and, when they finally returned to their trucks, Orlovsky said, "Now, my Eagles, after you clean up and rest for a few hours, we shall all meet at my apartment for a special dinner."

The Eagles were installed at the Hotel Metropol. Kuba shared a room with Otto. There was only one bathroom on the floor and they had to wait their turn to use the facilities. After they showered and cleaned up their uniforms and boots, Kuba produced the bottle of vodka that Tatyana had given him and they both had a drink. They talked about the parade for a while and then fell asleep on their beds. A sharp knock on the door awakened them. It was past four o'clock in the afternoon. Kuba, in his underwear, answered the door. A young sergeant was standing there at attention. He saluted and then said, "Captain, Sergeant Gregory Peshkov reporting for duty. I have been assigned as your adjutant."

"What is going on?" Kuba asked, in surprise.

"I don't know, Comrade Captain. Something to do with your new assignment."

Kuba looked at Otto, who was getting out of his bed. He had a funny grin on his face. Kuba asked him what was so amusing and Otto replied, "What did I tell you? It's a desk job for you."

At that point, the sergeant interrupted, "Comrades, they are expecting you down in the lobby in fifteen minutes. Your vehicles are about to leave for General Orlovsky's quarters."

Hurriedly they dressed and went down to the lobby and there found the entire group. They boarded a special truck equipped with benches. Kuba looked at the streets and houses of Moscow during the half hour trip and did not see a single war damaged building. He knew that the German troops had come within eight miles of the city, but the only visible damage was in the outskirts, the University section. General Orlovsky occupied a three-bedroom apartment on the top floor of a six-story building in the Pushkino section of Moscow. He was a widower, and his daughter acted as hostess. Several tables were set up in the living room, loaded with ham, caviar and a host of Russian dishes. Several side boards were filled to capacity with bottles of vodka and Caucasian wines. It was quite a party. They were eating, drinking, singing partisan songs and recollecting particular events from their life in the forest behind enemy lines. The party lasted all night. Neighbors complained. At one time there were Soviet militia men, police, in the room. By then, everybody was quite drunk. Kuba remembered that one policeman was let out of the apartment with a very bloody nose. Pasha sported the beginning of a shiner on one eye and Risa Orlovsky, the general's daughter, a girl of about twenty-seven years, took care of Pasha's nose, in her room.

Two days later, at seven in the morning, Kuba was awakened by someone shaking him rather hard. He sat up groggy, feeling a heavy hangover and looked at Otto, all dressed and holding a wooden suitcase in his hand. Kuba stood up and looked at him with a question in his eyes.

"Oh, I got my orders. Back behind enemy lines in Germany," Otto explained.

The door opened and Sergeant Gregory came in with a steaming pot of tea. He poured two cups and handed them to Kuba and Otto, then left the room and returned in a few minutes with bread, butter and sliced herring. They sipped the tea and munched on the bread. Finally, Otto got up and said, "I am due at Pushkino Air Base at eight-thirty!" The two comrades embraced. No words were spoken, but each one knew what the other was thinking. Otto was the first to speak, "Well, my brother, don't forget our three years behind the enemy lines. You might still get a chance to write it all down, the good and the bad." When he said it, Otto nodded his head in Gregory's direction and suddenly Kuba understood the meaning of Otto's words. He glanced at Gregory, who was busy gathering the dishes, Otto saluted and left.

Kuba stood there for a while, thinking about the meaning of Otto's peculiar nod. Could it be that Gregory was an NKVD agent? The sergeant left the room carrying a tray with dishes. Kuba took a shower, shaved and got dressed, wondering what his next assignment would be. Gregory returned a few minutes later and handed Kuba a sealed envelope. Kuba ripped it open. It contained instructions from the Special Security Section of the Ministry of Defense. Kuba was to report to a Colonel Lavrentyev at the Ministry at ten o'clock in the morning.

In the lobby, Kuba met Pasha and Toliya, both in regular army uniforms and both leaving for the front. They came over to Kuba and told him that the rest of the group had already left for their new assignment. Sanya, for some reason, was led away by two NKVD men. They could not find out what was wrong and Pasha told Kuba, "Do not try to find out! Everyone is on his own!"

Kuba went to his appointment, without making any inquiries, and arrived at the Ministry at the appointed time. He was led into Colonel Lavrentyev's office. He was a tall man, about six feet, two inches, from Novosibirsk and was an officer of the KGB, Commissariat of State Security. He motioned Kuba to a chair and continued looking through some papers and making notes here and there. Finally, he looked straight at Kuba. He had brown, penetrating eyes and Kuba felt uneasy. Surprisingly, his voice was very soft. "Captain, you are temporarily assigned to this section. You will be installed in an office on the second floor. Your adjutant has received his instructions, and he will occupy your outer office. Your first job is to write evaluations of every original member of the Special Group No.258 – Orlovsky, the Eagles. You must write down everything that you can remember about them: their behavior, conversations, habits, sex life and everything else that you can think of. You will find all the necessary material in your desk. If you have any questions, you may call me on the phone. Is everything clear?"

"Yes, Comrade Colonel!" Kuba said.

"Good! Your adjutant will show you to your office. That is all."

Gregory, the adjutant, was waiting for him in the corridor. They descended to the second floor and entered Kuba's new office which consisted of two rooms. The first room was about nine by ten feet, with a small, wooden desk, a telephone, some filing cabinets and three chairs. This was Gregory's office. A door on the opposite wall led into Kuba's office which was considerably larger. It contained large, wooden desk with a conference table set up against it, forming the letter "T" and several wooden chairs around the table and three filing cabinets against a wall in one corner. A window faced the street. The desk was equipped with a telephone and a buzzer button to summon Gregory, an inkwell and several pencils. The walls were decorated with portraits of the Soviet leaders.

Kuba sat down in a chair behind the desk and looked through the desk drawers. He found a stack of preprinted forms with the names of each member of the Orlovsky group at the top and specific questions on the left side of each page. There were about eight pages in each questionnaire. He pulled out the first questionnaire and placed it on the desk. The name at the top was Colonel A. F. Nikolsky. He looked at it, thinking about the commander of his partisan group and remembered that there had been a lot of friction between Nikolsky and Sanya, his assistant. Sanya had been resentful of the fact that Nikolsky had a seventeen year old mistress, a Jewish girl from a different partisan group, a relationship that lasted several months during 1943. Also, there was the question of some missing documents which had disappeared from an underground hiding place in the forest. Kuba had a hunch that Sanya had taken the documents. Maybe that was the reason for his arrest by the NKVD.

Kuba reached into his pocket for a cigarette and did not find any. He pressed the buzzer on his desk and Gregory entered and stood at attention. "At ease!" Kuba said. "Do you think you can buy cigarettes someplace?"

"Yes, Comrade Captain. There is a commissary downstairs," he replied, and left the room. Kuba tried to figure out the reason for the questionnaires. Suddenly it came to him. Of course! It is a part of the Soviet system to keep track of its entire population from birth to death, a way a dictatorship controls its people. The war had interrupted that process and thousands of people were beyond Soviet control during the period of German occupation. Therefore, the purpose of these questionnaires was to fill the gap.

There was a knock on the door. A short, pudgy, first lieutenant with a huge, dark mustache entered. He carried a heavy briefcase, saluted and said, "I am First Lieutenant Maxim Svierdlov, paymaster for this section, and I bring you an envelope containing your military back pay since 1942, Captain. Also, here is your PRAVDA that you did not pick up this morning. You know the rules here. You are to pick up your paper on the way in"

Kuba ripped open the envelope and counted out twenty-seven hundred rubles, his military pay for three years of service behind enemy lines, about three hundred American dollars. Kuba signed the receipt for the money and Svierdlov picked up his briefcase and left. Kuba sat there and stared at his desk. That was the first money that he actually had handled in at least three years.

Gregory returned with a package wrapped in newspapers. He unwrapped the package and produced six packs of cigarettes and a bottle of vodka, a broad smile on his face. Kuba handed him a thirty ruble note, three chervontsy in Russian. The sergeant looked at him, smiled and said, "I did not pay for it. There was a general who took care of it, once I told them who it was for."

"What was the general's name?" asked Kuba.

"Oh, his name is Major-General Tatarin. He is in charge of the second section of National Security and is the father of a Lieutenant Tatyana Tatarin, a nurse somewhere on the Polish front. She has written to him about you."

Kuba was surprised. He wondered what Tatyana had written to her father about him, but he had no time to think about that now. He picked up a pen and began writing his report, starting with Nikolsky's questionnaire and suddenly it dawned upon him that at this moment many partisans, like himself, were probably doing the same thing; writing reports about their comrades.

October came and the weather was getting cold. Kuba received winter uniforms, still lived at the officer's quarters in the hotel, made a few friends, both male and female, and attended a few parties. His job was very dull and boring. During the first week of October, he received an invitation from General Tatarin to come to dinner at his apartment on the next Sunday.

Gregory came in with a new stack of papers for Kuba to work on, reports about people that Kuba had never heard of. There were usually two or three reports about the same person, written by different people and Kuba's job was to cross check those reports and write a new one on that basis. It was an endless task and Kuba was getting restless. He asked Gregory to sit down for a while and when he was seated, Kuba offered him a cigarette.

"Tell me, Sergeant, where do you live?" asked Kuba.

"At the non-com quarters in the Lenin section of the city." Gregory was of above average height, light brown hair, brown eyes which seemed to be always smiling as if to hide much more knowledge than he let on. He was very correct in his behavior and performance of duties. Kuba had a feeling that Gregory somehow managed to watch him constantly. He also noticed that whenever he had visitors or spoke on the phone, Gregory turned an ear in his direction and listened.

"How long have you lived in Moscow?" Kuba asked.

"About four months. I was wounded at the front near Kursk and after my release from the hospital, I was assigned to this section," Gregory replied.

"Did you make some friends here?" Kuba said.

"Oh, yes. And I have a girl. We get together in the evenings and have a good time," said Gregory.

Then Kuba asked the most important question, "How long do people work in this section and where do they go from here?"

"Officers work here about six months and are then sent to the liberated territories," Gregory answered.

Kuba thought about that for a while, dismissed the sergeant and started working on some papers. He was thinking that maybe he would have a chance to leave the Soviet Union and return home to Warsaw.

Chapter Twenty-Nine

Kuba found the Tatarin house and climbed up to the third floor. It was one of the better buildings in Moscow, had flowerpots on little tables on the landings, and was occupied entirely by high ranking officers. Kuba looked at his watch, four o'clock. The watch was Government Issue, made in Gorki and about the size of a small shoe paste box. The people called them "aviation watches" because you could show the time to a passing aircraft pilot. In Russia this was a daring joke.

Kuba knocked on the door. It was made of massive oak, unpainted and quite new. He waited a few minutes and knocked again. The door opened and there was Tatyana. She had on a pink dress and looked very small. Kuba could not believe his eyes! Now he knew why the general had invited him to dinner. They embraced and Tatyana kissed him hard on the lips, her tongue darting out from between her teeth.

"Oh my darling how I missed you," she said softly moving her hands up and down his back.

"I missed you too very much, my dear Tatyana," Kuba said after he recovered from this very pleasant surprise. His spine was tingling as he remembered their brief encounter near the Bug River. He looked into her eyes and his desire for her was overwhelming. Tatyana sensed his feelings, kissed him again and said, "Later, darling."

She took his hand and led him into a large room where there were about a dozen people, men and women. The men were all high-ranking officers and the women were wives of the officers. A tall man in a general's uniform came forward.

He was gray haired with high cheekbones and distinct Mongolian features. Tatyana presented him as her father. Kuba saluted, but the general came over and gave him a bear hug, then took Kuba to the side and started pouring a drink for him from the sideboard. The apartment was much larger and more elaborate than General Orlovsky's apartment. A small Russian woman with characteristic weather beaten features of the Siberian people on her face came into the room carrying a tray of food. She put the tray on a table and came over to Kuba and Tatyana.

She looked at Kuba for a few minutes and then said, "So, you are my daughter's young man. Welcome to our humble quarters."

Kuba was flabbergasted. He did not know that Tatyana had gone so far as that. Her mother kissed him on both cheeks and continued. "My husband has contacted our people in the Kazan region and a proper ceremony will take place prior to your marriage. Meanwhile, my husband told me that you are being transferred to the west. That is all right, because Tatyana is also returning there."

Kuba tried to say something, but he could only stand there with his mouth open. Tatyana gripped his hand and said, "They are always three steps ahead." Kuba could think only about one thing. He was being transferred to the west, closer to Poland. Then he remembered what Tatyana's mother had said about a wedding. He grabbed Tatyana's hand and took her aside. Then he turned her around to face him and asked her, "What is all that talk about a wedding?"

"Oh, forget about that! I told my father that when we made love, I said to you 'Uchla Hamm!' which means in my father's Central-Asian dialect, I hereby marry you!" said Tatyana, smiling.

Kuba did not say anything. However, he decided to be on guard from now on. He knew that his transfer to the west had been arranged by General Tatarin. The evening proceeded according to the general's plans. Everyone ate and drank to their limits. Tatyana insisted on taking Kuba to his quarters in the general's car and then spent most of the night with him. She left about five o'clock in the morning. Kuba poured himself a stiff drink and went to bed.

THE ODYSSEY OF A PARTISAN

When he arrived at his office in the morning, Gregory greeted him with a big smile, picked up a pile of papers and placed them on Kuba's desk. Among the papers, Kuba found his travel orders and an assignment to the coach building section of the Soviet railroad at the station of Baranovichi. Gregory came into his office with some fresh coffee and said, "Comrade Captain, I received my orders, too. I am going with you."

During the next two weeks, Kuba was with Tatyana almost every evening; they went to the opera, ballet and the Bolshoi Theater several times. They were particularly impressed by the opera "And Quiet Flows the Don" by Mikhail Sholochov. "The music and songs are magnificent!" Kuba said.

"Yes, and it takes you right into the story so that you become like a participant," Tatyana replied.

"Tell me more about the story. I read part of the book in Polish when I was about twelve and I don't quite remember."

"Well, the story is about a Cossack family and particularly two brothers in that family. They lived in a village on the shores of the mighty River Don. The events begin during the latter part of the last century. There is a lot of romance, as you can see, and animosity between the two brothers and the rest of the village. Then World War I came and the two brothers, both officers in the Czarist army, went to the front against Germany. They were real honest to God Russian soldiers!"

"But look, Tatyana, here they are joining the anti-Czar revolution," Kuba remarked.

"Oh, yes, and that is how they went home to their village, and then they joined the new Bolshevik system of life!"

"Oh yes, and then problems began with the new Proletarian Government, which the Cossacks did not understand."

"Kuba, they finally accepted the new life. Look at those happy Cossacks on the stage riding against the "White Ottomans." There were about forty Cossacks on horseback on the stage. Kuba marveled about the technique of a rotating stage, but he recalled something about the author of the book, Mikhail Sholochov.

"Tatyana, tell me honestly, didn't Comrade Stalin order the imprisonment of Sholochov for that book?"

Tatyana looked at him suspiciously for a while and then she said, "Yes, because the end of the story criticized the early Soviet regime very badly! But since then everything is straightened out. Sholochov was released from prison and everything is all right."

They toured all the museums and art exhibits in Moscow and at the end of October Tatyana came to Kuba's office with two passes to visit Leningrad. Kuba remembered his visit to that city in 1941 when the German forces had surrounded the huge city except for the Lake Ladoga approach. The two got to Leningrad by way of a military transport. Leningrad!!! The second city (after Rome) of a thousand years, only its name was Petersburg (the city of Peter the Great!).

Tatyana and Kuba walked through the streets observing the buildings. They went across the Nyevskiy Prospect and looked at the row of museums.

"Let's go to the Hermitage!" Tatyana said. The Hermitage was not touched seriously by the blockaded state of the city. All the treasures were still there. They looked at the images of Peter the Great, the founder of the city, and all the following czars, including Yekaterina the Great. "What do you think of our heritage?" Tatyana asked.

They walked through streets that were covered with rubble, dead bodies of men and animals and rats. Huge Norwegian rats!!! "Look at those animals. They are big enough to consume a human being!" Tatyana said.

"I was here in 1943 in fall. My dear, believe me, those animals were devouring human carcasses in broad daylight! I was sick weeks after that. You asked me about your heritage... I respect it and I love it. Don't forget that I am also Slavic, in spite of the fact that I am a Jew. I love your culture, music, art and everything else. I am glad that our cultural exhibits were not stolen by the Nazis or eaten by the rats. Now you know what I think. If you still like me, you have to live with my ideals!"

Kuba was really excited and his forehead was wet with perspiration. Tatyana held him in her arms tightly and said, "That is the way I love you, Kuba. You are your own human being!"

During the second week of November, Kuba and Gregory left Moscow for Baranovichi. Before he left, Kuba had a final meeting with Tatyana. She told him that she was leaving in three days for the city of Lida, about thirty miles from Baranovichi.

About sixty percent of the city of Baranovichi had been destroyed by aerial bombs and artillery fire. Hardest hit was the area around the railroad depot. All buildings were demolished. When the train pulled into the station, Kuba noticed that some reconstruction was already in progress and that offices were housed in converted box cars which were also the living quarters for the railroad personnel. The maintenance shops were in the open, however, some temporary roofing was being constructed to protect the equipment from rain and snow.

Kuba, followed by Gregory, who carried their meager belongings, went to find the chief of the depot, a Colonel Genady Petrov, and found him in one of the box car offices. Kuba reported to him and handed over his orders. Petrov was of above average height with black hair and a mustache. He read Kuba's orders and then looked at the young, bemedaled captain with a certain amount of respect.

"So you are the 'Orlovyets' Kuba?" Petrov said and they shook hands.

"Yes, Comrade Colonel. I spent a few years in this area," said Kuba.

Petrov looked at him for a long time, and then said, "You know, Kuba, you are somewhat of a legend around here. Did you really make your way into the ghetto and kill the traitor who betrayed you and your family?"

A wave of memories swept through Kuba's mind. He remembered how he and Gibke found his little son Victor among the victims that night. He could plainly see the dead faces of the other inhabitants of his house and the sneering, repulsive face of Steinbeck! Slowly he returned to reality.

"I did what I had to do, Comrade Colonel. I could not go on living if I did not do that. This man had my wife and infant son killed for the sole purpose of continuing his own life," Kuba said.

"That is true," Petrov said, "and I believe you were nominated for the 'Hero of the Soviet Union Medal,'" Petrov said, holding a grip on Kuba's arm.

"Oh, I don't know about that. I have enough medals right now," Kuba said and sat down on a chair in Petrov's office, suddenly embarrassed.

Petrov showed him some blueprints for the reconstruction of the depot and asked for any suggestions. Kuba took the prints and told Petrov that he would like to study them before he made any comments. Petrov then suggested that he would show Kuba to his quarters, a railroad car divided into two rooms, containing some furnishings and a few bottles of liquor on a board. Petrov asked Kuba if it was alright and Kuba said that it was not exactly Moscow, but it was alright.

The Colonel then invited him to dinner that evening and left the two of them to unpack. They took their meals at the cafeteria, which consisted of three box cars. Kuba asked about Jewish survivors in the city and finally found a Lieutenant Goldsmith who told him that some Jewish partisans lived in the northern section of the city.

The dinner at Petrov's quarters was typically Russian and good: roast pork, real black bread and jellied pig's feet. Petrov's wife was a charming Ukrainian woman in her middle thirties. They had a twelve-year-old son who wanted to know everything about partisans. After about three hours, Petrov got slightly drunk and Kuba took that opportunity to say good-bye.

Valeriya Petrov squeezed his hand and smiled at him with a peculiar twinkle in her eyes. It was a little past seven in the evening when Kuba reached the north section of town. There were many people on the streets and Kuba looked into each face, in the hope of recognizing someone. As he rounded a corner, he came face to face with Chaim Stolovitski, his old friend and comrade from the ghetto underground.

Chaim cried out, "Kuba is that you? My, you look fancy in that uniform!"

"Yes Chaim, it's me. I just arrived from Moscow today."

"Well, let's go to my house. You will find a few old friends there." The house where Chaim lived was actually only half a house. The other half had been demolished. There were three rooms, occupied by about fifteen people, mostly from the Baranovichi ghetto. They were surprised to see Kuba, particularly in a captain's uniform and with all the medals. Kuba had a rough time answering all the questions which were being fired at him until midnight. Kuba told them about his new assignment and learned that several of his friends, including Chaim, worked on the railroad. Chaim and another friend, Moniek Dubkovski, accompanied him back to his quarters and on the way, Kuba was told about a new movement among the Jewish survivors which was concentrating on getting Jews out of Russia and into the "liberated" parts of Poland, with the hope of eventually reaching Palestine or the United States. Of course, all this involved a lot of money; the main obstacle at the moment. Kuba promised to visit them as soon as possible.

During the following weeks, Kuba worked on the reconstruction plans for the depot. He shared a box car office with a dozen engineers and draftsmen and was paid at the rate of seven-hundred-fifty rubles per month, barely enough to survive. For the first time, Kuba became entangled in Soviet bureaucracy; each report, document, drawing and blueprint had to be prepared in quintuplicate and approved by a large number of various officials and this state of affairs hindered the progress of the reconstruction efforts. However, there were occasions when that bureaucracy worked very swiftly, as when the Soviet troops occupied the industrial parts of Poland and southern Europe. They dismantled German-built factories and shipped the machinery back to Russia.

Eventually these trainloads of machinery passed through Baranovichi. The equipment in the machine shops and maintenance shops of the depot were old and dilapidated, mostly of English manufacture. When the first trainload of machinery arrived in Baranovichi, there were no manifests accompanying the cargo. The various department heads met with Petrov and a decision for a quick exchange action was made. Special teams of workers examined the contents of the cars in the train and whenever they found suitable equipment in a car, or on a platform, they marked the car with a large letter "B," meaning, in Russian, "bolnoy," or sick, and were diverted to a special siding in the depot. The machinery, consisting of engine lathes, mills, shapers and other equipment, all in excellent condition, was then unloaded and the old equipment was loaded into the cars in their place. The cars were then returned to the train and continued on their trip east.

Kuba witnessed several such procedures. Later, he was to learn that the same thing had happened to lend-lease equipment, even food and clothing, sent by the American people for the people of the Soviet Union.

New Year's 1945 came. There was a New Year's party at the depot and for that occasion, a special, large tent was set up and old oil drums were converted into stoves and placed in several locations within the tent. In spite of the cold outside, these stoves heated up the tent quite well. There were tables set up with drinks and some food, consisting mostly of bread and scrambled eggs.

It had snowed all day and the plywood sheets, which had served as a floor in the tent, were wet and slippery. The snow stuck to the boots of the people and, of course, it fell off their boots and melted on the floor and after an hour, the floor was a slushy mess. There was an orchestra consisting of an accordion, a violin and a balalaika. People were eating, drinking, dancing and there were speeches and toasts. The men were dressed in their uniforms and regulation overcoats and the women were bundled up in their warmest clothing with "babushkas" covering their heads. It was a very joyful atmosphere in the tent.

Petrov, in the company of a major, came over to Kuba and took him aside. "Captain, this is Major Vasili Bunin, the political commissar of the depot. As you know, we do not have, as yet, a chairman in our railroad workers union here. At a meeting today, it was decided that you should have that position. Our people here like you and they remember your war record."

Kuba was aghast. He did not like that turn of events at all. That meant that he would be watched very closely from now on and might even spoil his plans for a return to Poland. He looked at

Bunin's hard, almost cruel face and decided to play along for the time being.

He turned to Petrov and said, "But, Comrade Colonel, I thought that a chairman is elected by the members."

"That is correct," Bunin said, "you will be elected at a meeting next Wednesday." That ended the conversation. Colonel Petrov proposed a drink and they went to the closest table to get it. They were drinking from metal cups and this gave the alcohol a peculiar taste. By midnight, everyone was drunk and several arguments and fights erupted. Kuba saw Petrov hit someone on the side of the face with the butt of his pistol. At that moment, Gregory appeared at Kuba's side and both left for their box car home.

The union meeting took place at six o'clock on Wednesday evening, held in a half-finished maintenance building, and was a typical example of Soviet democracy. There were several propaganda speeches, a few questions and answers and then a young machinist, a member of the "Komsomol," Community Youth Organization, read from a piece of paper the names of nominees for chairman, secretary and lower functionaries of the union. Kuba's name was listed for the post of chairman and there were no other candidates. The vote was unanimous and the meeting was adjourned.

Several office buildings were already rebuilt and Kuba's new office was in one of those new buildings. He began to learn the purpose and meaning of Soviet trade unions from several brochures on the structure and duties of the Soviet trade union organization provided him by Major Bunin.

Back in his room Kuba looked through the literature, given to him by Bunin, while Gregory was pouring some drinks. "Tell me, Gregory, you were born in this country and you know its structure. Explain to me the working of the Soviet trade unions."

"Well, Captain," Gregory began after placing a drink in front of Kuba, "I am going to recite to you everything I learned in school about our unions. The highest leadership of the organization rested with the All-Union Central Council of Professional Unions, or the initials, in Russian, VCSPS, which controlled all trade unions. On the next level down, the hierarchy of the Soviet trade unions, were the central councils of the individual states, or 'republics' as the Russians called them; for example, the Ukrainian Republic, Belarusian Republic, Russian Republic, Armenian Republic, and so on, and then came the city committees, factory or plant committees, below the central council. Each committee, with a membership of more than four hundred, had a paid chairman. This procedure was repeated for each trade or profession."

"Well how did it work on the individual level?" Kuba asked.

"Each unit from the Central Council down, was divided into specific sections, which included: the Socialist Competition section; a Social Security section, which concentrated only on hospitalization and recuperation; a section for Communist propaganda; a section for physical and military education, and so on. The most significant of these sections, the Socialist Competition, an activity also known as the Stachanov movement, originated during the first Five Year Plan in the early twenties. It was started by Alexei Stachanov, a coal miner who began to double and even triple his daily production quota by rearranging his work procedure. The government and the Communist Party picked up the idea and began to implement it throughout the Soviet Union and Stachanov became a national hero. The movement became the main task for the trade unions in the Soviet Union, by organizing production competitions between various departments of a plant, then between plants, industries, etc. The production quotas were raised and workers who did not meet their quotas were fined by losing part of their pay. For being late to work, five or ten minutes, people were fined twenty-five percent of their paycheck. In case of a repetition of the same 'offense,' the workers were sentenced to three years in forced labor camps."

"How is the rate of pay decided upon?" Kuba asked.

"Except for white-collar workers, everyone in the Soviet Union got paid on the basis of piece work. It would seem that with the increase in production due to the Stachanov movement, people would earn more money. However, that was not the case, because the per piece quotas were down graded every few months and then the workers did not receive any reward for their effort. Furthermore, it is impossible for anyone in the Soviet Union to change jobs voluntarily. The people become virtual slaves at their assigned places of employment. Also, it was illegal for people to travel to other cities, unless they obtained a special travel permit from the NKVD. All these activities were the main task and purpose of the trade unions in the Soviet Union."

This became Kuba's job and he hated it from the very beginning and decided to find a way to escape from the Soviet Union to Poland at the first opportunity. Such an opportunity was becoming available to many Polish citizens in the Soviet Union because a Communist-backed provisional government was set up in the Polish city of Lublin and the Soviet government began a repatriation program for Poles. Kuba hoped that somehow, in spite of his military rank, he would be able to take advantage of that situation.

On January 18, Gregory told Kuba that he had received a vacation permit and that he was going to visit his family, leaving on Saturday the 20th. Kuba decided to buy a present for him, but the only place to buy anything in those days was the black market, an open black market, called "Kolchak" in Russian. One was located not far from the house where Kuba's partisan friends lived, so the next day Kuba went to the "touché" and bought a jar of honey, a few packs of cigarettes and a bottle of vodka, paying almost three hundred rubles for these items. As he was about to leave, someone took his arm. He turned around to face his friend Chaim Stolovitski.

He smiled at Kuba and said, "Shalom aleichem, Kuba. How are you? We were expecting to see you sooner. There is a lot of important news that you should know about." Kuba smiled at Chaim and the Hebrew greeting. He knew that Chaim and most of the other Jewish partisans in his group were Zionists.

He replied, "Aleichem shalom. What is the latest news?"

"Why don't you come over for dinner tomorrow, Saturday at six o'clock, then you will find out many interesting things and developments," said Chaim. Kuba promised to be there for dinner and the two friends parted.

Gregory was surprised by Kuba's gift. "Oh, Comrade Captain, that is unexpected. That will keep me all the way to my home town."

"Gregory, you know that I like you very much and we became good friends and also we do understand each other."

"Yes, Comrade, we do understand each other and I wish you personally all the luck in the world.

"You are a real friend," Gregory replied and shook hands with Kuba. The following morning Gregory left by train and Kuba had a feeling that he would never see him again.

Chapter Thirty

Kuba arrived at Chaim's house and found about twenty or twenty-five people already in the house: Chaim Stolovitski and his new wife, the two Dubkovski brothers, Lazar Segal and his wife and many others. He received a very warm welcome, and there was a surprise for him. In the second room was Colonel Nikolsky, who was on a special meeting with his old unit and to give out Medals for Bravery. He was quite drunk and did not pay any attention to the conversations which took place and soon after, went to sleep in an alcove on the second floor of the house.

All the partisans were gathered in the living room and talking quietly. Kuba learned that all of his friends had already obtained repatriation permits and were to leave for Poland within ten days. They used their own names without any problems. Kuba asked Chaim what he thought of Kuba's chances for obtaining such a permit. Chaim gave Kuba a very candid look.

"Kuba," he said, "in your case we have a problem, three problems actually. First, is the fact that you are a highly decorated captain of a special partisan unit. Second, is that you are your father's son, and third, you're with the trade union, very tricky. We had a traitor among us by the nickname of "Katsap"[5] who revealed your true identity to the KNVD. You cannot leave under your own name."

Kuba thought uneasily about the "Katsap" case and Nikolsky's visit. He knew that Nikolsky was high up in the KGB, Commissar-

---

[5] Editor's note: *Katsap* is an anachronism for Russian soldiers which surfaced from arabic *kassab* or butcher. –ED

iat for State Security, and recalled a remark that Nikolsky had made earlier in the evening. "Kuba," he said, "is on his way to becoming like his father." He had not replied to that remark, pretending to be involved in a conversation with a young woman who was sitting next to him. Remembering his past few months, Kuba knew that he would have to leave the Soviet Union as soon as possible.

It was already past midnight when Chaim said to Kuba, "Let's go for a walk." They walked along a deserted street lined on both sides of the street with the ruins of buildings. Kuba wondered about the people who had lived in those houses before they were destroyed. What had happened to them? Where are they now? It seemed like thousands and thousands of people had disappeared from the face of the earth; first, at the hands of the Nazis and their Sonderdienst and, now, at the hands of the Soviet regime. There were rumors circulating about uprisings among Soviet soldiers who were now observing how people lived outside of the Soviet Union. Kuba saw trains consisting of sealed box cars, heavily guarded, which carried troops from the front lines into the interior of the Soviet Union, most likely towards forced labor camps. Every day, hundreds of people were being arrested by the NKVD in the cities, in factories and on the railroad. These people just disappeared.

The two men walked for a time in silence. Kuba remembered a Jewish official of the railroad, the chief of personnel, a short and chubby man who looked almost grotesque in his uniform, named Moisey Weinstein. Kuba got to know him quite well. Moisey was a family man with a wife and two children, living somewhere in Russia. Moisey fixed up living quarters for them and was saving most of his food rations, stashed away in a large foot locker which he kept so that his family would not go hungry when they joined him. One day, the NKVD searched Moisey's quarters. They arrested him for hoarding. He disappeared, never to be heard from again.

Chaim pulled sharply at Kuba's coat and this brought Kuba back to reality. "What is the matter with you?" he asked, looking at Kuba closely. "I have been talking to you and you were not listening!"

"I am sorry. I was thinking about all the people who have vanished from this city," Kuba said.

"Kuba, now listen carefully. There is only one way for you to escape. Do you know Misha Murski, who runs the lumber mill outside of town?"

"Yes, I have met him. The railroad runs there and there are some tracks which go to the mill. I heard that he just got married," Kuba said.

"That is the one," said Chaim. "He can help you. Let's go over there right now."

"Isn't it late now for visits?" Kuba asked.

"No. For this visit the time is just right," Chaim replied. The lumber mill was located three miles outside of town, next to the railroad tracks. Chaim told him that Misha and his wife lived in a little house on the premises. In addition to running the mill, Misha was also heavily engaged in the black market and in obtaining false documents. He even had a photo lab and print shop stashed away at the secluded lumber mill. Chaim knocked on the door in a way that sounded like a signal. The door opened almost immediately and Misha, a tall, blonde man of about twenty-five, came out and after a short greeting, asked them to enter. They came into a very comfortable room, furnished with two couches, some overstuffed chairs and a table and benches. Misha offered them some tea and they sat down at the table. They spoke quietly because Misha's wife was asleep in the next room. Chaim explained briefly Kuba's unique situation and then added,

"We don't know how much time Kuba has left. Therefore, he must get out of here and into Poland as soon as possible." Misha nodded his head but did not say anything for a long time. He studied Kuba's face for a few minutes before he replied.

"I understand your situation, Kuba. I cannot give an answer right now. We had a visit from the local police, today, looking for a printing press. Somebody has talked to them and I have a hunch who it was. Of course, they did not find anything."

They were silent for a few minutes. Finally, Misha got up and began pacing the floor. He stopped in front of Kuba and said,

"Why don't you stop by here at noon on Monday. We will have lunch and see what can be done. I may have to go into hiding myself soon."

Chaim and Kuba walked briskly back to town. Before the two friends parted, Chaim said, "He will do it, Kuba. It might cost a little more, but he will do it. He usually charges around two thousand rubles. If you need some money, let me know. Good night, Kuba."

Kuba arrived at his quarters about four o'clock in the morning, sat a while and thought about the complicated situation in which he found himself. He missed Gregory and his hot tea. The wind picked up and it was snowing heavily.

At about six-thirty in the morning, Kuba was awakened by a persistent knocking on his door. He was immediately alert. Did he wait too long with his escape plans? Dressed only in a long, Russian nightgown, he went to the door. It was bitter cold in his box car. He had not bothered to start a fire in the stove the previous night.

Shivering and in his bare feet, he asked, "Who is it?"

"Tatyana Tatarin." Kuba unlocked the door and looked at the girl standing there, bundled up in furs and felt boots. Tatyana pushed past him into the box car and started laughing.

"Look at my hero, turning blue from cold. Get back into bed and I will warm you up instantly!" Kuba went back to bed, shivering, and covered himself. In the dim, early morning light, he watched Tatyana undress, piling all her clothes on the table. She slipped under the cover of his bed completely nude. She made him take off his silly nightgown and said, giggling, "Now let's start warming you up!" Kuba slept badly after that. He had a nightmare in which he saw himself once more in the interrogation cellar of the Moscow prison. He felt like there was a heavy weight on his chest and he had difficulty breathing. He woke up. The pressure was caused by Tatyana laying on him and kissing him hard on his lips. The room was warm. There was a fire in the stove and the aroma of fresh-brewed coffee filled the air. Tatyana was wearing one of his shirts and nothing else.

Kuba jumped out of bed and asked, "Where did you get the coffee?"

"I brought it with me and some sausage also," she said, smiling. They were sitting on the bed and drinking coffee. The shirt that Tatyana was wearing was not buttoned and her full breasts were exposed. Kuba felt a desire mounting in him for her and he put the coffee on the floor. She followed his example instantly and then took off the shirt making those animal noises almost immediately after he entered her.

Later Kuba got out of bed and looked at the girl. She was lying on her side with her back towards him, pretending to be asleep. Kuba smacked her on her bottom and said, "Time to get dressed, you little animal."

"Okay, boss," she said and sat up. Kuba went to the wash basin in the corner. He passed the single window and tried to look outside. It was impossible because the window pane was frosted over, the ice forming a beautiful design. He heated some water in a bucket and started to wash up, but Tatyana came over and took the soap from his hand.

She started washing him and said, "After I wash you, you will wash me." Afterwards, Kuba was putting on his uniform and Tatyana was frying some sausage. They ate breakfast and got dressed.

They spent the day touring the depot and walking through the city and Kuba introduced Tatyana to some people at the depot. In the evening, they went to the railroad worker's club where movies were being shown on Sundays. They returned home around nine o'clock in the evening because Tatyana had to leave on the six o'clock morning train for Lida.

As they were eating sausage and egg powder omelets for dinner, Tatyana said, "My parents are coming for us in May. Father will arrange a month's furlough for you." Kuba kissed her on the cheek, but did not dare to say anything. He felt sorry for the girl, but he knew that if her dream came through, it would spell disaster for her and her entire family; a reality in the Soviet Union, and there was no way that he could explain that to Tatyana.

It was a cold, crisp Monday morning. Kuba stood with Tatyana on the platform, near her train, talking quietly and Kuba promised to visit her in a few weeks. The conductor and station master walked by, saluted and smiled knowingly at Kuba. There was a sharp whistle from the locomotive, announcing the departure of the train. The two embraced and kissed each other, then the train began to move and Kuba helped Tatyana to board her car. "Well, dear Kuba," Tatyana yelled to him from the moving train, "I will write to you tomorrow and you write to me."

"I will!" Kuba yelled back. Tatyana was yelling something else to him, but Kuba could not hear that, because the train was moving away swiftly. Suddenly Kuba felt very lonely. He thought to himself, *Now the third important person in my life left me. First Franca and Victor, then Rachel and now Tatyana... But Rachel, Rachel... she is alive somewhere! And if she is alive I shall find her.* Kuba could see Rachel's angelic face in front of him as he was walking home from the railroad station.

At his office, Kuba looked over his work load for the day. A number of grievances and complaints from people in various departments of the depot and a list of people who did not work all week, meaning Kuba would have to talk to all of these people and try to straighten out the situation. He had a horse and sleigh assigned to him, so he took his briefcase, containing all the complaints and began making his rounds. A few minutes before noon, he pulled up before Misha's house at the lumber mill. Misha's wife, a tall, somewhat plump woman with blonde hair and a very pleasant face, opened the door for him. "Please come in. Misha will be here in a few minutes."

Her name was Sonia and she spoke in Yiddish to Kuba in a ringing, melodic voice, like a singer. She offered him some tea and told Kuba about their worries. "I overheard your conversation Saturday night, and I know of your problems as well. I think that Misha has found a way to help you," she added.

Misha was twenty minutes late. After greeting Kuba, he said "I had a visit from the NKVD just now. They were just asking around. I have a feeling that the place is being watched."

Sonia served some herring, bread and butter for lunch and they ate in silence as Misha was absorbed in his thoughts. After lunch,

Misha got to his feet and said to Kuba, "I must talk something over with Sonia. It will only take a few minutes and then I will tell you what we are going to do."

Misha, Sonia and Kuba all lit cigarettes and looked out the window, which was scrubbed free of frost. He thought, if the house is under surveillance by the NKVD, then they knew that he was present and that would worsen the situation.

After five minutes, the Murskis returned to Kuba. Misha sat down next to Kuba and came right to the point. "It will cost you three thousand five hundred rubles. You will receive all necessary documents and travel permits in a name of your choice within two weeks. It has to be done somewhere else, not here, and that is why the price is so high. There is one more provision. You will take Sonia with you as your wife. She has relatives in Lodz, Poland, and I will come later. In this way, she will be safe regardless of what might happen to me. If this is acceptable to you, I shall take a picture of you now for the documents."

Kuba was slightly taken aback by Misha's request. He thought about it for a while and decided that there was no other way. He would have to get the money somehow. "It is all right with me," Kuba said.

"Good. Let me get the camera." Misha went into the kitchen, pulled up a linoleum tile from the floor and opened a trap door to a cellar. He went down and returned shortly with an old German camera on a tripod. He took Kuba's picture, using a magnesium flash. "I will get you some civilian clothing and you will have to change your clothes on the train when it is safe," Misha said.

"How will you let me know when everything is ready?" Kuba asked.

"It would be best that you do not come here again. Give the money to Stolovitski and I will get it from him. When everything is ready, Sonia will come to you with the documents, railroad tickets for Warsaw and clothing. You will then both leave immediately. By the way, don't leave now through the main gate. There is another gate on the north side of the mill. Go that way." Kuba found the gate and a deserted, narrow road through a forest, leading toward the city. He reached his office without incident.

Kuba had two more places to visit before completing his rounds and quitting time. He arranged his papers for those visits and started putting on his overcoat when the door opened and Bunin came in without knocking. Bunin was in his fifties, short, gray hair with thick glasses which magnified his eyes so that he looked like an owl. He was an old-line Bolshevik and he did not trust anyone. Kuba had the feeling that Bunin was always watching him. "Are you leaving?" Bunin asked.

"Yes, I have to visit two sections of the locomotive department."

"Do you mind if I ride with you? I have to talk to you about some very important things that came up."

"That's fine," Kuba replied. However, beneath his calm, he worried. It might mean trouble, after all. Bunin was the Party Commissar on the railroad depot. They were riding in the sleigh and Bunin starting talking, "Congratulations on your Medal for Bravery."

"Thank you."

"You are a very unique person; a good engineer, a good soldier and now an excellent chairman of the trade union and your name was mentioned in a report in <u>IZVESTIA</u> last month. The All-Union Congress of Trade Unions will take place in Moscow and it has been decided that you should be a delegate. Next week, I will bring you an outline for your speech. You work on it and it will be of great honor to us."

Kuba thought about it. It could be a trick to get him into the wolf's den without any problem. Does that mean that the end is near? After a while, he gave the only safe answer. "It will be a great honor to serve in that capacity, Comrade Bunin."

When Kuba returned to his room, his quarters looked very neat. Tatyana had cleaned and washed everything. He was suddenly very hungry, so he went to the cupboard and started looking for some food. He found bread, sausage and a bag of "vermishel," which Tatyana must have left. As he was closing the cupboard, he noticed a package on top of the cupboard. He took it down and examined it; there was something wrapped in newspapers. He unwrapped the package carefully and found two large pieces of fine, black leather for boots, two thick pieces of leather for soles and heels and a note. The note was signed "Tania," for Tatyana.

My dear Kuba,

In these boots you will be the envy of every officer in the Red Army. Have them made up right away.

Love, Tania.

Kuba stood there for a long time, looking at Tatyana's note, with mixed emotions. He loved the girl, but he was not in love with her. That might come later, if they were married. However, in view of the obvious facts, their future looked very bleak. If he were arrested and became a political prisoner, Tatyana, her father and the rest of their family would also fall into disgrace and, eventually, be arrested. No, there was no other way. He must disappear from the Soviet Union.

Tuesday evening, Kuba took the package with the leather to Chaim Stolovitski. He asked Chaim to sell it for him and Chaim agreed to do so. Friday evening, Chaim met with Kuba and handed him four thousand seven hundred rubles and Kuba gave Chaim three thousand five hundred rubles of it and asked him to keep it for Misha who picked up the money that same evening. Kuba had made his decision, the second step toward freedom. The first one was his Monday meeting with Misha and Sonia.

Chapter Thirty-One

Katsap was an old time member of the Jewish section of the Polish community party. He was in his mid thirties, burly with a full head of kinky hair. During the war he belonged to one of the non-combatant partisan units in Belarus, acting in the capacity of political commissar. On Sunday afternoon, Katsap was standing in front of a major of the local NKVD office in Baranovichi, reciting his report. "And furthermore, I overheard Kuba talking to Stolovitski and the other partisans in that house about a possible escape to Poland. From this conversation I obtained more proof that Kuba is actually the son of Samuel Mordecai, 'Comrade Arthur' of the Jewish 'Bund' party and member of the Polish government in exile."

The major opened a drawer in his desk and took out a photograph of 'Comrade Arthur.' "Who is this man?" he asked.

"It looks like Captain Kuba," Katsap answered. Kuba was a spitting image of his father, mustache and all. The major handed Katsap an envelope containing two hundred rubles.

"Remember to report all developments in person immediately!" Katsap left the room and the major pressed a button at the side of the desk. Bunin entered the room.

"Well, Comrade Bunin," the major said, "your information was correct. You may give Kuba these travel orders tomorrow. They will be waiting for him in Moscow."

In an adjoining office, a young woman, former member of an active Jewish partisan group, recorded mentally all the conversations that took place in the major's office. That evening she reported everything to Chaim Stolovitski.

On Monday the 29th, Kuba was sitting behind his desk, going over the routine tasks for the day, when Bunin entered his office without knocking. He put in front of Kuba a folder containing about thirty hand-written pages and said, "Here is the outline for your speech. Study it well. After you absorb it, we will discuss it in more detail later on in the week. Don't forget that the great Stalin will be there." Kuba picked up the folder and glanced at the first page. Bunin continued to talk, "Here are all your necessary travel orders, permits and tickets. You will leave for Moscow on Tuesday, February 7. In a few days, I will bring you a special travel allowance." Bunin dropped a heavy envelope on the desk and left the room. Kuba pushed aside the folder and opened the envelope which contained a permit from the NKVD in Kuba's name, a delegate's I.D. card to the Congress of Trade Unions, a reservation card for the Metropol Hotel and a one-way ticket to Moscow.

Kuba stared at the ticket for a very long time. One thought continued to cross his mind: *That is my death sentence for being the son of a prominent anti-communist! THIS IS MY DEATH SENTENCE!* Kuba got up and put the documents, along with the folder of Bunin's speech outline, into his briefcase and went out to his sleigh and took off on his daily visits to the various departments of the depot.

At half past eleven, Kuba pulled up in front of Stolovitski's house. Chaim opened the door for him and embraced Kuba with a hearty "Shalom!" Then he said, "Kuba, it is great that you showed up. I was trying to figure out how to get hold of you today."

"What happened? What is all the excitement?" Kuba asked.

"Kuba, listen to this. Moniek, Lazar, I and the rest of our households are leaving for Poland tomorrow morning and from there we shall make our way to Palestine. Just imagine, in a couple of months, we will be in Eretz Israel, fighting for the land of our forefathers!"

"That is great news," said Kuba, but his spirit began to sink. Chaim looked at him for a while, then left the room and returned with Moniek Dubkovski.

They looked at Kuba and Moniek asked, "What is the matter, Kuba? You turned so pale all of a sudden." Without a word, Kuba opened his briefcase and handed him the envelope with the documents. Moniek took out the papers and spread them out on the table and Chaim and Moniek examined the documents in detail.

They were quiet for a while, and then Chaim spoke up, "That is cutting it very short for you, Kuba. Unless you want to wait until your return from Moscow."

Kuba jumped up impatiently, looked at his friends and almost screamed out the words, "Look again at the documents. Do you see there a return travel permit or a return ticket?" The two bent over the documents and looked in disbelief.

Finally, Chaim said, turning pale, "What does that mean?"

"It means that Katsap's big mouth condemned Kuba to prison or death!" yelled Moniek as he hit the table with his fist. After that, they sat quietly trying to figure out a solution.

Chaim got to his feet. "We must get in touch with Misha. I will send the Pinski boy from next door to bring him here. How much longer can you stay here with us, Kuba?"

Kuba looked at his watch and said, "Oh, about one hour." "That's fine," said Chaim and he left the room. Moniek went to the kitchen and returned with a bottle of vodka and glasses and handed one glass to Kuba.

"L'chaim, to life," he said softly.

Stolovitski returned shortly and joined them in a drink and at twelve-fifteen a sleigh pulled up in front of the house and Misha got out of the sleigh and walked toward the house. A boy of about twelve got out from the other side and ran toward the house next door.

Misha came in and looked at the long faces of the three ex-partisans, turned to Kuba and said, "Your passport and repatriation permits are ready, but I am waiting for the NKVD travel permit to Warsaw. It will be authentic, then Sonia will get the railroad tickets and you are all set."

Chaim placed Kuba's official documents in front of Misha and said, "Look at this, Misha. This is Katsap's doing. Kuba has to get out not later than February 7, and you better hurry up with the rest of the stuff. I understand that Sonia is now involved in that situation. Well, forget about monetary gains and do something fast!"

Misha listened and became very excited. He paced the floor for a few minutes, then stopped in front of Kuba and said, "Kuba, I know what that means. I will step on this *sukin syn* (SOB) from the NKVD to process your papers immediately. Don't forget that Sonia's security is now tied to you. So help me, I will carry this out. My own life depends on it." After that statement, Kuba left at once. He was late and he hoped that no one at the depot would notice. When he returned to his office, he found a letter from Gregory, his adjutant, informing him that his next assignment was in Leningrad.

So, Gregory has a new assignment, meaning that Kuba no longer exists. Gregory, whom Kuba considered a true friend, in spite of his KGB affiliation, took the risk of writing to him. How Kuba wished that he were here right now, and to hear his standard statement, "Comrade Captain, between us everything is in order." The letter in itself did not pose any threat to Kuba as far as the NKVD and Bunin were concerned. However, it carried a message for Kuba, which he could not afford to ignore. On Wednesday, Kuba found a reason to travel to Lida, which was in his district and did not require any special permits. He spent a few hours with Tatyana at the huge hospital complex and told her that he was scheduled to go to Moscow the following week. Tatyana showed surprise, because, her father was unaware of this. He would have let her know. Kuba thanked Tatyana for the leather for the boots, but did not mention what he had done with it.

He returned to Baranovichi and when he got back to his room in the box car after midnight, he found the room in disorder. Someone had been there, searching through his belongings but nothing was missing. Next morning, when Kuba reached his office, he noticed a strange man standing at the corner of the building, trying to light a cigarette. The man had a gun strapped to his waist. After that Kuba began to wear his gun every day.

Saturday morning, Bunin came into Kuba's office and asked Kuba if he had read the speech. Kuba replied in the affirmative: he had read it on the train back from Lida and had penciled in a few insignificant remarks. He handed the speech to Bunin, who looked it over and seemed to be satisfied. Then he dropped a bundle of money on Kuba's desk and said that it was for his extra expenses in the capitol of the Soviet Union. Kuba counted the hundred ruble notes, and it amounted to two thousand rubles, hardly enough to spend two days in Moscow. Kuba looked at Bunin, who was avoiding his stare, and in spite of his better judgment, asked a critical question. "Comrade Bunin, am I being watched or investigated?"

"My dear comrade, you are being guarded against the enemies of the Soviet Union. After all, you are one of our war heroes." He thought a lot about Bunin's evasive answer to his question, certain now that he was marked for a quick Soviet disappearance.

When he got to his quarters that evening, there was another shock waiting for Kuba. Tatyana was waiting for him, hidden behind the box car and when he unlocked the door, she ran inside, like a scared rabbit. "What happened?" asked Kuba, after locking the door behind him.

"I don't know," she said. "Father was suddenly ordered back to the front in Germany." Kuba did not say anything. He was now certain, more than ever, that there were no secrets from the Soviet regime. Tania fixed up a meal from Kuba's supplies and after Kuba made certain that everything was locked up, they went to bed. Tania watched with tearful eyes as Kuba placed his gun under the pillow. They embraced and spent half of the night in sleeplessness, just listening to each other's heartbeat. When it began to turn gray outside, Tatyana said, "My mother is moving back to Kazan next week."

Kuba kissed her on the temple and they finally fell asleep. Tatyana stayed over Sunday. Early Monday morning, she got up, washed and dressed and Kuba also got up. He meant to take her to the station, but she stopped him and said, "No, my dear, it is better if no one sees us together." Before leaving, she embraced Kuba and began to cry. It the first time Kuba had seen her cry. She pressed her face to his and whispered, "I know that I shall never see you again, my darling, but I will never forget you. This is our Soviet lot." They kissed each other many times and then she broke away and ran out into the crisp cold of the winter morning.

On Monday, February 6, 1945, Kuba went to his office, as always. He plowed through his daily routine, trying not to think about past events. He met Colonel Petrov in the hall and they exchanged a few words about the situation at the depot. He did not show any sign of disturbance, as far as Kuba was concerned. Kuba spent a few hours in his office, putting all his reports in order, then got into his sleigh and started for the various departments of the depot. He ate lunch alone at the railroad cafeteria, thought about Misha and wondered if everything was all right. He had some meetings in the afternoon and there were no further disturbing events. Back in his room, Kuba did not bother with dinner and ate some cold sausage and bread. He was very nervous and he could not go to sleep. This was his last night in Baranovichi, one way or another. He poured himself a glass of vodka and started packing his few belongings into a small plywood suitcase, then got out a piece of paper and started to write a letter to Tatyana. He knew that he would never mail the letter, but he could not help himself. He had to pour out his feelings on paper.

When he was half way through, he started thinking and said to himself, "If I survive all this, I will write everything down for future generations to know how it really was." Suddenly there was a knock on the door. Kuba looked at his watch. It was a few minutes past midnight. He pulled out his gun and took off the safety catch. "Who is it?" he asked.

"Sonia. Sonia Kurskaya," came a whispered reply. Kuba unlocked the door and Sonia came into the room, bundled up in a fur coat with a babushka on her head and carrying a small suitcase and a package of clothes for Kuba. He locked the door after admitting her and turned around. Her face was pink from the frost and excitement. She put the suitcase down, opened her coat, reached into her dress between her breasts and pulled out a paper wrapped package and handed it to Kuba. He asked her to sit down and poured a glass of vodka for her. He unwrapped the package and found there a passport in the name of Arthur Zielinski, a repatriation permit to Poland, a NKVD travel permit to Warsaw, Poland, and a railroad ticket for the same destination. All the permits stated that he was traveling in the company of his wife, Sonia. Kuba examined the documents with a pounding heart. Could it be true? Would it work? He looked at Sonia and he could tell that the same questions crossed her mind.

"We will make it, Sonia," he said and kissed her on the cheek.

"I know that with you, we will make it," she replied. Sonia took off her coat and sat down on the bed, sipping vodka. Kuba asked her if she was hungry, but she replied that she could not eat a thing, she was too excited.

Kuba knew that the Moscow-Warsaw train was leaving Baranovichi at seven-thirty in the morning and that the express train for Moscow would leave at seven-forty in the morning, ten minutes later. That would work out just right; no one would question his presence at the station at that hour because of his scheduled trip to Moscow.

Suddenly, he turned to Sonia and said, "Can I see your documents?"

Without a word, she reached into her bosom and produced a small leather wallet and handed it to Kuba. He looked at her passport in the name of Sonia Zielinski and all other documents were in the same name. Her travel permits stated that she was traveling in the company of her husband, Arthur. It looked very good. Kuba handed the wallet back to her and sat down at the table, staring at the floor when Sonia spoke.

"You now, Kuba, that Chaim, Moniek and the rest of their group are in Warsaw right now."

Kuba looked up at her. She looked very tired and worried. He took a sip from the glass and said, "Why don't you go to bed, Sonia, I will sleep in the other room."

"Oh, no Kuba," she replied. "You can sleep here with me. It's cold in there, and besides I trust you."

Sonia undressed, leaving on her bra and panties, and got under the blankets. Kuba paced the floor for a while. Then he turned off the lights, undressed and got into bed, next to Sonia. She snuggled up to him, kissed him on the cheek and fell asleep almost immediately.

Kuba awakened at five-thirty and was surprised to find his left hand resting on Sonia's bare breasts. She must have taken off the bra during the night. He got out of bed, washed up and shaved and could hear Sonia getting up. While she was washing up, Kuba made some tea and when they were sitting at the table, Kuba said, "We will leave at seven o'clock, you will go first and board the train. I will follow a few minutes later, but, of course, I have to go to the officer's car. As soon as we are out of this railroad district, I will change into the civilian clothes you brought for me. Then I will go back through the train and find you. If there are any problems with me, do not try to approach me. It might be dangerous."

"I understand, Kuba, and I will do exactly as you have told me."

Kuba took out the rest of the sausage and bread, divided it into two parts and they ate breakfast. He watched Sonia eat and thought of last night.

As if reading his thoughts, Sonia looked up and blushed deeply. She gave Kuba a warm smile and said, "About last night, Kuba, nothing bad happened. I was cramped in that bra, so I took it off. You were sound asleep and I felt very safe with you. I feel safe with you now and I will always have that feeling, no matter what happens." She got up from the table, came around to Kuba, put her arms around his neck and kissed him on the mouth. Then she said, "Besides, according to those documents, we are husband and wife." And she started laughing.

Chapter Thirty-Two

At a quarter to seven, Sonia got up and said, "Kuba, I had better go now. After all, it is a ten to fifteen minute walk to the station." Kuba got to his feet and they embraced. "Be careful, Sonia, and I will see you on the train."

"Don't worry about me. You are the one to be careful. If something happens to you, I will get off the train and get Misha." She kissed Kuba, picked up her suitcase and went outside. Kuba watched her walk toward the distant station. There was no one nearby and Kuba was sure that she was not observed leaving his quarters. He returned to the room. The first thing he noticed was the unfinished letter to Tatyana. He burned it in the stove. Then he opened his suitcase and placed the clothing in it which Misha had provided for him. He looked around the room and remembered the evenings with Gregory and, of course, the nights and days with Tatyana.

At five minutes past seven Kuba, dressed in his uniform, picked up his suitcase, went outside and locked the door, put the key in his pocket and looked around. There was not a soul in sight. He began to walk toward the station. He arrived at the station at seven twenty five. There were about a dozen passengers in the station. The train for Warsaw was on track number one, and the train for Moscow was on track two. Both trains were side by side, facing in opposite directions. The station master greeted Kuba and they shook hands. "So, you are off to Moscow." It was more a statement than a question.

"Yes, Comrade," Kuba replied with a smile. Kuba walked between the trains until the Warsaw bound train began to move. He looked around. There was a brakeman standing at some distance, but he did not look in Kuba's direction. Kuba jumped on the moving train and made his way to the officer's car in front. He opened the door to the first compartment, stepped inside, and stopped in his tracks. The compartment was occupied by a general-colonel and two other high-ranking officers.

Kuba excused himself and started to leave when the general called out to him, "Please come in." Kuba saluted smartly and closed the door, put his suitcase on a shelf overhead and introduced himself. The general and the others introduced themselves, in turn. There was a long, unfolded table in the center of the compartment, loaded with food, several bottles of vodka and a deck of cards. Kuba sat down next to a brigadier general and a conversation began about various things, particularly the war. Someone poured a glass of vodka for Kuba. The general-colonel's name was Osipov, traveling from Moscow to Warsaw, as were all the other officers in the car. Kuba sipped the vodka and glanced at a jar of caviar on the table. Osipov said to him, "Eat something, Captain."

Kuba thanked him and spread some caviar on a piece of bread. The train was rolling at a high speed, passing snow covered fields, forests and villages. The clickety-click of the train made Kuba sleepy but he could not afford that now, so he looked out the window. After they finished eating, Osipov proposed a game of poker. They pushed aside the food and started playing. Kuba was a little rusty at the game, not having played it since his college years. After a while, he started winning, and he found in the game an avenue of escape from reality and played on for about two hours. The train slowed down occasionally, and even stopped for some periods of time because all tracks were rebuilt after the destruction to them and the train was forced to travel along available tracks, sometimes north and then south and finally west again. The officers in Kuba's compartment must have been up all night on their ride from Moscow and no doubt had consumed a great amount of vodka. They showed signs of weariness and the game broke up.

Osipov stretched out on his seat and was asleep in a minute. The others followed suit. Kuba leaned back in his seat and closed his eyes. He had won about forty-five hundred rubles in the game and considered that a good omen, but he could not fall asleep. Suddenly, he sat up.

Sonia was somewhere on the train and she was probably hungry by now. He should change his clothes and become a civilian so that he would be able to travel under his new identity and join Sonia. But, how could he do that now? He was a part of this elite group of Soviet officers. If he changed into civilian clothes and disappeared from this car, that would cause suspicion on the part of the authorities and could become very dangerous.

Then he began to think about another danger that lurked in his path: What would happen when they arrived at the Soviet-Polish border and the border guard would ask him for his documents? He didn't have any permit to travel to Warsaw in his own name. Ah, Warsaw! His hometown, his family, the house on twenty-six Novolipie Street... These thoughts flashed through Kuba's mind and brought tears into his eyes. He placed his palms on his face and wept quietly. After a while, he came to a decision. If the border guards questioned him, he would pretend to be drunk and say that he boarded the wrong train at Baranovichi. After all, he had travel documents for Moscow. He thought about it for a long while and then decided to go find Sonia. He got to his feet and looked at the table. There was a lot of food there. He picked up a few pieces of bread, spread some caviar on them and placed thick slices of cheese on top, then wrapped them in a cloth napkin and put it into his pocket. His companions were sound asleep and snoring.

Kuba left the compartment and walked through the train cars toward the back of the train and found Sonia in the sixth car from the officer's car, leaning back on her seat, in a crowded car, full of repatriated Poles. Kuba touched Sonia's face and she opened her eyes, startled. "Oh, Kuba! Is everything all right?"

"Yes, Sonia, let's go out into the corridor." She got up quickly and they went out. Kuba handed her the food and she began to eat at once.

"You think of everything, don't you, Kuba?" she said with a smile.

"Listen, honey, we have a big problem. I cannot change into civilian clothes. I am in the company of high-ranking Soviet officers. If I suddenly disappear from their company and am found in civilian clothes with false documents, it would be like committing suicide."

Sonia stopped eating, her eyes swelled up with tears and she buried her face into Kuba's chest. She spoke very quietly. "Oh, my dear Kuba, what is going to happen?"

"Don't worry, dear, everything will be all right. I worked out a plan and it will work, but, I will not be able to be with you here. We will meet in Warsaw when we detrain. I will bring you food whenever I can." He kissed Sonia on the forehead and left quickly. The officers in the compartment were still asleep. Kuba sat down in his seat and closed his eyes. He could see Warsaw again. Then something began to bother him. The Russians had taken the city three weeks before, on January 15, 1945, but, the Red Army had stayed on the shores of the Vistula River, opposite Warsaw since August 1, 1944. The people of Warsaw, including the Jewish survivors of the ghetto uprising in April of 1943, revolted against the Nazis, anticipating a quick capture by the Russians. But the Red Army just sat there in the suburb of Praga, across the river, and watched as the Nazis put down the uprising, killed a great number of the population, destroyed the city and hung from lamp posts about forty-two-thousand freedom fighters. Kuba thought about that and realized that the Soviets were actually giving the Nazis a free hand to liquidate the intellectual and fighting spirit of the Polish people, so that they could dominate the country after the war. He looked out through the window and recognized the countryside. They were approaching the city of Slonim. He remembered his activities, only a few months ago, in the area surrounding the city and knew that the next stop would be Volkovysk and then the new border between Poland and the Soviet Union.

At Slonim, they were diverted to a side track and waited there for about five hours while a maintenance crew fixed some demolished tracks ahead. It seemed, he thought, that a Polish resistance organization, the Polish Home Army, had been active in this area against the Russians.

Osipov and his friends began waking. The general asked why the train was not moving and Kuba told him what he had learned. The three officers went to the bathroom to clean up and Kuba, realizing that Sonia must be hungry by now, put together a couple of sandwiches and went to find her. She greeted him, as before and told him that she had made some friends amongst the fellow travelers and seemed to be more relaxed.

In the corridor, Kuba gave her the food and said, "Sorry, that is the best I could do under the circumstances. In a few hours we will cross the border into Poland. That is all that matters right now. I will try to get you something to drink.

"It is not necessary. A woman in there has a whole kettle of cold tea and I did drink some," Sonia said.

Kuba returned to his car and the train again began to move, very slowly. Some people with picks and shovels were standing alongside the tracks and watched the train go by. Someone must have brought in a new load of food to the officer's compartment because the table was loaded with ham and other meat cuts.

"Let's eat, Comrades," the general said. "Comrade Stalin provides for his officers. The Polish dogs out there cannot disturb us. By the way, Comrade Captain, did you talk to those people out there in Polish?"

"Yes, Comrade General," Kuba replied.

"Did they trust you in that uniform?"

"Not much."

"That's Polish dogs for you," the general said with a chuckle.

After they ate and drank, the general proposed another game of poker. They played for about an hour, and then one of the officers said, "What is that city we are passing now?"

Kuba looked out the window. A flood of memories went through his mind. "That is Volkovysk," he said. Fifteen minutes later the train came to a stop. They reached the official Polish border.

Kuba poured himself a drink of vodka, and the others did the same. He was nervous but tried to appear calm. There was a lot of activity on the train. Kuba looked outside and noticed several Soviet border guards walking alongside the train. There was a commotion in the corridor and the compartment door opened.

A first lieutenant of the border patrol stood in the doorway and behind him stood three more border guards. Kuba leaned back in his seat and faked being slightly drunk. The lieutenant entered, looked at Osipov, saluted, then asked the general for forgiveness and left, closing the door behind him. Kuba sat up. Osipov, undisturbed by the interference, urged them to continue the game and about one hour later, the train began to move again. Kuba looked out the window and realized that they were now in Poland. He suddenly felt very tired. The game was breaking up so Kuba climbed up to a berth and fell asleep instantly.

The train stopped suddenly and Kuba almost fell off the berth. It was dark outside. He looked at his watch. It was past three o'clock in the morning and the train had just pulled into the city of Bialystock. He went out into the corridor and came face to face with the conductor, who saluted him, and Kuba asked him how long they would be stopped at Bialystock. "Forty-five minutes, Comrade Captain!"

Kuba went through the interconnecting doors to the back of the train and found Sonia asleep on the seat and the other passengers asleep on the two tiers of the upper berths. He sat down next to Sonia and she woke up, startled.

Kuba took her hand in his and said in a whisper, "Look, Sonia, we are in Bialystock right now. In four hours from now, we will be arriving in Warsaw. I will try to get away from my companions and change into civilian clothes and when we come to Warsaw, you get off the train and look for me. I am in the sixth car up toward the front. If you see me in civilian clothes, you can come right over to me and we will take it from there, but, if I am in my uniform, you will have to observe what is going on around me and follow wherever I go. Eventually, I will get rid of my company and then you can come to me, but remember, speak to me only in Polish."

"Yes, Kuba, whatever you say, I will follow," she said and squeezed his hand.

Kuba went back to his car. The officers were still asleep so he went out on the platform and started pacing alongside the train. When he came to Sonia's car, she stepped down and joined him.

"I watched you since you left your car," she said and they walked alongside the train as they talked.

When they turned back and came half the distance of the train, they met General Osipov on the platform. He looked at them, smiled, and said, "You found yourself a nice looking girl."

The sky was turning gray. Sonia went back to her car and Kuba caught up with General Osipov. The general asked him if he played chess. Kuba answered, yes, so they went back to their car and the general produced a chess set. They played the game until early in the morning and then both of them went to sleep.

The train stopped near the ruins of a small town. Polish soldiers and railroad workers were standing on both sides of the train. Kuba got off and walked toward the locomotive. A wet snow was falling and the cold air was tickling Kuba's nostrils. A group of workers were fixing the tracks ahead. Kuba watched the activities and thought about his immediate future. Suddenly, there was machine gun fire not too far away to the left. The people were not disturbed, glancing once in that direction and then continuing with their work. About an hour later, the train began to move and shortly afterwards it pulled into the city of Ostrow Mazowiecki where the train was diverted to a side track. Osipov and the other officers went into the half demolished station where Kuba got off the train and joined them. They got some hot tea from the stationmaster and sipped it while watching military transports passing the station in both directions. Kuba refilled his cup with tea and went out to the train.

"Where are you going?" asked one of the officers.

"Oh, he has a girl on the train," said Osipov and all three started laughing. Kuba got on the train and gave the tea to Sonia. He sat there with her until the train began to move again. The landscape changed. The train passed more and more towns and villages, all showing various stages of destruction. Kuba recognized the names of many towns as the train approached Warsaw. There was a lot of activity at the various stations and many passengers were waiting for trains. Railroad workers were busy at their jobs, and there were vendors, dozens of them standing behind makeshift tables loaded with various items from food to household goods. Kuba bought a pack of cigarettes, paid with Russian money and received change in brand new Polish banknotes which the Soviet government had issued for Poland.

At six o'clock in the evening, the train stopped at a temporary station in Praga, a suburb of Warsaw on the east side of the Vistula River. That was as far as the train could travel because all bridges across the Vistula were destroyed and passengers for other cities in Poland had to cross the river by sleigh or wagon over a pontoon bridge. The terminal was constructed with plywood and salvaged lumber from the demolished buildings. It was wet and drafty inside the terminal. "Would you like to come with us to the Red Army Officers Club on Saska Kempa?" the general asked Kuba.

"No, thank you, General," Kuba answered. "I have orders to proceed to the city of Lodz."

The three officers got into a sleigh and were driven away. After the officers left, Kuba went to look for Sonia.

There were hundreds of people milling around in the terminal. The center of the station was taken up by long benches on which people were sitting or even sleeping, while clutching their possessions in their arms. A Polish lieutenant saluted smartly and as Kuba approached, Kuba returned the salute and spoke to the officer in Polish. The lieutenant smiled and replied in Russian, "I am Russian, on special assignment to the Polish Army."

"I understand," said Kuba and walked away. Thinking about the Russian in Polish uniform, Kuba came to the conclusion that as far as he was concerned, Poland was only a way station and he would never be safe here.

He found Sonia and said to her, "I must change my clothing. Let's go outside and see if we can find a place where I can do it safely. The restrooms are crowded with people." They went outside through a door in the back of the station. It was already dark and there were no lights burning in the building. Kuba spotted a small shed, probably used for storage of tools. He turned to Sonia and said, "You stay here on guard and I will change my clothes behind the shed."

There was a large, wooden box behind the shed. He put his suitcase on the box and changed into the civilian clothes which he had been carrying. The clothes were somewhat too large for him, but it had to do for the time being. As they returned to the terminal Kuba asked, "Sonia, do you have the address of your friends in Warsaw?"

"Yes, right here in my pocket," she replied. Kuba took the slip of paper from her and memorized the address. They went out in front of the terminal where all the sleighs and wagons were lined up, hired a sleigh for two-hundred and fifty rubles, and took off across the pontoon bridge for Warsaw.

Sitting in the sleigh under a blanket, Kuba leaned over to Sonia and whispered, "You see, we made it."

"I was sure that we would," she replied and kissed him lightly on the cheek.

They reached the western shore of the Vistula River and proceeded in a northwestern direction and arrived in Warsaw proper. Kuba looked around at the city where he was born and could not believe his eyes. The city was in ruins. Here and there, parts of brick walls and chimneys were standing, like witnesses to the bestiality of the German invaders. Kuba could not recognize the area through which they were passing, although he had lived here for twenty years. The city, as far as the eye could see in the gray light of the moon, was completely devastated. They traveled about five miles to the northern outskirts of the city and came to a street with several houses almost undamaged. The driver stopped in front of a two story house. "That is the house," he said.

Kuba got out of the sleigh and checked the number on the house near its gate. Then he said to Sonia, "Go knock on the door and see if your friends still live here." Sonia went to the door and knocked. About five minutes passed before anyone answered the knock. Kuba noticed a window shade being pulled to the side and someone looked out at Sonia. Finally, the door opened and a woman came out. She and Sonia talked briefly. The woman went back into the house. Soon, a tall, burly man of about fifty came out, embraced Sonia, and then came over to the sleigh. Sonia introduced the man to Kuba as Cousin Jan. He picked up the two suitcases and Kuba paid off the driver and went into the house. When they were inside and the door locked, Jan introduced them to his wife and two other couples.

The back of the house was demolished and boarded up, leaving three rooms and a kitchen. Jan's wife asked Sonia about Misha and when he planned to come to Warsaw. She then went into the kitchen and returned with a bottle of vodka, filled glasses for everybody and proposed a toast. "Next year in Jerusalem! L'chaim!"

They drank and then Jan's wife and one of the other women went into the kitchen, returning with plates of food and placed them on a table in the center of the room. They all took places around the table and began to eat. Kuba looked at his watch. It was nine o'clock Moscow time, which made it seven in the evening in Warsaw.

Jan looked at Kuba, smiling and said, "You made it just in time for dinner." The meal consisted of dried fish, cheese, potatoes, herring and bread. Kuba learned that they had all survived the ghetto uprising in Warsaw and Jan, a partisan, had come from Baranovichi.

One of the men, by the name of Halperin, appeared to be very familiar to Kuba. He was sure that he had seen him before the war and Halperin, in turn, was watching Kuba. After dinner, he came over to where Kuba was sitting with Sonia and said, "Now I remember who you are. You are the son of Samuel Mordecai."

"Who are you?" Kuba asked him, somewhat sharply.

"Oh, I was a teacher in the Jewish folks-schule (public school) and a member of the Jewish Labor Bund. Your father was a great man and the bravest person in our world."

Sonia got to her feet, took Halperin's arm and said, "His name is now Arthur Zielinski and he would be in great danger if the communists ever found out who he really is. Please do not forget that!" All of them looked at Kuba in silence. No words were spoken, but everyone understood the meaning of Sonia's statement.

Halperin said to Kuba, "A group of ghetto fighters from the 'Bund' live not far from here. I will take you to them tomorrow, if you wish."

Kuba listened to these words and began thinking: Who survived the Holocaust? Let's see...there is Hana Kastel, Marek Edelstein, Gabriel Fryszman, Maius Wierbman in America, Janek Silberman somewhere in China or Japan and Mietek Kornstein in the Soviet-created Polish Army. And then he began wondering about his own family: His mother Golda, sister, Ryvka, grandmother Dvoyra and his Aunt Tema and Uncle Abram. What happened to them? And where is Rachel? It was past midnight when they finally went to bed. Jan brought in two straw mattresses and put them on the floor in the front room, side by side, the beds for Kuba and Sonia.

They turned down the kerosene lamps and went to bed, but, Kuba could not fall asleep. He was lying there on the straw mattress thinking about his past. What was he to do next? He decided to go to the "Bund" club the next day and find out who of his old world was still alive. He turned and twisted under his blanket until the early morning hours.

Kuba turned and felt Sonia pressing against him, and put her arms around him and said, "You cannot find any peace, Kuba. It is all over. You are not in Russia anymore."

She pressed her body hard against his body and he relaxed enough to fall asleep. He could feel her working hard on him to show some response, but he just drifted off into a dream. Sonia had kept him in her arms until Jan's wife knocked on the door in the morning. They got dressed, ready to face the new day.

They spent the day talking about the ghetto uprising and the activities of the Jewish underground after 1943. Kuba learned from these people that his friend, Gabriel Fryszman, the husband of Hana Kastel and father of a son, was killed by the Nazis during a raid on their partisan camp. Gabriel was awarded the Medal of Heroes of Poland by the Polish government in England. He learned also that Bernard, the father of his friend, Janek Silberman had been one of the leaders of the Warsaw resistance movement and active also during the period after the ghetto uprising.

At six o'clock in the evening of that day, Halperin and Kuba arrived at the "Bund" club. Kuba wore his old uniform, which Sonia had modified by sewing some cloth over the buttons and shoulder pads, which had identified his rank. The civilian suit, which Misha had sent to him, was so bad that he did not care to take any chance wearing it. They arrived at the club in fifteen minutes. Halperin knocked on the door and said something aloud. The door opened and they walked inside. The club consisted of one room that was all that was left of the building. There were about two dozen people assembled there. Because of his appearance and the fact that they did not know him, the people looked at Kuba with suspicion. He looked around and spotted a familiar face, Yashunski, the son of a friend and an associate of his father.

Kuba walked over to him and said, "Yashunski, I know that you don't recognize me, but I am the son of Arthur," using the underground name of Kuba's father. Yashunski, a tall man with a black beard, broke out in a smile, grabbed Kuba in his arms and said, "Of course! You look just like your father. We have received notice that you were coming here. Now we can notify our friends in London and New York that you have arrived!"

Kuba was surrounded by people whom he did not recognize but they all knew of him. Yashunski finally took him aside and said, "We are moving our quarters to Lodz next week. Marek Edelstein and Hana and many others are on their way there right now. Bernard Goldstein left this morning. Meanwhile, you can stay where you are. Halperin is a reliable man. We will contact you tomorrow. By the way, what name do you go by?"

"Arthur Zielinski," Kuba replied.

Yashunski looked at him and smiled, "That is a good name. We heard about your activities behind Nazi lines from people who returned from the Soviet Union. Your father would have been proud of you."

Walking alongside Halperin, Kuba thought about Yashunski's last words and he recalled the times when he had spoken, mentally, to his father and mother, during some difficult moments in his life behind enemy lines. They seemed very near now, his mother's tear-streaked face telling him, "Take revenge for our lives and blood, my son. You are the only one who can do it."

He could still see the face of his father in the background of a snow-covered forest, while he was riding back from a difficult assignment, "You did right, my son! My heart cries for you because you couldn't save your own wife and son...but soon you will start a new life and create a new family with a good woman as your wife, and have sons to carry on our name!"

Three days later all arrangements were made for Kuba's departure to Lodz. He said goodbye to his new friends and Sonia walked out with him to the sleigh that was to take him to the station.

"Thank you, Kuba, for all you have done for me," Sonia said.

"Thank you, Sonia. I hope that Misha will join you soon."

"I hope to see you again." There were tears in her eyes. They kissed and Kuba got into the sleigh.

Sitting in the cold railroad car, Kuba observed the countryside and the towns and villages that they passed by. Every town and village was either completely destroyed or heavily damaged. It looked as if the entire country was in ruins.

Kuba arrived in Lodz the following morning. Except for the Jewish section the city showed very little damage. The Germans incorporated the city into the Third Reich and that was the reason why it was preserved whole. Kuba went to an address on Piotrkovska Street which was given to him by Halperin in Warsaw.

It was a seven-story apartment building. Kuba climbed up to the third floor, found the right number and rang the doorbell. A young woman in her early twenties, with a dark complexion and burning dark eyes, answered the door. She looked at Kuba, started to say something and suddenly threw herself into Kuba's arms screaming, "Kuba! My God, it's Kuba!"

"Yes, Hanna, it's me!" The two let their emotions overtake them and cried openly. Hanna and Kuba grew up together, went to the same schools and belonged to the same organizations. Hanna was like a sister to Kuba and they loved each other since childhood. Kuba knew that Hanna married another classmate of theirs, Gabriel Fryszman, who was killed in action as a partisan. Hanna gave birth to a boy in the Warsaw ghetto during the uprising in 1943. Hanna took Kuba to her room. A little boy was sitting on the floor. He looked at Kuba with a smile on his face and when Kuba stretched out his arms the boy came to him immediately. Kuba picked him up and kissed him. "What is his name?" Kuba asked.

"Gabrish. He is named after his father." Kuba held the baby close to his chest and when he closed his eyes he had the feeling that it was his own little Victor in his arms. Hanna was watching him, and she must have seen something in his face.

"You had a little son of the same age as Gabrish, Kuba?" Kuba opened his eyes, looked at Hanna and only nodded affirmatively. Hanna put her hand on his shoulder, kissed him on the cheek and then embraced him and the baby.

"You must be starved," Hanna finally said. She went to a cupboard and placed some bread and sausage on the table then she left the room and returned shortly with a pot of tea and some cups. She put Gabrish in his crib and the two of them began to eat.

After a while, Kuba said, "You know, Hanna, I learned about the ghetto uprising from a Polish newspaper in Moscow. The editor of the paper was Wanda Wasilewska and I went to see her. She filled me in on some details and also told me quite a bit about my father's death. I would like to know about you and Gabriel and all our friends. If you can, please tell me. "

Hanna was silent for a long while. Her eyes were lowered and she seemed to watch the tea in her cup. Her face was rigid and there was a lot of concentration as if she were searching for the right words. Finally she let out a sigh and began her story.

"Gabriel was a squad leader in the Z.O.B. (Zydowska Organizacia Bojowa), the Jewish Combat Organization. We lived at my parents' apartment on Mila Street. You remember where. You were there many times. My parents were already deported to Treblinka at the same time that your mother and sister were taken there. On April 19, 1943, the German troops entered the ghetto in accordance with their plan to liquidate the remaining Jews of Warsaw. I was a member of Gabriel's squad and we took up positions at windows facing the street. When the German troops came nearer with their tanks and other vehicles, we opened fire. We pelted the tanks with Molotov cocktails and sprayed the street with our gunfire. Several tanks were burning and many German, Lithuanian, Ukrainian and other SS troops were killed. The Germans withdrew from the ghetto. We repelled many German attempts to enter the ghetto during the following few days. Finally the Germans employed artillery and their Luftwaffe. They began to destroy systematically every building in the ghetto with incendiary bombs and shells. Our house was the first one hit and we escaped over the rooftops to another section of the ghetto."

"What happened to your casualties? Did you take the wounded with you?" Kuba asked.

"Our casualties were very heavy. Most of the wounded chose to commit suicide on the spot. The less severely wounded continued to fight until they died."

"Where did you go from Mila Street?" Kuba asked.

"There were only five of us left and we headed towards Karmelicka Street. We had to cross Gensha Street and that was hell. The entire street was aflame. As a matter of fact the entire ghetto was a burning inferno. The smoke was thick and there was a heavy stench of burning bodies."

"Where did you finally take shelter?" Kuba asked.

"We joined a Zionist fight group on Novolipki. We took shelter in the ruins of a demolished house and fired at the enemy from there. We had to change our location quite frequently, because the German artillery fire was being concentrated on our positions."

"How long were you able to keep this up?" Kuba asked.

"We fought for ten days, and then our ammunition was gone."

"What did you do then?"

"We were hiding in ruins and even sewer holes. Finally the shooting diminished. The artillery stopped shelling us and there were no more aircraft over our heads. We hoped that we would be able to hide out among the ruins for a while, but then came the German mop up commandos with dogs and poison gas. They were all around us and getting closer. We descended into a sewer and moved away several blocks from our location. There we remained for several days."

"How did you finally escape from the ghetto?" Kuba asked.

"We were joined by a number of other surviving ghetto fighters and one day a girl came to us from the 'Aryan' side of Warsaw. She brought us a message from Vladka and Bernard. You know them. They were in contact with the Polish underground army. The message contained instructions for the group to follow the sewer canals to Prosta Street at the corner of Twarda Street. Two members of the Polish Socialist Party who were employees of the sewer system guided the group to a manhole at that location. Two trucks awaited the ghetto fighters at the manhole and in broad daylight we escaped from Warsaw and joined a partisan group in the Vyskov Forest near Warsaw."

Hanna fell silent and Kuba closed his eyes, reliving her ordeal. He thought of all his brave friends in the ghetto who perished in such an uneven fight. But he also felt enormous pride for being a part of such a valiant Jewish generation. His own experiences seemed to be diminished by the enormity of the ghetto uprising.

"Tell me, dear Hanna, how did Gabriel die?"

Hanna wiped some tears from her eyes and continued her story. "Shortly after we joined the partisans, Gabriel went on a mission with some others and they were caught in an ambush. The fight lasted only a few minutes and my Gabriel was killed."

"What did you do then?" Kuba asked.

"I was very pregnant and our friend Celek took me back to Warsaw where I found shelter in Bernard Goldstein's hiding place. He was like a father to me and he was the one who delivered little Gabrish." She was silent for a while and then added, "Can you imagine? There was still sporadic fighting going on in the ghetto."

"What happened after the provisional government was established in Poland?" Kuba asked.

"We were recognized as freedom fighters for Poland and many of our living and dead were awarded the highest military medals by the government."

It was getting late and Kuba got to his feet. Now he had to think about his own existence. He had a couple thousand rubles and not much else of material value. He must find some lodging and some sort of job if possible.

"Hanna, how do I go about finding a place to live?" he asked.

"Don't worry about that. We will bring in a cot here and you can stay with me for as long as necessary."

And so it was. Kuba remained with Hanna. He treated her as a sister and helped her take care of little Gabrish. Several months passed. Germany surrendered unconditionally. The world was celebrating the allied victory and General Eisenhower went to Moscow to receive the Soviet Medal of Victory.

One sunny day in May of 1945, Kuba was walking with Hanna, pushing a baby carriage with little Gabrish in it, down Piotrkovska Street, when he was approached by three Soviet officers.

One of them yelled, "This is our captain!"

Kuba pushed Hanna and the baby aside, ran into the street behind a street car and continued running alongside the car for several blocks. The Russians spread out and ran after him. They were soon joined by other Soviet soldiers and Polish policemen. The car turned into a side street and Kuba followed it. He thus lost sight of his pursuers. He crossed the street and walked up to another street car which was heading in the opposite direction. The street car came to a stop at the corner and Kuba boarded it, paid for a ticket and took a window seat. There was a newspaper on the seat next to Kuba's. He picked it up and half covered his face with it, as if he was reading. The street car turned into Piotrkovska Street and Kuba noticed a big commotion. There were many Soviet and Polish military police on the sidewalks, looking into stores and hallways and checking the identities of many people. Two Polish policemen boarded the street car in which Kuba was riding. Kuba's pulse quickened. He tried to remain calm as he reached into his hind pocket and pulled out his Beretta pistol. He released the safety and held the pistol in his right hand hidden by the newspaper. His brain was racing.

"They will not take me alive!" he was thinking. "I will not die in some Soviet prison after all these years of fighting the Nazis!"

The policemen were slowly crossing the street car from front to rear. Kuba pretended to be deeply absorbed in the paper he was reading. The policeman closest to Kuba gave him a passing glance and continued to walk toward the rear. The two policemen stopped at the rear platform and looked back at the passengers. Just then a police vehicle pulled up and the driver said something to the policemen. They got off the street car and crossed the street quickly. The street car continued on its way. Kuba caught a glimpse of Hanna and the baby carriage, entering their apartment building.

Kuba got off several blocks further and walked back by way of another street. He entered through a rear door and ran upstairs. Hanna opened the door for him and gave a cry of surprise. Kuba realized that he was still holding the gun in his hand. He put it in his pocket and closed the door behind him.

Hanna was extremely worried. She locked the door of her room and looked Kuba deep into the eyes. "What happened? Why were the Russians after you?" she asked.

"You see, my dear, I did not have a chance to tell you everything that happened to me in the Soviet Union. Some months ago the Russians found out who my father was. I also learned that they had been investigating my background for some time. An order for my arrest was issued and I escaped to Poland using an assumed name."

"What would happen to you if they would apprehend you?"

"A torturous interrogation and then --execution."

"Oh, my dear, what should we do?" Hanna said and her eyes filled with tears.

"Listen, Hanna, it is clear that if I remain here, you and Gabrish will be in extreme danger. We must find a way for me to leave the city as soon as possible...tonight!" Kuba said.

Hanna was pacing the floor for several minutes, and then she stopped suddenly, picked up her handbag and said, "Kuba, I am going out for a little while. You lock the door after me and don't open it for anybody. I have my key with me. Keep an eye on Gabrish." She kissed him on the lips and departed quickly.

Kuba put Gabrish in his crib and began to pack his few belongings. For the first time in his life he felt completely lost. He did not know how to get out of the city now. The Russians knew that he was in Lodz and they would be watching the railroad station and bus terminals. He knew that he must get away in a southwestern direction toward the border with Czechoslovakia. From there he would make his way to Austria and eventually France. He finished packing and sat down on Hanna's bed. He counted his money and was surprised that he had more than he thought. Over three thousand rubles --equal to sixty-five American dollars. He leaned back on the bed and began to think. He must have dozed off. It was past eight o'clock when he sat up startled. Someone was unlocking the door. He reached in his pocket and felt the assuring coolness of his gun. Hanna came in and locked the door behind her.

She sat down on the bed next to Kuba and took his hand in hers. "Listen, Kuba," she said. "Our friend Bolek is driving a truck to Wroclaw tonight to pick up a load of lead letters for the printing shop of the newspaper where he is employed. He will pick you up at ten o'clock." She opened her bag and took out a small card and handed it to Kuba. "Here is a certificate that identifies you as an employee of that newspaper. It is made out in your new name."

Hanna's voice was so full of assurance that Kuba relaxed completely. He read and reread the certificate and then put it in his pocket. Hanna left the room and returned shortly with a plate containing a big part of a smoked ham, some bread and mustard. They ate in silence, absorbed in their own thoughts. After dinner Hanna got a paper bag and placed the leftover ham and bread in it. Then she extracted something from her handbag. "Here, Kuba, take this food with you so that you won't starve on the way. And this was sent to you by the Jewish Labor Bund committee. You will need it." She handed him two U.S. banknotes amounting to fifteen dollars.

"Thank you very much. Some day I will repay you for your love and kindness, my little sister." He kissed her on both cheeks.

At a quarter to ten Bolek entered the apartment. He extended his hand to Kuba and the latter shook it heartily. "Well, Kuba, if you are ready, we can leave now. Two Polish Socialist comrades are waiting in the truck. They are keeping an eye on the street to make sure that it is safe for you to leave."

Kuba picked up the sleeping Gabrish and kissed his forehead. He then took Hanna in his arms and again they both shed some tears. "I am sure that we will meet again soon," he told Hanna.

The trip to Wroclaw was uneventful and Kuba slept most of the way. In Wroclaw, he met many old friends from Warsaw and began a search for possible surviving relatives, but there were no encouraging signs. He lived with some people from the Polish city of Bendzin, who had known his father. There were rumors every day about possible survivors of Kuba's family, but none of the rumors checked out. He then went into a deep state of depression, thinking more and more about suicide because he could not find any reason to go on living.

Kuba spent his days walking the streets of the city and thinking. Wroclaw was a large city with a main railroad junction, and many viaducts crossing the railroad tracks. He walked across those bridges, holding his right hand in his pocket; his palm wrapped around the Beretta pistol, thinking about how to end it all.

One day, while Kuba was walking across one of the viaducts, he came face to face with two girls coming toward him. He did not pay too much attention to the girls, but something made him turn around and look after them as they passed. One of them turned around also and looked at Kuba, standing there. "Kuba! Oh, Kuba darling! I found you! I found you!" she cried and came running to fall into his arms.

It was Rachel, the girl that was foremost on his mind since her disappearance after a Nazi raid on her partisan camp back in 1943, while he was on a mission with his partisans against the German garrison in Nesvizh. Rachel was the girl to whom he pledged his love and devotion and who shared his hut in the forest camp near the Wygon Lake. Now she was in his arms, sobbing quietly while tears streamed down his cheeks. There was a warm feeling in Kuba's heart, somehow he knew that Rachel would survive and they would meet again.

"What are you doing here?" Kuba asked. "How did you find me?"

"Oh, Kuba, look. This is my sister Esther. She survived a very severe German concentration camp. When the war ended I returned to my home town, Slavkov hoping that you might show up there. I found Esther and she also had the feeling that I would return to our place of birth."

"But what did you mean when you said that you found me? How did you know that I would be here?" Kuba asked somewhat puzzled.

"Darling, let's go home to our apartment. There I will tell you everything. I knew that I would find you in Wroclaw somehow!"

The two girls shared the two-room apartment with two other girls from their home town. Rachel took Kuba to the room which she shared with her sister. They sat on the bed and looked at each other for a long time.

"Rachel, how did you know that I was in Wroclaw? You kept on saying that you found me. Tell me what happened to you since that afternoon in 1943. Please, I must know!"

Rachel lowered her head into the palms of her hand and sat silently for a long time. Finally she raised her head, put her arms around Kuba's neck and kissed him passionately on the mouth.

"My dear, I was taken to a concentration camp called Ludwiksdorff, just across the German border with Poland. They put me to work as a spot welder in an ammunition factory. The fact that I look so 'Aryan' and mastered the German language perfectly helped me enormously. During the last two years I was transferred three times to different concentration camps. My lot was much better than that of the other women because the Germans thought that I was half German. All that time I was thinking about you and your combat activities against the Nazi murderers. Somehow I knew that you were still alive. My darling, you were my first man and all my love and compassion belongs to you only. Some highly placed Germans tried to take me out of the camps and include me in their households, but I refused always, stressing the point that I am pure Jewish and I wanted to remain with my people regardless of what their lot might be."

"Where were you when the Russians arrived?" Kuba asked.

"I was in a camp in Gorlitz. I worked in a big munitions factory where stocks for rifles and machine guns, etc. were also produced. The Soviet troops liberated that camp in May."

"How did the Russians treat you?" Kuba asked.

"The first units were very sympathetic and helpful, but they were soon replaced by other troops. These soldiers were mostly drunk, wild and they raped every woman they could lay hands on."

"What did you do?"

"When I saw what was going on, I and another girl hid in one of the barracks under a bunk. We spent about ten hours there. It was terrible! It was filthy and there were lice crawling all over."

"And then what happened?" Kuba asked.

"All the Soviet combat troops finally left the area and a medical corps took over the camp. There were many Jewish doctors among them. They examined every camp inmate, and I was sent to a hospital to be treated for malnutrition. After I regained my strength I volunteered to stay on at the hospital as a nursing aid. There were many Soviet combat casualties at the hospital and I helped take care of them."

"How did you get along with the Soviet patients?" Kuba asked.

"Great. There were many Jewish soldiers and I spoke Yiddish to them. Now, Kuba, I must tell you the most extraordinary thing that happened to me. There was one Jewish lieutenant who told me that he was a partisan in Belarus until 1944. One day he produced a photograph of his group. 'This was my partisan group,' the soldier said, 'we were on a special mission with the famous "Orlovsky" group and a TASS photo-journalist was there. He took that picture and we later received copies.'"

Rachel began to cry again. She put her arm around Kuba's neck and buried her face in his shoulder then she proceeded. "I took the photo from his hands and looked at it. AND YOU KNOW WHAT?!!! THERE YOU WERE, RIGHT IN FRONT. You were sitting on a horse with your submachine gun across your lap. My heart was pounding and I asked the soldier if he knew who this man is."

"'Oh sure. That is Comrade Kuba. He made quite a name for himself fighting the Nazis.'" Rachel paused for a while and then she continued. "I asked him if he knew what happened to you. 'I heard from my co-partisans that Kuba left the Soviet Union and is now somewhere in Wroclaw.' That did it. I quit my job, went into Poland, first to Slavkov where I was reunited with my sister Esther, and then we came to Wroclaw."

Kuba lowered his head into his hands and cried, but this was a sweet feeling full of joy. He found his place in the new, postwar world. It actually happened! His father's prophecy came true. There would be a continuation of their name. Kuba and Rachel were married that same day.

Epilogue

Kuba was driving north along Foothill Boulevard. He turned right on Densmore Street and then left to his house. There on the front porch of their home was his beautiful wife, standing and waiting for her husband. Their two sons were busy with their homework somewhere in the house. Kuba recalled the years behind enemy lines, and Rachel --the biggest gift of his life. Kuba got out of his car and kissed Rachel. Tomorrow would be another day and he would then have to tackle the problem of Soviet participation in the forthcoming space symposium.

Joseph, New York, 1946 *Adele (Rachel), Joseph's second wife, Poland, 1945*

Made in the USA
San Bernardino, CA
22 November 2017